Realist Evaluation in Practice

Health and Social Work

M<small>ANSOOR</small> A.F. K<small>AZI</small>

SAGE Publications
London • Thousand Oaks • New Delhi

SAGE Publications Ltd
6 Bonhill Street
London EC2A 4PU

SAGE Publications Inc
2455 Teller Road
Thousand Oaks, California 91320

SAGE Publications India Pvt Ltd
B-42, Panchsheel Enclave
Post Box 4109
New Delhi - 100 017

Library of Congress Control Number available

A catalogue record for this book is available from the
British Library

ISBN 0-7619-6995-0
ISBN 0-7619-6996-9 (pbk)

Typeset by C&M Digitals (P) Ltd., Chennai, India
Printed in Great Britain by Athenaeum Press, Gateshead

Contents

1. Introduction   1

2. Contemporary Perspectives in Practice Evaluation   10

3. The Realist Evaluation Paradigm for Practice   22

4. An Example of Qualitative Research Methods in
   Realist Evaluation   42

5. Quantitative Methods: Evaluation of Family Centres   62

6. A Realist Evaluation of Practice: the NSPCC's
   Shield Project and Intensive Analysis   95

7. The Shield Project: Extensive Analysis in Realist Evaluation   110

8. Patterns of What Works, For Whom and in What Contexts   137

9. The Contribution of Realist Evaluation for Practice   158

   References   168

   Index   176

List of Figures

Figure 3.1 The realist effectiveness cycle   29

Figure 5.1 Walpole case 11   68
Figure 5.2 Westtown case 10   69
Figure 5.3 Southgate case 20   70

Figure 6.1 K's outcome measures   105
Figure 6.2 K's outcome measures   105
Figure 6.3 K's outcome measures   106
Figure 6.4 H's outcome measures   107

Figure 8.1 The interaction of causal machanisms in
realist evaluation   148

List of Tables

Table 3.1   Change in majority of scored ADLs in Oakes Villa   38
Table 3.2   Destination of clients at discharge from Oakes Villa   38
Table 3.3   Result of DCC scores   40

Table 4.1   Schedule of repeated interviews   46
Table 4.2   Changes in outcomes matrix: template analysis
             of first interviews   47
Table 4.3   Changes in outcomes matrix: template analysis
             of second interviews   48
Table 4.4   Changes in enabling mechanisms matrix:
             template analysis of first interviews   50
Table 4.5   Changes in enabling mechanisms matrix:
             template analysis of second interviews   51
Table 4.6   Changes in disabling mechanisms matrix:
             template analysis of first interviews   52
Table 4.7   Changes in disabling mechanisms matrix:
             template analysis of second interviews   53
Table 4.8   Changes in content matrix: template
             analysis of first interviews   54
Table 4.9   Changes in content matrix: template
             analysis of second interviews   55
Table 4.10   Changes in context matrix: template
             analysis of first interviews   57
Table 4.11   Changes in context matrix: template
             analysis of second interviews   58

Table 5.1   Distribution of cases and numbers
             included in the evaluation   67
Table 5.2   Comparisons between the first and the last scores,
             and effect sizes   72
Table 5.3   Parents' self-esteem (PCSEQ) outcomes
             cross-tabulated by age of child (in years)   73
Table 5.4   Parents' self-esteem (PCSEQ) outcomes
             cross-tabulated by gender of child   73

Table 5.5   Parents' self-esteem (PCSEQ) outcomes
             cross-tabulated by gender of the parent(s)
             working with the family centres   74
Table 5.6   Parents' self-esteem (PCSEQ) outcomes
             cross-tabulated by the racial origin of the child   74
Table 5.7   Parents' self-esteem (PCSEQ) outcomes
             cross-tabulated by profession of the referrer   75
Table 5.8   Parents' self-esteem (PCSEQ) outcomes
             cross-tabulated by the reason for referral   76
Table 5.9   Parents' self-esteem (PCSEQ) outcomes
             cross-tabulated by type of service provided at
             the family centres   77
Table 5.10   Observation of Child Rating Scale (OCRS)
             outcomes cross-tabulated by age (in years)   77
Table 5.11   Observation of Child Rating Scale (OCRS)
             outcomes cross-tabulated by gender of the child   78
Table 5.12   Observation of Child Rating Scale (OCRS)
             outcomes cross-tabulated by gender of the
             parent(s) working with the family centres   78
Table 5.13   Observation of Child Rating Scale (OCRS)
             outcomes cross-tabulated by the racial
             origin of the child   79
Table 5.14   Observation of Child Rating Scale (OCRS)
             outcomes cross-tabulated by source of referral   79
Table 5.15   Observation of Child Rating Scale (OCRS)
             outcomes cross-tabulated by reasons for referral   79
Table 5.16   Type of service provided and OCRS outcomes   80
Table 5.17   Parent-child interaction (PCIS) outcomes
             cross-tabulated by age of child (in years)   81
Table 5.18   Parent-child interaction (PCIS) outcomes
             cross-tabulated by gender   81
Table 5.19   Parent-child interaction (PCIS) outcomes
             cross-tabulated by gender of the parent(s)
             working with the family centres   81
Table 5.20   Parent-child interaction (PCIS) outcomes
             cross-tabulated by the racial origin of the child   82
Table 5.21   Parent-child interaction (PCIS) outcomes
             cross-tabulated by sources of referral   83
Table 5.22   Parent-child interaction (PCIS) outcomes
             cross-tabulated by reasons for referral   83
Table 5.23   Parent-child interaction (PCIS) outcomes
             cross-tabulated by type of services provided by
             the family centres   83

Table 5.24   Parents'/carers' CSQ8 scores   84
Table 5.25   Parents'/carers' CSQ8-1 scores cross-tabulated by
             racial origin   85
Table 5.26   Parents'/carers' CSQ8-1 scores cross-tabulated by
             reasons for referral   85
Table 5.27   Parents'/carers' CSQ8-1 scores cross-tabulated by
             type of service provided   86
Table 5.28   Referrers' CSQ8 scores   87
Table 5.29   Referrers' CSQ8-1 scores cross-tabulated by
             racial origin   87
Table 5.30   Referrers' CSQ8-1 scores cross-tabulated by
             reasons for referral   88
Table 5.31   Referrers' CSQ8-1 scores cross-tabulated by
             type of service provided   88
Table 5.32   Patterns through odds ratios and relative risk   91

Table 7.1   Shield child BRIC outcome and effect size   119
Table 7.2   The effect sizes of changes in the parent,
             school and carer BRIC scores   119
Table 7.3   Self-concept effect size   120
Table 7.4   The effect size of changes in CAM and CAF scores   120
Table 7.5   Results of AI reliability tests and the effect size   121
Table 7.6   Effect size of change in Hare Self-Esteem Scores   122
Table 7.7   Effect size of change in A-COPE scores   123
Table 7.8   General case outcome: whether assessment was
             completed or not   124
Table 7.9   Engagement of the child/young person in the
             programme   125
Table 7.10   Engagement of either parent in the programme   125
Table 7.11   Assessment sessions held with the
             child/young person   126
Table 7.12   Assessment sessions held with either parent   126
Table 7.13   Number of days in assessment work and
             multi-disciplinary meetings held   127
Table 7.14   The extent to which the requirements of the
             assessment model were met   127
Table 7.15   Contexts in the circumstances of the
             children/young people ($n = 49$)   129
Table 7.16   Mechanisms and changes in the mechanisms
             ($n = 49$)   130
Appendix 7.1 Matrix of qualitative review templates against
             requirements of the model met and assessment
             completed   133

Table 8.1   Significant correlations between assessment
             completed and other outcomes, content
             variables and mechanisms   141
Table 8.2   Significant correlations between engagement
             of the child/young person in the programme
             and other outcomes, content variables
             and mechanisms   143
Table 8.3   Significant correlations between engagement of
             either parent in the programme and other
             outcomes, content variables and mechanisms   145
Table 8.4   Binary logistic regression with mechanisms   150
Table 8.5   Binary logistic regression in relation to contexts   151
Table 8.6   Binary logistic regression analysis of contexts
             impacting on the outcome of assessment
             completed (final step in the forward–conditional
             method)   153
Table 8.7   Binary logistic regression analysis of contexts
             impacting on the outcome of engagement of
             either parent (all three steps in the
             forward–conditional method)   153

This book is dedicated to my wife Shahida, my sons Jehan and Shan, and to my daughter Shammy

Acknowledgements

I am indebted to Colin Robson and Nigel Parton for their helpful guidance throughout this enterprise. Particular thanks also to Ray Pawson and Nick Tilley for sending me a copy of their historic book that set the ball rolling. In the development of the realist evaluation paradigm, my thanks also to the colleagues from all over the world who have helped in the development of ideas and strategies – Ilmari Rostila, Mikko Mäntysaari, Tuija Lindquist, Riitta Haverinen, Marja-Riitta Kilponen, Björn Blom in Finland and Sweden; Bruce Thyer, Tony Tripodi, Jeane Anastas, Kevin Corcoran, Wayne Paris in the US. Above all, this book would not have been possible without the practitioners who took up the challenge to integrate the realist evaluation paradigm in their practice – the NSPCC Shield Project's past and present workers, namely, Ann Ward, Valerie Charles, Martin Walker, Karen Higgins, Lisa Wilkinson, Judith Walsh, Diane Duckworth, Baseer Mir, Tina Zawada and former managers Sue Woolmore and Gerry Hudson. I am particularly grateful to Ann Ward for her work from the practitioner's perspective (Chapter 6). For the adult rehabilitation programmes at Oakes Villa and Barton, my special thanks to Kathleen Firth, Avril Henson, Sandra Lickess, Robert Taylor and Ann Ward; for the family centres' example, my thanks to all the family centre workers and, in particular, their manager Margaret Buckley and my co-evaluator in the project, Martin Manby. For the Lifeline example, many thanks to Lucy Spurling, Maggie Rogan and Claire Goodhind, and, in particular, Dawn Lawson and Claire Fraser for their help in the template analysis. For the development of the inferential statistics used in all the examples, I am indebted to the Calderdale and Kirklees Health Authority statistician John Varlow for his help in working out how the database should be set up, and what tests would be appropriate, as well as for calculating the odds ratios and relative risk in particular. For the references from Scandinavia and the translations, my thanks to Ilmari Rostila, Björn Blom, Stefan Morén and Anna-Lena Perdal. I am also grateful to colleagues in my other realist evaluation projects which have not been used as examples in this book, but which have helped in the development of the paradigm for practice, namely, Moray Council Children's Services, Leeds Social Services' Therapeutic Team, and Kirklees Education Social Work Service, to name a few. I am also grateful to many other colleagues in the Society for Social Work and Research, the American

Evaluation Association, and the European Evaluation Society, and to those who have attended the 'Evaluation for Practice' series of conferences, for the exchanges of ideas and experiences. My thanks also to other colleagues who have participated as researchers in the various projects, Shahida Kazi, Treena May and Robert Taylor. More recently, I am indebted to Finland's STAKES (The National Research and Development Centre for Welfare and Health, Helsinki) for my appointment as a consultant, and to over a hundred social workers at social services departments in Helsinki and Korso who are now beginning to integrate realist evaluation procedures outlined in this book into their practice. I am also grateful to colleagues at Seinajoki Polytechnic in Finland for their participation in developing realist evaluation. Finally, I am grateful to Sue Frost, Dean of Human and Health Sciences at this University, for her encouragement and guidance.

Confidentiality

In all of the examples, pseudonyms, letters of the alphabet or numbers are used to protect the identity of service users. In all the evaluations, informed consent was obtained from all participants. All the agencies where these evaluations took place have been named and identified with their permission.

Preface

This book is the culmination of work dating back to 1990, when I was Education Officer (Pupil Welfare) and head of a newly-formed Performance Review Team at the Rochdale Local Education Authority near Manchester in England. Having moved to the University of Huddersfield, I was able to develop evaluation strategies with Joe Wilson at the Kirklees Education Social Work Service, Kathleen Firth at Oakes Villa Rehabilitation Unit, and Michelle Hayles at the West Yorkshire Probation Service. The extensive use of single-case evaluation led to contacts with Bruce Thyer and other colleagues from the Society for Social Work and Research (SSWR) in the USA. By 1995, the Centre for Evaluation Studies (and later also the Centre for Applied Childhood Studies with Nigel Parton) at the University of Huddersfield began a series of 'Evaluation for Practice' international conferences, and I was also influenced by the conferences of the SSWR, the European Evaluation Society (EES) and the American Evaluation Association (AEA). Having used outcome studies extensively, it became apparent that this was a foundation that needed to be built upon. How could we determine the content of the services that were found to be effective, and the contexts in which they were effective? I was influenced by Juliet Cheetham and other colleagues who were then at Stirling, and began to apply the pragmatic approaches. At the 1997 EES conference in Stockholm, I presented a paper in the same session as Ray Pawson and Nick Tilley. Their paper on realist evaluation appeared to provide some answers, but it did not become clear until they sent me their newly-published book. Having worked with social work, health, education and probation practitioners and developed the empirical practice approach of integrating research methods into practice, I began to continue with this emphasis, and began to integrate the realist effectiveness cycle where it was possible. This book presents the findings from the first several evaluations where the realist paradigm has been applied, based on my PhD thesis.

1

Introduction

This publication aims to outline and develop a framework for the application of the new, emerging realist paradigm in evaluation research in practice, and applies it to social work practice in particular and to the practice of human service programmes in general. This paradigm is reported to have the potential for an evaluation strategy that not only systematically tracks outcomes, but also the mechanisms that produce the outcomes, the contexts in which these mechanisms are triggered, and the content of the interventions (Kazi, 2000a; Pawson and Tilley, 1997b). According to realism, human service programmes introduce interventions that interact with the other causal mechanisms in the contexts of service users to produce outcomes. The purpose of realist evaluation is reportedly to investigate 'what works best, for whom, and under what circumstances' (Robson, 2002: 39). However, to date the realist paradigm largely remains at the level of a philosophy of science (Bhaskar, 1998; Sayer, 2000), and as a manifesto for evaluation research (Pawson and Tilley, 1997b; Robson, 2002). As the title suggests, this publication attempts to develop an approach for the integration of realist evaluation into the practice of human services, and the methodologies that can be used for realist evaluation. Practice examples are provided from a number of studies to substantiate the potential contribution of realist evaluation for practice.

To date, there is a dearth of published examples of realist evaluations in any area of human service practice which can demonstrate the utility of the paradigm or the processes and methodologies that can be used to actually achieve an investigation of 'what works best, for whom, and under what circumstances'. The paucity of examples is exemplified by the fact that the advocates of realism tend to use the same few examples as illustrations (e.g., Pawson and Tilley's, 1997b example of crime prevention measures which also appears in Robson, 2002 and Sayer, 2000). This publication attempts to make a contribution by providing real examples and helping to develop ways in which this philosophy of science could be translated into an evaluation paradigm for practice. In particular, this publication develops realism as a paradigm for practitioner-evaluators, with the development of a realist effectiveness cycle which can be integrated into the practice of human services in a partnership between internal evaluation (that is, what the agencies themselves do) and external evaluation (that is, evaluations carried out by academics and external consultants). In this way, the findings from evaluation can be directly utilised to influence the future development of programmes.

Evaluation for Practice

The pressures on social work practice to demonstrate effectiveness have continued to grow in the last two decades. The pressures from changes in the legal and societal context mean that social work is no longer taken for granted and that its worth has to be demonstrated (Parton, 1994). In Britain, the Children Act 1989 and the Community Care Act 1990 both included requirements for planning in response to need, and reviewing progress. The purchaser–provider split, the growth of the voluntary and private sectors alongside the public sector, and the introduction of competition for contracts also made monitoring and evaluation more central in social work practice. The current British government has continued this trend with an emphasis on 'league tables' which rank health and social services according to performance. There is a growing emphasis on evidence-based practice and clinical effectiveness (Powell, 2002). The resources are finite, and yet the social needs are complex and in a state of flux. Evaluation research is one way to make social programmes accountable and to enable politicians, agencies and practitioners to make hard choices in the allocation of scarce resources. The analysis thus far has concentrated on the question of accountability and demonstrating the merit and worth of social work. There is another dimension to this – the need to develop and improve the content of social work practice itself, so that it is better able to meet the needs of its clients and the wider society.

According to Mark, Henry and Julnes:

Evaluation assists sensemaking about policies and programmes through the conduct of systematic inquiry that describes and explains the policies' and programmes' operations, effects, justifications, and social implications. The ultimate goal of evaluation is social betterment, to which evaluation can contribute by assisting democratic institutions to better select, oversee, improve, and make sense of social programmes and policies. (2000: 9)

Robson adds: 'Evaluation is often concerned not only with assessing worth or value but also with seeking to assist in the improvement of whatever is being evaluated' (1993: 175). Therefore, there are two main purposes of evaluation research – providing evidence of the merit and worth of social work practice, and striving to improve practice itself to respond to the changing needs and contexts, for the betterment of society. Whether emphasis is placed on one or the other of these purposes may depend on the paradigmatic influences that are inherent in the effectiveness inquirer's activities. For example, from a critical theorist perspective, Shaw adds another purpose in evaluation for practice: 'Evaluating in practice is not limited to determining whether social work is effective, but must be a means of empowerment and social change' (1996: 189).

The epistemological debates in philosophy and in other sciences are also reflected in social work research, with perspectives ranging from the 'empiricist' view that effectiveness can be demonstrated through empirical evidence of effects, to the 'humanist' or interpretivist position that effectiveness can be demonstrated through the subjective perspectives and the meanings attached to such perspectives (as described in Shaw, 1996: 21).

In response to these developments in the philosophies of science, there has been a growth in research methods' textbooks and other publications addressing the need for social work to demonstrate its effectiveness (Newburn, 2001). Most of the authors have tended to be university-based, but these publications also reflect a developing partnership between academics and social work practitioners. For example, Macdonald (1996) is one of a number of publications on effectiveness from Barnardos – a children's charity and a voluntary social work agency; and Everitt and Hardiker (1996) is a British Association of Social Workers' publication. Kazi (1998a) and Fuller and Petch (1995) directly address practitioner research, and Shaw (1996) has a number of examples from practice. These and other publications are contributing to the development of effectiveness strategies that can be applied to human service practice, by both practitioners and researchers.

This book also seeks to make a modest contribution to the development of evaluation research in contemporary practice in social work, health and other human services. The book begins properly in Chapter 2 with a critical analysis of contemporary paradigmatic approaches to the evaluation of practice, including the extent to which each approach is able to 'capture' the breadth and depth of the effectiveness of practice. In the main (but not exclusively), the recent publications referred to above reflect the influences of some of the main paradigms from the philosophies of science. Each of these approaches can be credited with the contribution it has made, and continues to make, to various aspects of practice effectiveness – this can be substantiated through an analysis of the ontology, epistemology and methodologies (Guba, 1990) associated with each paradigm. At the same time, each of these paradigms also has its limitations, and this critical analysis will attempt to show the extent to which any one of these paradigms can address the complexities of practice effectiveness.

Paradigms and Influences

The term *paradigm* is used a great deal in this book, and therefore it is important to clarify what this means from the start:

> Close historical investigation of a given speciality at a given time discloses a set of recurrent and quasi-standard illustrations of various theories in their conceptual, observational, and instrumental applications. These are the community's paradigms, revealed in its textbooks, lectures, and laboratory exercises. By studying them and by practising with them, the members of the corresponding community learn their trade. (Kuhn, 1970: 43)

The recent publications in social work effectiveness research (reviewed in more depth in Chapter 2) encompass the main contemporary paradigms, as Kuhn suggests. However, like most of the terms used in this book, precision in definitions is not possible, as concepts tend to be used in different ways, and the definitions shift according to the way a term is used. Kuhn is credited with the introduction of the notion of the paradigm, but Masterman (1970) notes that he used the term in 21 different ways. In this book, the term *paradigm* is used in the sense of a 'set of beliefs about the nature of the world and the individual's place in it' (Mark, 1996: 400). In an operational sense, paradigms are characterised by the inquirer's world view, or his/her outlook with respect to the existence of reality, the theory of knowledge, and the way one conducts an inquiry. In the practice of evaluation, discrete boundaries cannot be drawn for each paradigm (Kazi, 2000a; Shaw, 1996; Trinder, 1996), as the evaluator is likely to cross many a boundary. Nevertheless, paradigmatic influences can determine the selection of evaluation questions and the selection of research methods to deal with those evaluation questions.

The Realist Evaluation Paradigm

> Realism is ... a common-sense ontology in the sense that it takes seriously the existence of the things, structures and mechanisms revealed by the sciences at different levels of reality ... the task of science is precisely to explain 'facts' in terms of more fundamental structures, and in the process it may reveal some of these 'facts' ... to be, in part, illusions ... we may not yet, and never finally, know whether it is true or false. (Outhwaite, 1987: 19–20)

The term *fallibilistic realism* was first suggested by Donald Campbell in a personal communication (Manicas and Secord, 1983); and it is also used by Anastas and MacDonald (1994) (and more recently by Anastas, 1999) who were the first to introduce this perspective in social work effectiveness research. However, if we include texts in the Finnish language (see Rostila and Kazi, 2001), then Professor Mikko Mäntysaari (University of Jyväskylä, Finland) wrote about realism in relation to social work a few years before Anastas and MacDonald. This perspective is also known by other terms, such as *scientific realism, transcendental realism, referential realism* or generally as a *realist* view of science or even as *post-positivism* (Fraser et al., 1991; Phillips, 1990). Archer (1998), Bhaskar (1998) and Robson (2002) prefer the term *critical realism*, emphasising realism's critical role in social research. In the application to evaluation for practice, this author prefers the term *realist evaluation*, which is similar to *realistic evaluation* (Pawson and Tilley, 1997b).

However, *realistic evaluation* implies a tendency whereas *realist evaluation* is a more emphatic description of this new paradigm in evaluation research.

Realist evaluation is based on the work of the philosophers Roy Bhaskar (1997, 1998) and Rom Harre (1984). Mark, Henry and Julnes (2000) and Pawson and Tilley (1997a, 1997b) have developed the realist paradigm as a legitimate evaluation research perspective in its own right. Anastas (1999), Kazi (1998a, 1999, 2000a, and 2000b) and Rostila (2000, 2001) attempt to apply this perspective in the evaluation of social work practice; and in other human services, Porter and Ryan (1996), Tolson (1999) and Wainwright (1997) apply realism in health services.

Realist evaluation seeks to evaluate practice within the realities of society. Practice takes place in an open system that consists of a constellation of interconnected structures, mechanisms and contexts. Realism aims to address all the significant variables involved in social work practice, through a realist effectiveness cycle which links the models of intervention with the circumstances in which practice takes place.

Realist evaluation research is about improving the construction of models and, therefore, about improving the content of the practice itself. Evidence from data gathering is used to target and adjust the content of the programme in such a way that it can have a generative impact on pre-existing mechanisms and contexts, and help to bring about the desired changes. Objectivity lies not just in the use of outcome measures, but in the extent to which the model is analogous with reality. At each cycle, a better approximation of reality is obtained, as compared with the previous cycle. In this way, realism addresses all the dimensions and questions of effectiveness of practice, including contexts, the perceptions of all involved, ethics and values, and the content of practice. The multi-method data gathering addresses the questions of what actually works, for whom and in what contexts. (Kazi, 2000c: 317)

Underdevelopment of Realist Evaluation Methodology

The above definition provides a summary of this author's development of the realist paradigm in the evaluation of practice in human service programmes. However, a contention of this book is that whilst realism is developed as a philosophy of science, at the level of methodology this paradigm is relatively underdeveloped at this stage. For example, at the sixth annual conference of the International Association for Critical Realism (IACR) in August 2002, one of the three main themes was 'research using realism':

What constitutes critical realist empirical research? In what ways does a critical realist perspective influence or facilitate substantive research? We are particularly interested in papers providing answers to these and other questions in the best possible way – by reporting the results of substantive research undertaken from a realist perspective. (p. 1, http://www.criticalrealism. demon.co.uk/iacr/conference_2002.html)

The fact that this is still a major theme suggests that these issues are far from being resolved at the level of realist research designs generally, and the same is true for evaluation research. There are no complete published realist evaluations of human services; and to date, no account of dedicated methodologies that can be applied to investigate what works, for whom and in what circumstances. For example, Pawson and Tilley (1997b) outline the rules and framework for a realist evaluation, but they fall short of specifying the methodologies for investigating what they call mechanism–context–outcome configurations. Robson (2000) has a helpful section on mechanisms and how they influence programme design and evaluations, but again does not explicitly state the methodologies that may be appropriate for a realist evaluation. Robson (2002) does suggest that inferential statistics may be used, as well as qualitative methods as specified by Miles and Huberman (1994); however, no complete examples of realist evaluation are provided.

As Tolson explains, realist evaluation

> is an applied form of research which lends itself to the process of practice innovation through its contextual sensitivity. Accordingly it is complex and its methodological rules are still emerging. The apparent complexity will undoubtedly ease as this type of evaluation research matures and its practice is documented. (1999: 389)

Realism is methodological-pluralist, but the methods it can draw upon were developed either within the empirical or interpretivist paradigms that may not have the same ontological depth as realism. These issues are considered in Chapter 3, and then the rest of this publication provides examples of the application of realism in the evaluation of human services – with the aim of easing the complexity of realist evaluation, as indicated by Tolson.

Issues of Implementation and this Book's Contribution

Realism transcends the qualitative and quantitative divide, or the epistemological divide between empirical and interpretivist approaches (Mark, Henry and Julnes, 2000; Pawson and Tilley, 1997b). Nevertheless, realists continue to be influenced by these debates and express a preference for either of these approaches, at the methodological level, even within the stated methodological-pluralist approach in realism. For example, Sayer (2000) advocates intensive research (which he defines in qualitative terms), as the only way of achieving an explanatory critical realist inquiry. On the other hand, Lawson (1998) emphasises the need to investigate demi-regularities, and thereby advocates extensive research, with an emphasis on empirical methods. These preferences are within the paradigm of realism, as it is expected that the selection of evaluation questions, and how the research is conducted, depend upon the theoretical and methodological preferences of the inquirer. However, the preferences expressed by these two authors are of crucial importance at this stage when realism is still an emerging evaluation research perspective, and when there is a need to develop this paradigm further in its actual application to the evaluation of human services. Realism is relatively underdeveloped at the level of methodology at this stage; and therefore, the question remains – can you go further from 'what works' to 'what works, for whom and in what contexts'? These questions are addressed in the subsequent chapters of this book, with real examples of realist evaluation to contribute to the development of appropriate methodologies and to help ease the apparent complexities of realist evaluation.

Chapter 2 attempts to categorise the main evaluation research perspectives, and the contribution to practice evaluation made by each perspective. The empirical practice approach with a focus on outcomes provides a foundation for evaluation, and the other perspectives (that is, interpretivist and pragmatist) add building blocks to the process of evaluation. However, these approaches remain at either the 'black box' (outcomes only) or 'grey box' (outcomes with some components of process) levels. The 'white' (or preferably, 'clear') box evaluations are the potential contribution of the realist evaluation perspective.

Chapter 3 outlines some key concepts from the realist perspective that are relevant for the practice of evaluation. The outcomes of a programme can be understood in relation to the causal mechanisms that produce them, and the contexts in which they are triggered. Investigations of these mechanism–context–outcome configurations enable an account of the circumstances in which a programme may be more successful, and the circumstances in which it may be less successful. A framework for practice, or 'realist effectiveness cycle' is proposed that enables an integration of realist evaluation procedures into a programme's practice, and establishes a direct link between practice and evaluation in order to improve practice. The chapter provides an example from adult rehabilitation services where this cycle was beginning to be integrated, with the use of outcome measures in daily practice. When analysed with the other patient information in the agency's records, the 'black box' began to turn 'greyer', indicating the utility of realist perspective in encouraging a search for explanations beyond appearances.

Chapter 4 provides an example of the use of qualitative methods in realist evaluation. Five sets of repeated interviews from a project with the drug-using community are used to demonstrate the identification of mechanisms, contexts, content, and outcomes from the service users' perspectives. Template analysis was used to identify the patterns that emerged from the data. As an example of a 'grey box' study, a limitation was that outcomes were not systematically tracked, and therefore this example also remained at the beginning stages of the realist effectiveness cycle. The example also demonstrates that the use of a single method (whether quantitative or qualitative) may enable the identification of mechanism–context–outcome patterns, but tends to fall short of establishing the causal factors that may be responsible for change.

Chapter 5 demonstrates the use of quantitative methods within a realist perspective. Single-case evaluation was used with 155 service users in the family centres at Kirklees Metropolitan Council in Yorkshire, England. This intensive research with each case paved the way for one-group pre-test post-test designs across several outcome measures. In addition, the type of intervention, problems at referral, and contextual factors were also systematically recorded alongside the use of standardised measures, and this enabled the use of statistical analysis to identify some potential patterns in the data linking the outcomes to the circumstances of the service users and the type of service provided. Drawing upon the example of Duguid and Pawson (1998), a fairly extensive analysis was undertaken to identify these patterns, turning the 'black box' study 'greyer'. However, although the outcomes were systematically tracked, and it was possible to determine the outcome patterns associated with particular service-user circumstances, the causal mechanisms were not clearly identified at this stage. Again, the use of a single method has its limitations, and although this study has gone further in integrating the realist effectiveness cycle, the analysis falls short of turning the study into a 'clear box' type of evaluation.

The next three chapters 6–8 demonstrate prospective realist evaluation in practice, based on an evaluation of the NSPCC's Shield Project that provides services for young people who sexually harm others. The realist effectiveness cycle as described in Chapter 3 has been integrated into practice, and the findings from the first two years of this evaluation are used to demonstrate the utility of realist evaluation. There are no published reports of an evaluation where Pawson and Tilley's rules are implemented, and therefore this study may be one of the first of this kind. Chapter 6 describes the project and the way procedures have been applied to systematically track outcomes, mechanisms and contexts. Two case examples are used to demonstrate how intensive research is undertaken with each case, using both quantitative and qualitative approaches.

In Chapter 7, the data across the cases are analysed using both qualitative and quantitative methods. Some common mechanisms and contexts are identified from a literature review, from the qualitative data available, and from the perspective of the Shield workers. These mechanisms are systematically tracked both in terms of whether they are enabling or disabling in relation to the desired outcomes, and in terms of whether they are changing in a positive or a negative direction. The outcomes include standardised measures as well as process outcomes. The database may be used to identify patterns in relation to the mechanism–context–outcome configurations, as presented in Chapter 8. Inferential statistics are used to investigate what works, for whom and in what circumstances. First, bivariate tests are used to identify the intervention components and the mechanisms that may be associated with the outcomes. Second, a number of binary logistic regressions models are tested to identify the effects of the potential causal mechanisms, taken together along with the contexts in which they may be triggered.

The concluding Chapter 9 analyses some key features of realist evaluation for practice, and some limitations. A framework for realist evaluation in practice is proposed, and the potential contribution of realism for the practice of evaluation is presented. One reason why practice of realist evaluation is still limited following Pawson and Tilley's manifesto may be that the realist authors are too preoccupied with problems of the philosophies of science, and there is less emphasis on developing methodologies for practice. A contribution of this book is an attempt to change this emphasis, and to demonstrate the potential utility of realism as a perspective in the use of existing research methodologies that can be called upon to address the problems of realist evaluation.

2

Contemporary Perspectives
in Practice Evaluation

The pressures on human service programmes to demonstrate their effectiveness have continued to grow in the last two decades in Britain and there has been a growth in evaluation publications, particularly in the 1990s (Shaw, 1996). This chapter presents a brief critical analysis of each of the main contemporary evaluation research paradigms, including the contributions and limitations of each perspective in the evaluation of practice.

Social work interventions usually take place at the interface of the individual and social, where multiple factors and influences are continuously at work (Cheetham et al., 1992; Morén, 1994a, 1994b). This is also true of society in general and for other human services (for example, in health and in education) which work in the society, which is essentially an open system. For example, Outhwaite (1998: 289) refers to the 'general messiness and fluidity' of social structures. The complexities of practice for the human services are such that there are several dimensions in a continuous state of flux; for example, the content of interventions, the value base of practitioners, the outcomes of practice, the perspectives of all the different people involved, and the contexts of practice (Kazi, 1998a). The dimensions of practice that are targeted by the researcher, and the extent to which the complexities are addressed, may depend upon (a) the paradigmatic perspective of the researcher, and (b) the extent to which the particular perspective enables the researcher to address these complexities. As indicated in the previous chapter, the paradigmatic preferences of the inquirer may influence the selection of evaluation questions and the selection of research methods to deal with those evaluation questions.

Classification of Evaluation Research Paradigms

Guba (1990) provides a useful classification of the main research paradigms based on the epistemological, ontological and methodological frameworks. This classification is also used by Shaw (1999) to categorize the main research paradigms as (a) positivism, (b) post-positivism, (c) critical evaluation and (d) constructivist evaluation. However, any attempt to categorize the contemporary evaluation research perspectives is likely to be contentious. First, there is considerable overlap between the perspectives and therefore the boundaries that exist can only be indicative; and, second, the way these perspectives are classified will itself depend upon the perspective of the reviewer.

For example, Trinder (1996) identifies three main perspectives within British social work:

1 empirical practice and experiments (for example, Macdonald, 1996);
2 pragmatism and partnership (for example, Fuller, 1996; Fuller and Petch, 1995); and
3 politics and participation (for example, Everitt and Hardiker, 1996; Shaw, 1996).

This helpful classification is based on the manifestations in practice of the main research paradigms, but there are problems with the boundaries drawn here. 'Partnership' is a growing trend within empirical practice as well as within the perspective classified as 'politics and participation'; and, similarly, participation is also inherent in, say, the practitioner–researcher approach to empirical practice (Reid and Zettergren, 1999). If participatory evaluation is seen as a means of giving silent people a voice (Dullea and Mullender, 1999), then there are similarities here with both the consciousness-raising in critical evaluation and the worker–user collaborative evaluation in empirical practice (Kazi, 1998a).

Bearing in mind these limitations, this review classifies the main contemporary perspectives that influence the evaluation of practice research in Britain and the Nordic countries in Europe (American authors writing in British publications are also included) at the present time, as follows:

1 empirical practice (e.g. Bloom, 1999; Dillenburger, 1998; Hansson, 2001; Hansson, Cederblad and Höök, 2000; Kauppila, 2001; Kazi, 1998a; Kazi and Wilson, 1996; Kazi, Mäntysaari and Rostila, 1997; Macdonald, 1994, 1996; Saarnio et al., 1998; Sheldon, 1988; Thyer, 1998);
2 pragmatism or methodological pluralism (e.g. Blom, 1996, 2001; Cheetham, 1998; Cheetham et al., 1992; Fuller, 1996; Fuller and Petch, 1995; Kazi, 1997a; Lindqvist, 1996; Mäntysaari 1999; Markström, 1998; Sundman, 1993);
3 interpretivist approaches including critical theory and other participatory approaches (e.g., as in Carlsson, 1995; Dufåker, 2000; Everitt, 1996; Everitt and Hardiker, 1996; Forsberg, 2000; Shaw, 1996, 1998); feminist evaluation (Humphries, 1999); and social constructionism (Hall, 1997; Parton and O'Byrne, 2000; White, 1998);
4 post-positivist approaches such as scientific realism (Kazi, 1998a; Kazi and Mäntysaari, 2002; Pawson and Tilley, 1997a, 1997b; Rostila and Kazi, 2001).

The classification used here is not presented as a definitive position, but as an attempt to promote further discussions in this regard. It is based on (a) a review of British and Nordic publications mainly from 1995 to date, and (b) the dimensions of practice that are addressed by each perspective. For example, there appears to be no overt constructivism that does not recognise an external reality (as described by Guba, 1990) in the major British publications in this period. There are other prominent perspectives evident in American literature; however, this review is based on British and Nordic publications and the American authors who may be quoted here are those who are included in British publications (for example, Bloom, Reid, Thyer). As in Trinder (1996), the third category of interpretivist approaches is a mixed bag, encompassing several epistemologies. These positions locate themselves in dimensions of practice other than outcome-oriented positions (for example, White, 1998, emphasises the meanings that social workers use to understand their world), and therefore have similarities in their criticism of the limitations of outcome-oriented approaches and in the ways they deal with these. There are also other perspectives not included in this author's classification, such as Schön's work on reflexive inquiry (described in Shaw, 1996). Schön's reflective work, and the position of participatory evaluation, are not necessarily evaluation research perspectives in themselves, as reflection and participatory evaluation may be seen to permeate the other perspectives, for example, empirical practice (Kazi, 1998a; Reid and Zettergren, 1999).

Whatever classification is applied, the contemporary paradigms in social work research are a reflection of the developments and debates in the philosophies of social science. The basis for these controversies lies in the demise of foundationism (that is, the certainty of knowledge obtained from the senses) on which the earlier versions of positivism were based. Karl Popper, Kuhn, and others challenged the view that knowledge could be based on 'facts' as absolute truths (Popper, 1979). Scientific knowledge could not achieve absolute certainty in terms of facts, since observation was both theory-laden and value-laden; and, at best, scientific knowledge was probabilistic knowledge – what is known today is an approximation of truth – and such approximations change and develop as progress is made.

There is no certain way to compare a theory to theory-neutral reality and, therefore, the problem of science or knowledge cannot finally be resolved (Manicas, 1987: 263–4). The world cannot be known as it is, because it is mediated by socially- and historically-constituted practices. Therefore, the choice between competing theories (for example, theories of social support) depends upon a mixture of objective and subjective factors of shared and individual criteria in those making the selections. In other words, no research process can be perfect – there are always limitations – and the findings from research can be true only until further notice. Moreover, a degree of cognitive bias is present in all applications of research methods.

A number of anti-positivist paradigms have emerged from this realisation, holding different ontological and epistemological positions, and these are also reflected in the contemporary publications in British and Nordic social work research. If the philosophy of science holds that truth and certainty are not attainable, then, at the level of ontology (that is, theories about the nature of being), one has to make choices; either one takes the position that there is a reality out there in the world, and that one can use the reflection of this reality as a standard to strive for (no matter how imperfect); or one can take this lack of certainty to its ultimate conclusion, that there is no reality which can be used as a standard, and that there are therefore many truths which are all equally true even if they are contradictory. The first position is known as realism; the second is that of a particular trend in constructivism which holds that realities exist in the form of multiple mental constructs and that there is no reality external to these constructs (Guba, 1990: 27). In Britain, such non-realist perspectives tend to be under-represented in practice research. Unfortunately, the present author was unable to locate an explicit 'non-realist' position in the literature reviewed, and is therefore unable to explore this position in the detail it deserves.

Empirical practice approaches deal with limitations in the apprehension of reality by the application of reliability and validity tests; interpretivist approaches focus on perspectives and meanings of reality through language and narratives; while scientific realism offers a cyclical evaluation that attempts to link knowledge with reality. These various approaches to reality are all represented in contemporary British and Nordic social work evaluation literature. As for which perspective is dominant in practice, Trinder (1996) notes that most Department of Health-funded research in Britain is in fact pragmatist, based on non-experimental quantitative methodologies including surveys, a view also confirmed by American reviews of the products of social work research (see Fraser et al., 1991). More recently, Powell (2002) indicates that most social work research in Britain continues to be located within the pragmatic approach.

Empirical Practice Movement

Reid and Zettergren describe the main features of the empirical practice approach as:

(1) stress on case monitoring and evaluation through single-system designs and more broadly the application of scientific perspectives and methods in practice; (2) application, to the extent possible, of interventions whose efficacy has been demonstrated through research; and (3) the development of new knowledge by practitioner–researchers using single-system designs. (1999: 41)

Empirical practice tends to be associated with positivism; however, it is not possible to describe positivism in the sense of a single paradigm or a single description that captures the essence of positivism. Outhwaite (1987: 6–7) notes at least twelve varieties of positivism, and therefore any single description of positivism as a paradigm will not be able to do full justice to all these variants. In social work circles, positivism is identified with methodology rather than regarded as a perspective; and those who promote, say, randomised controlled trials or single-case designs, or those who want to apply outcome measures to effectiveness in order to provide evidence for testing interventions, tend to be associated with a single entity called positivism – which is itself a victim of incorrect assumptions.

An example from the contemporary British literature is Humphries' assertion that a 'principle of conventional research is neutrality towards the objects of research – a position of being value free' (1999: 121), implying that all proponents of empirical practice in social work assume that observation is theory-free. Within the epistemological debate, an assumption is made that empirical practice in social work is associated with foundationist positivism which believes in the certainty of objective knowledge as true reflections of reality, or in the certainty of causal links between phenomena (for example, White's, 1998 reference to naive realism). In fact, this author has not found any publication within the empirical practice movement in social work (either in Britain or the USA) that advocates a foundationist approach. Reid and Zettergren (1999) refer to the neutrality of single-case designs in the sense that they can be used within any kind of theoretical model; suggesting, in other words, that this methodology can be used by a practitioner with any theoretical orientation. This is usually interpreted to mean that empirical practice advocates that something could be theory-free or completely objective. However, there appears to be no explicit trend within the empirical practice movement that argues for a foundationist position, i.e., that external reality can be apprehended in a theory-neutral sense.

If we define empirical practice in terms of an emphasis on evidence-based outcomes, then, in British and Nordic social work practice research, there appear to be two main movements associated with the empirical practice perspective. First, there is the promotion of single-case evaluation procedures that could be used by practitioners to ascertain the effects of their practice through the measurement of user outcomes (Bloom, 1999; Dillenburger, 1998; Kazi and Wilson, 1996; Kazi, Mäntysaari and Rostila, 1997; Sheldon, 1988). This author's work to promote the use of single-case evaluation by practitioners in a variety of settings has been reported elsewhere (Kazi, 1996; 1997a; 1998a). Second, there is the promotion of randomised controlled trials (RCTs) which seek to establish causal links between the programmes and their effects with greater confidence. Examples of this trend are the recent publications of Barnardo's, the biggest children's charity in Britain (Macdonald, 1996; Oakley, 1996).

The Contribution of Empirical Practice

In the 1970s and 1980s, most effectiveness strategies were dominated by empirical practice or outcome-oriented approaches. That is because (a) the empirical practice perspective was the first to recognise the need for providing evidence of effectiveness and to develop effectiveness strategies (for example, by drawing a distinction between an intervention and its effects); and (b) its focus on outcomes lends itself to an emphasis on effectiveness in the (albeit narrow) sense of social work practice causing a desired effect, and to an attempt to test the intervention's effects. In the early stages, the epistemological debate within research circles centred around whether it was possible or even desirable to address effectiveness questions, given the complexities of social work (Jordan, 1978; Sheldon, 1978); latterly (although the earlier questions are by no means resolved), this debate has moved on to how effectiveness questions can be addressed, to the extent that researchers critical of empirical practice are attempting to develop alternative effectiveness strategies which are largely accepted as equally rigorous (Everitt and Hardiker, 1996; Shaw, 1996).

Limitations of Empirical Practice

A major limitation of empirical practice is its tendency to concentrate on effects, to a virtual exclusion of consideration of the content of the intervention that is tested, as suggested by the philosopher Medawar: 'The weakness of the hypothetico-deductive system, insofar as it might profess to offer a complete account of the scientific process, lies in its disclaiming any power to explain how hypotheses come into being' (1982: 135).

Even if randomised controlled trials are used, this central limitation remains. Oakley (1996) provides examples of RCTs which, whilst providing a robust examination of the effects of a social programme, also fail to address the content of the programme itself. For instance, RCTs were used to test the effectiveness of social support for pregnant women. Oakley provides an extensive analysis of the types of outcomes and the characteristics of the random groups, but little information about the nature of the social support programme itself, nor any evidence of a dynamic approach to the development of the social support. This limitation is not just a question of methodology that needs to be addressed in future applications. Whilst some improvements could be made, the central issue is one of paradigm, the ontology and epistemology of the inquirer using the methodologies.

This limitation of virtually ignoring content is at the heart of the positivist influences in the empirical practice paradigm. In the North American literature, various approaches have been proposed by empirical researchers to deal with this limitation, for example, change process research, and intervention design and development as described by Fortune and Reid (1999), but there is no comparable development in the contemporary British and

Nordic practice evaluation literature, although the trends towards pragmatism and/or realism described below do attempt to deal with this particular limitation. A further shortcoming of empirical practice is that contexts of practice are also virtually ignored. Concentrating on the outcomes at the surface level, empirical practice approaches are limited in addressing the full complexities of social work practice.

In summary, empirical practice emphasises evaluation activities based on outcomes and concentrates almost exclusively on the effects of practice as defined in terms of measurable outcomes. Future successes cannot be guaranteed not only because of the inadequate descriptions of content which make replication difficult, but also because typically there is no analysis of contexts which are inherently unpredictable.

Pragmatism or Methodological Pluralism

Central to the pragmatist position is the desire to 'get on with the job' of effectiveness research. Fuller's (1996) position, for example, is to place the needs of practice first, thereby considering the epistemological debates to be a waste of time since the issues debated around the comparison of theory with theory-neutral reality cannot be resolved. Such a stance has led to a charge that pragmatism is essentially an anti-intellectual trend in social work research, and that it is an 'unashamedly empirical approach to research, steering a course between the scientific empiricism of the positivist project and the messier politicised approach to research of participative/critical researchers' (Trinder, 1996). It has also been attacked as 'anything goes' (Macdonald, 1996). In fact, the advent of the pragmatic approach to mixing methods is a consequence of the epistemological debate, in the sense that this debate has helped (a) to recognise the limitations of the methods associated with each paradigm, and (b) to enable the realisation that qualitative methods are acceptable and can be combined with quantitative methods to present a more comprehensive approximation of reality.

At first sight, this pragmatic position appears to be similar to the 'many ways of knowing' position of American authors such as Hartman (1990) which implies that both realism and relativism can be accepted as potentially true approaches. Fuller's pragmatism, on the other hand, does draw a line. Fuller, for example, accepts that there is a 'real world' (1996: 58). Furthermore, the methods used at the Social Work Research Centre at the University of Stirling in Scotland are largely non-experimental quantitative methodologies, together with some qualitative approaches such as case studies, hence reflecting a basis in neo-positivist methodologies, but practised within what appears to be a realist ontology which recognises both the complexities of social work and the limitations of positivism in addressing these complexities. In this sense, the methodological pluralism expressed in Fuller (1996) does not imply philosophical pluralism. Ontologically, pragmatists tend to draw the line at relativism, and therefore, at least at the level of ontology, it is not 'anything goes'.

Cheetham et al. (1992: 20) describe this pragmatic approach as 'eclectic, not wedded to a single alliance', and explain that, because of the 'diversity, occasional elusiveness and the generally shifting sands of social policy in action', adherence to a single approach 'would risk leaving much social work activity unresearchable'. Feasibility is an important factor in the selection of methods; one should begin with the evaluation questions and then select a method (or a combination of methods) which can be applied appropriately to address them. Typical methods are secondary analyses (the study of records), monitoring devices (some measures), questionnaires, interviews, scales and schedules, observation, and diaries with a largely quantitative base, but with some efforts at gaining qualitative insights (Fuller and Petch, 1995). The mixing of methods in effectiveness studies as reported in Kazi (1997a; 1997b; 1998a; 1998b) where single-case evaluation was combined with other methods in the evaluation of social work programmes, was influenced by the pragmatic approach advocated by colleagues in Stirling. The data obtained through the use of both empirical and naturalistic approaches enabled the author to draw more informed inferences regarding effectiveness.

Advantages and Limitations of Pragmatism

Through a methodological-pluralist stance, the pragmatist takes on board the advantages of empirical practice and attempts to compensate for its limitations through triangulation. The definition of effectiveness is still understood in the empirical practice sense of drawing a distinction between the intervention and its effects, and these effects are empirically tested with the use of both quantitative and qualitative methodologies. At the same time, the content is analysed with greater insight. In this way, pragmatism can dig deeper into the complexities of practice; more objective outcome data are combined with a wider range of subjective perspectives of all the parties concerned, and the context is also taken into account to some extent if desired. Therefore, the pragmatic approach of realist methodological pluralism can establish connections between the outcomes and the processes of practice, including issues of ethics and values as well as the wider perceptions of all the parties involved. In addition, it digs into the context a little deeper than the empirical practice approach, but only if the pragmatist feels that it is desirable or necessary to do so.

A limitation of methodological pragmatism is that it may concentrate on the needs of stakeholders or the needs of practice, and therefore fail to capture the effectiveness of a programme in a more comprehensive way. This is particularly so if the inquirer tends to become essentially methodologically-driven or considers feasibility to be the main criteria. In terms of its explanatory powers, methodological pragmatism may concentrate on the expressed needs of the participants in negotiating questions of inquiry, and may fail to capture the main features of the mechanisms that influence the effectiveness of programmes in an open system. These pitfalls will ensure that, although the explanation of reality may be improved when compared with empirical practice, the effectiveness of practice will be apprehended at best only partially.

In summary, the pragmatic, methodological-pluralist approach recognises the limitations of both empirical practice and interpretivist approaches, and attempts to provide a perspective that goes beyond the consideration of either outcomes or interpretivist insights. However, the pragmatic focus means that concentration is on what is seen to be desirable and appropriate at any time.

Interpretivist Approaches

In contemporary practice evaluation literature, the main interpretivist approaches include critical theory, social constructionism and feminist evaluation.

The critical theorist paradigm of research is described by Everitt and Hardiker (1996) and by Shaw (1996). It is politically-oriented inquiry that includes movements aimed at the emancipation of oppressed people, including feminist, neo-Marxist and other forms of participatory inquiry. 'Evaluating in practice ... is not about reflective rigour in empowering but concerns a practice which is legitimated only through the test of whether it empowers and emancipates ... Effectiveness is truth' (Shaw, 1996: 110). The task of the inquiry is to raise people (mainly service users, and to some extent also practitioners – but, it is implied, not managers) from the various forms of false consciousness they have due to their oppressions, to a level of true consciousness which helps to emancipate oppressed people and enables them to transform their situation. Therefore, the ontology is by definition critical realist ('true' consciousness), coupled with a subjectivist epistemology which relates the inquiry's activities to the values of the inquirer (Guba, 1990).

Social constructionism is distinct from Guba's (1990) contructivism in that it does retain a 'subtle' realism (Hall, 1997; Parton and O'Byrne, 2000; White, 1997, 1998), and hence accepts that there is an external reality. Parton and O'Byrne describe the social constructionist perspective as similar to the construction of a building, but the construction of social reality takes place through language and narratives. White's (1998) research found that the social workers' constructs had important implications for their practice with children and their families. Feminist evaluation is a kind of critical research that emphasises women's experiences, conscious partiality, the view from below, change of the status quo, and conscientisation (Humphries, 1999).

Interpretivist researchers can utilise several epistemologies; for example, Shaw (1999: 23) describes his position as a 'combination of a strong version of the fallible realism of post-positivism, the constructed character of reality, and the central role of political and personal interests'. Shaw (1996: 115–6, 1998: 207–9) combines critical theory with Schön's reflexive approach and Popperian falsifiablity as well as other influences.

Typically, the interpretivist evaluators apply a dialogic approach that helps participants achieve greater self-knowledge and self-reflection. Understanding comes by change and change comes by understanding. The methodologies may include both empirical analyses and historical hermeneutics, but hard data are not considered to be any better than soft data. The interpretivists' preference is for qualitative approaches that enable the inquirer to dig deeper into the underlying values, meanings and interpretations of the participants (Popkewitz, 1990). The process of scientific enquiry is not technical or procedural, but is embedded in values, ethics, morality and politics.

Contributions and Limitations of Interpretivist Approaches

Interpretivist approaches go further than empirical practice in addressing the content of practice, the ethics and values, the multiple perspectives, and to some extent the contexts as well. Critical theorist, social constructionist and feminist researchers not only have the advantages of a realist methodological-pragmatic approach, but also provide an additional emphasis on the perceptions of users and practitioners. They emphasise ethics, values and moral issues, and attempt to make such issues part of the process and outcome of practice. When combined with methodological pragmatism, critical theory can add a richer dimension to effectiveness research, as this author found in an evaluation of a mental health advocacy service. Standardised outcome measures were combined with semi-structured surveys and focus groups based on a critical theorist standpoint, providing a richer account of the process of advocacy, its effects, and the perceptions of the participants; at the same time, the process of research itself contributed to develop the consciousness of the mental health service users.

A limitation of interpretivist approaches is that they tend to concentrate on the needs of stakeholders and their perceptions, and therefore may fail to capture the effectiveness of a programme in a more comprehensive way. There is a tendency to be suspicious of attempts to measure effects of services; this in part explains Shaw's (1998) heavily critical stance towards single-case evaluation, even where this methodology is no more than a systematic tracking of client outcomes. This tendency to exclude the consideration of outcomes means that interpretivist researchers may not capture the main dimensions of practice as described earlier. They may concentrate on processes and in-depth perceptions of people with regard to human service programmes but without an investigation of the outcomes achieved by the programme. More recently, a pragmatist turn in critical and participatory dialogic enquiry has been advocated, 'alongside a more creative use of conventional research skills' (Powell, 2002: 30).

In summary, interpretivist approaches developed largely in opposition to empirical practice, in the form of several epistemologies such as critical theory, feminist evaluation and social constructionism (e.g., Carlsson, 1995; Dufåker, 2000; Forsberg, 2000; Parton and O'Byrne, 2000; Taylor and White, 2000). However, these perspectives tend to be suspicious of outcome-based methodologies, and therefore their focus may be one-sided in capturing the main dimensions of practice.

The Three 'Boxes' of Evaluation and Realist Evaluation

Each of the above three perspectives has its limitations, based on emphasis on one or the other element of the complexities of practice; at the same time, each has an important role to play in addressing these complexities, and each sets out to achieve this goal in its own way. Another way of categorising the evaluation strategies is to consider the three 'boxes' of evaluation. Adapting Michael Scriven's terminology of 'black box', 'grey box' and 'white box' evaluations (Scriven, 1994), 'black box' evaluation is where the researcher concentrates on evaluating a programme's effects, without addressing the components that make up the programme. Such research is crucially important, and stands in its own right; this is the role of much empirical practice research. 'Grey box' evaluation is where the components of a programme are discerned, but their inner workings or principles of operation are not fully revealed; this is the contribution of much pragmatist and interpretivist research.

As indicated in the previous chapter, another post-positivist perspective is emerging in social research, that of realist evaluation (Pawson and Tilley, 1997a, 1997b). Realism attempts Scriven's 'white box' (he probably meant 'clear box') evaluation, which not only addresses the effects, but also the inner workings and operations of the components of a programme and how they are connected. This new, emerging paradigm appears to have the answers for dealing with the apparent limitations of these other contemporary perspectives, but as yet there is no report of a completed study in social work or health where this perspective has been applied. The studies described in this book make a contribution in this regard, and there are some other examples of turning the 'black' box 'greyer' in British, North American and Nordic literature (for the latter, see Kazi et al., 2002a).

For example, Duguid and Pawson (1998) also refer to the three boxes, when they describe their efforts to make the 'black' box 'greyer'. Kazi (2000a) also presents an account of the Centre for Evaluation Studies' activities as classified into the three boxes. When the purposes of evaluation are categorised within these three types of approaches, or 'boxes', it is apparent from Scriven (1994) that that empirical practice which concentrates on the evaluation of effects or outcomes forms the basis in each type of box. Other methods are added to address the wider questions, but it is assumed that empirical practice, as in the form of the 'black box', remains. In this sense, the other perspectives add building blocks to the process of evaluation. Apart from the proviso that a study of outcomes forms the basis for evaluation that may be contentious for some in the interpretivist school of thought, Scriven's three boxes are helpful in categorising what each perspective contributes to the needs of practice evaluation. The 'three boxes' approach also implies a preference for an inclusive approach where one perspective does not have to destroy another in order to create a niche for itself within the boxes (Kazi, 2000a; White and Stancombe, 2002). A further implication is the challenge to develop a 'white box' or 'clear box' evaluation that suggests a fairly comprehensive evaluation for practice. The next chapter addresses these issues in more depth, outlining the principles of realist evaluation, and the chapters that follow may indicate the path towards a 'clear box' evaluation for practice.

3

The Realist Evaluation
Paradigm for Practice

The previous chapter classified the main contemporary perspectives in terms of what each paradigm can contribute for practice evaluation. This chapter outlines some key principles from the emerging realist paradigm in evaluation research, and indicates how they may influence the practice of evaluation. Although as yet there are no research methods dedicated to the practice of realist evaluation, these principles may affect the purposes of evaluation, the selection of the methods available, and the way they are applied. For example, according to the principles of realist evaluation, human service programmes introduce interventions that interact with the other causal mechanisms in the contexts of service users to produce outcomes. Even in circumstances where the relevant mechanisms affecting the programme outcomes are not yet identified, the realist inquirer may strive to analyse the available data in the search for explanations, and to pave the way for the identification of the relevant mechanisms in the future. A practice example from adult rehabilitation is included later in this chapter, as a forerunner for the foregoing chapters that concentrate on the methodology that may be required in the quest for a 'clear box' evaluation. We now turn to some key principles of realist evaluation.

Ontological Depth: Beyond Appearances

Klee defines an ontological issue as 'one involving the very being of things, their existence, their possibility, necessity, or contingency and so on' (1997: 247). According to Klee, in relation to these ontological issues, a realist 'is anyone who holds that there are objective facts of the matter independent of the conceptual frameworks' (1997: 248), or in other words, that objective reality exists outside of the mind, and that it can be approximated. Therefore, at the level of ontology, the realist perspective is inclusive of all three perspectives described in the previous chapter (empirical practice, interpretivist and pragmatic approaches), with the exception of some interpretivist approaches that do not accept this realist view of being.

However, realism goes further than the other paradigms in recognising that the world is an open system or a constellation of structures, mechanisms and contexts. Realism distinguishes between the *real*, the *actual* and the *empirical* (Sayer, 2000). The *real* exists regardless of our understanding of it, and constitutes the realm of objects, their structures and powers. The *actual* refers to what happens if and when these powers are activated. The *empirical* is the domain of experience that can refer to either the real or the actual. In other words, some real structures may not be observable, but they can be inferred by reference to the observable through empirical inquiry. However, human observation is theory-laden (Manicas, 1987), and what is empirical depends upon our knowledge and perspectives; but what is concrete does not – the crucial difference is between the *appearance* and the *essence*. Reality does not consist simply of experiences and actual events; rather, it is constituted by structures, powers, mechanisms and tendencies that underpin, generate or facilitate the actual events that may or may not be experienced. Therefore, the realist evaluator may not be satisfied with appearances, such as the achievement of a programme outcome with the majority of service users, but seek to investigate the essence – for example, an explanation of why the programme was successful with the majority, but not with the minority, and to identify the potential causal mechanisms that produced the outcomes. The realist evaluator would not be satisfied with the findings of an evaluation at any point in time, but seek to develop new explanations and new discoveries, in order to develop an understanding beyond the appearances.

Inherent in realism's stratified reality is the concept of *embeddedness*. Realism refers to the embeddedness of all human action within a wider range of social processes as the 'stratified nature of social reality. Even the most mundane actions make sense only because they contain in-built assumptions about a wider set of social rules and institutions' (Pawson and Tilley, 1997a: 406). The activities of persons in society may be seen as a set of interacting, interwoven structures at different levels. Causal powers do not reside in the events or the behaviours of particular objects, variables or individuals, but in the social relations and organisational structures which constitute the open system. One action leads to another because of the actions' accepted place in the whole (here, realists tend to use the example of the signing of a cheque which is accepted for payment because of its place in the banking system – as in Pawson and Tilley, 1997b; Robson, 2002). Persons are complex particulars and the events of interest – for example, programme outcomes associated with human services – are the result of complex transactions of many different kinds of structures at many different levels. Establishing the existence and properties of these things, and the construction of confirmable explanatory theories about structure and their properties, are the products of both theoretical and experimental work, that is, they are the products of realist evaluation research.

Realism's stratified ontology also includes the concept of *emergence* – that is, that the stratification of structures in the open system continually gives rise to new and emerging phenomena. Emergence is inherent in the concept of *structures*, which is defined as 'a set of internally related elements whose causal powers, when combined, are emergent from those of their constituents' (Sayer, 2000: 14). Therefore, human service programmes and their effectiveness can best be understood in relation to the structures and elements that exist, and in relation to how the interventions of services interact with other elements within this stratified reality. The concept of emergence implies that situations in which programmes operate are continuously changing, and therefore the programmes have to respond to these changes. What works in one time–space location may not work in another time–space location as the circumstances change: '… one of the defining features of society is its morphogenetic nature, its capacity to change its shape or form' (Archer, 1998: 195). Evaluation research in the real world takes place in a fluid context, that is, in an open system which is mutable, messy and fluid (Outhwaite, 1998). Therefore, realist evaluators may not be satisfied with a description of the programme outcomes achieved, but aim to identify how a programme's interventions interact with the existing circumstances to produce the outcomes, and how the patterns of interrelationships may be transformed or change over time.

Retroduction or Investigation of Causal Mechanisms

The identification and investigation of the potential causal mechanisms that influence a programme's desired outcomes are a crucial part of realist evaluation. 'The aim is not to cover a phenomenon under a generalisation (this metal expands when heated because all metals do) but to identify a factor responsible for it, that helped produce, or at least facilitated, it' (Lawson, 1998: 156). In the realist world view, social work or human service programme outcomes cannot be explained in isolation; rather, they can only be explained in the sense of a mechanism that is introduced to effect change in a constellation of other mechanisms and structures, embedded in the context of pre-existing historical, economic, cultural, social and other conditions. This process of explanation, known as *retroduction*, enables the realist inquirer to investigate the potential causal mechanisms and the conditions under which certain outcomes will or will not be realised.

> On the transcendental realist view of science … its essence lies in the movement at any one level from knowledge of manifest phenomena to knowledge produced by means of antecedent knowledge, of the structures that generate them. (Bhaskar and Lawson, 1998: 5)

In this way, effectiveness of the programme may be apprehended with an explanation of why the outcomes developed as they did, and how the programme was able to react to the other underlying mechanisms, and in what contexts. This analysis may provide not only evidence of effectiveness, but also an explanation that may help to develop and to improve both the content and the targeting of future programmes.

Causality and Explanation in Realist Evaluation

The ontological depth of realism has implications for both causality and explanation in evaluation research: 'realists analyse causality in terms of the natures of things and their interactions, their causal powers (and liabilities). The guiding metaphors here are those of structures and mechanisms in reality, rather than phenomena and events' (Outhwaite, 1987: 21–2).

Unlike conventional approaches that strive to isolate systems from extraneous influences in order to observe causal relations (such as the use of randomised 'intervention' and 'no intervention' comparison groups), a realist analysis of causality strives to account for the interaction of various causal tendencies within the complex and open systems among which we live. Therefore, a realist inquirer will not be satisfied with the findings from a randomised controlled trial, but regard them as a regularity that still has to be explained by demonstrating the existence and functioning of a mechanism that produces the regularity. This is one of the ways in which the realist *retroduction* differs from the conventional research approaches to findings from the processes of deduction and induction.

In both the positivist and interpretivist traditions, researchers regard the processes of research to be either inductive, or deductive, or both in the sense of moving from one to the other. *Induction* is the process of inferring theories or laws from data; whereas *deduction* involves developing hypotheses which are then empirically tested through an analysis of the data (see Anastas, 1999: 15; also Crabtree and Miller, 1999: 167 suggest that both processes can be used in constructing codes in qualitative template analysis). In realist research, the central mode of inference is neither induction nor deduction, but retroduction which investigates the potential causal mechanisms as explained above. The process of retroduction operates under a logic of analogy and metaphor and draws heavily on the investigator's perspectives, beliefs and experience; and at the same time, it is based on empirical evidence (Lawson, 1998). However, as there are no research methods dedicated to retroduction, in fact the realist inquirer may use methods that involve induction, deduction or a combination of the two, in the investigation of the causal mechanisms. In this way, realists utilise both the subjective and objective processes of evaluation research.

Realist evaluators seek to investigate the causal properties of structures that exist and operate in the world – it is in this sense that the realist view of causation is generative rather than successive (Pawson and Tilley, 1997b). In an open system, events are not the outcome of a connection between two variables (for example, the intervention and outcome variables in a comparison group design); rather, they are the outcome of structured processes and complex causal configurations that operate at many levels and at the same time. Sayer explains: '... causation is understood ... as the necessary ways-of-acting of an object which exists in virtue of its nature. That is, causation is not conceptualised in terms of a relationship between separate events 'C' and 'E', but in terms of the changes in each of "C" and "E"' (1998:124).

Both Sayer and Pawson and Tilley (1997b) use the example of gunpowder. The causal powers of gunpowder are activated in certain conditions with a spark; and in these conditions and with the contingency of a spark, it will *necessarily* explode. Because these conditions are independent of the causal powers, the succession of events cannot be known just on the basis of the knowledge about the causal powers. 'The essential characteristic of law-likeness is not universality but *necessity*' (Sayer, 1998: 125). These laws are not understood as universal empirical regularities in patterns of events, but as statements about mechanisms that may or may not be triggered in particular contexts.

The establishment of a causal link (even if it is inferred with maximum confidence as indicated in Macdonald, 1996) by itself does not have explanatory power; at best, it is a probabilistic description that requires analysis at a deeper, structural level to be fully understood. If it can be proven that a human service programme caused a desired effect, the experiment can only demonstrate what happened in the past; it cannot prove that the same relation will hold in the future. Therefore, the purpose of realist scientific explanation is not just to predict; it is to explain and to improve the explanation. The goal is to understand how the phenomena under study react or change in the presence or absence of other antecedent or concurrent phenomena in an open system. These theories are empirically assessed and, when found to be empirically adequate, are themselves explained in turn, in the cognitive unfolding of explanatory knowledge (Lawson, 1998). From the realist perspective, this is the process of retroduction, whereas what is contributed by other forms of inductive and deductive research may be fundamentally descriptive.

> According to fallibilistic realism, the goal of science is not to describe causal connections between variables in static contexts but rather to understand the fundamental properties of phenomena by describing them and how they act in the presence of other phenomena in closed or open systems. The goal of science, then, is to describe properties rather than to declare propositions: it is to understand and explain phenomena well enough to know what they are like and how they will act.... (Anastas and MacDonald, 1994: 24–5)

Identifying Mechanisms

In the realist view of causation, the notion of underlying *mechanism* is central. 'A mechanism is ... an account of the makeup, behaviour, and interrelationships of those processes that are responsible for the outcome. A mechanism is thus a theory – a theory that spells out the potential of human resources and reasoning' (Pawson and Tilley, 1997a: 408).

These theories are subject to empirical tests and new ones emerge that require further tests. Therefore, science does not consist only in doing experiments; scientists are also involved in developing an adequate and a self-consistent system of concepts with which to understand the world as revealed in the results of experiments. For the realist inquirer, the question is not just that the programme works, but what it is about the programme that makes it work, and why it works with some people and not with others.

Pawson and Tilley (1997a: 409) note three identifiers of the mechanism in relation to social programmes: (a) reflecting the embeddedness of the programme within the stratified nature of social reality; (b) taking the form of propositions that will provide an account of how both macro and micro processes constitute the programme; and (c) demonstrating how programme outputs follow from the stakeholders' choices and their capacity to put these into practice.

Identifying mechanisms involves an attempt to investigate how a programme actually changes behaviour, and the basic realist claim is that initiatives always work in a weaving process that binds choices and capacities together. The generative mechanism (or the programme of intervention in a human service) cannot be explained in isolation from the context in which the programme operates. Programmes impact upon pre-existing conditions, and an important task of the inquirer is to investigate the extent to which these mechanisms and contexts enable or disable the intended change in outcomes. Contexts include not only physical structures, but also the prior sets of social rules and cultural systems that may form an important part of the explanation for the success or failure of the social programme.

The basic task of social inquiry is to explain interesting, puzzling, socially significant outcomes. Explanations take the form of positing some underlying mechanism that generates the regularity and thus consists of propositions about how the interplay between structure and agency has constituted the outcome. Within realist investigation there is also investigation of how the workings of such mechanisms are contingent and conditional, and thus only fired in particular local, historical or institutional contexts (Pawson and Tilley, 1997a: 412).

Application of The Realist Evaluation Paradigm

Realism aims to penetrate beneath the observable outputs and inputs of a programme. This is the first of the rules for realist evaluation developed by Pawson and Tilley (1997b: 215–19), who argue that a realist evaluation also needs to address:

1   how the causal mechanisms that generate social and behavioural problems are removed or countered through the alternative causal mechanisms introduced in a social programme;
2   the contexts within which programme mechanisms are activated and in which programme mechanisms can be successfully fired;
3   what the outcomes are and how they are produced;
4   context–mechanism–outcome pattern configurations, that is, what works, for whom, and in what contexts;
5   teacher–learner relationships with practitioners and others to test and explain the context–mechanism–outcome configurations;
6   permeability – intrusion of new contexts and new causal powers during the evaluation of a programme's effectiveness.

Although a researcher or a researcher–practitioner may not be able to apply all the above rules in the evaluation of practice, with such a perspective one may be more aware of limitations of the research that is attempted, and also more aware of its exact contribution to practice, and what needs to be addressed in the future. Based on the analysis of data to date including outcomes, mechanisms and contexts, programmes are developed as models of intervention targeted to achieve the desired outcomes. A multi-method strategy may be applied to test the extent to which these models of intervention are analogous with reality, and the data collection and analysis may directly contribute to the further development of these programmes of intervention as well as their future targeting.

The Realist Effectiveness Cycle in Practice Evaluation

Realist practice evaluation based on the above principles aims to address the significant factors involved in human service practice, and this process may be implemented through a realistic effectiveness cycle (Figure 3.1) which links the models of intervention with the circumstances in which practice takes place. A cycle is selected as, unlike natural sciences, 'instead of running straight ahead in pursuit of new knowledge, they (social sciences) move around in small circles and spend a lot of time re-inspecting the starting block' (Outhwaite, 1998: 290).

The starting point in Figure 3.1 is theory that includes propositions on how the mechanisms introduced by a programme into pre-existing contexts can generate outcomes. This entails theoretical analysis of mechanisms, contexts and expected outcomes, using a logic of analogy and metaphor (Bhaskar and Lawson, 1998). Theoretical explanations are characteristically analogical, for example, scientists began looking for a virus for mad cow disease as previous ailments in cattle tended to be caused by a virus (Lawson, 1998). In the same way, in evidence-based practice theoretical constructs may be based on what is known about the particular areas of work. The practitioner may draw upon prior knowledge of causal mechanisms

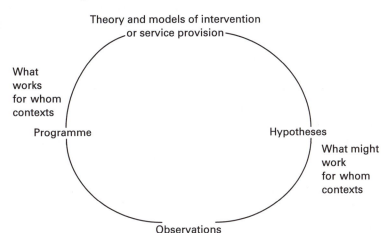

Based on existing assessment of mechanisms, contexts, outcomes (M, C, O)

Theory and models of intervention
or service provision

What
works
for whom
contexts

Programme

Hypotheses

What might
work
for whom
contexts

Observations

Multi-method data collection on M, C, O

Figure 3.1   *The realist effectiveness cycle*
Adapted from Pawson and Tilley, 1997b. Source: Kazi, 1998a, 1999

which may account for the effectiveness or otherwise of models of intervention in particular contexts. The model of intervention may include an
assessment of personal, social and environmental difficulties and a programme of intervention designed to fulfil expectations of change.

The second step on the cycle consists of hypotheses that would typically
address the following questions:

1   what changes or outcomes will be brought about by a programme's
    intervention?
2   what contexts impinge on this?
3   what social, cultural and other mechanisms in the pre-existing environ-
    ment would enable these changes, and which ones may disable the
    programme?

The next step on the cycle is the selection of appropriate methods of data
collection to help return to the concrete – and here, realists may be committed methodological pluralists and do not rule out anything that addresses
real entities. The realist inquirer may identify the evaluation research methods
that can address the questions raised by the theory and the hypotheses, and
that can also provide data on the theoretical propositions, the identified
mechanisms, and the identified outcomes of the programme. It is here that
a plausible connection may be made between the social programme model
and its likeness with reality – or, to put it another way, provide evidence of
the programme of intervention's ability to change reality.

Further on, we return to the actual programme of intervention, in order to make it more specific as an intervention of practice. This specificity is based on the findings from research methods to date, that is, an investigation, so far, of what works and in what circumstances, to target the programme better, and to improve its content to meet the needs of the users it is actually aimed at. The programme may be directed at one person, a family, a group, a community, or an entire population – it may be based on explanations, so far, of the role of particular mechanisms embedded in particular contexts to ensure that the programme has maximum impact.

Next, but not finally, we return to the theory – not finally, because the cycle may continue its journey of explanation. The theoretical basis of the programme of intervention may be developed further, the hypotheses may be based on explanatory evidence thus far, the data collection methods may be developed and applied more appropriately, and the programme may be developed accordingly, and returning to theory, and so on. The practitioner has her own models of practice that she follows in making assessments as well as service delivery to a client or a client group (for example, see Briggs and Corcoran, 2001, for an account of the contemporary models of social work practice). The realist effectiveness cycle enables a dialectical relationship between this model and the realities of practice, which enables the refinement and development of this model based on the realities of practice. It is based on empirical evidence gathered through research methods that can also be used as evidence of effectiveness, and to make judgements about the merit and worth of practice, but such use is a by-product – the main purpose is the development and improvement of the models of practice.

Implementing the Realist Effectiveness Cycle

Based on the principles of realist evaluation, a programme may integrate the above effectiveness cycle by introducing research methods to systematically track the following:

1   changes in **outcomes**, including changes in the levels of risk – this can be done through appropriate outcome measures (for example, from Corcoran and Fischer, 2000; Fischer and Corcoran, 1994) which may be used repeatedly before, during and after the intervention. The outcome data will also include qualitative data from the interaction with the service users. The integration of outcome measures into practice will facilitate the use of single-case designs and/or comparison group designs to systematically track client progress over time, and the findings may be shared with service users and other stakeholders;

2   changes in the **models of intervention**, or the content of the programmes implemented. This can be done using qualitative strategies, for example, in regular focus group meetings with the team of service providers, and on a regular basis as part of the supervision and review

arrangements within a programme team's practice. Realist evaluators may strive to ensure that this becomes part of the routine recording systems, and one way of doing this may be to create a menu of the possible components of interventions to systematically track changes in the content over time;

3   changes in the **contexts** of service users, for example, levels of social deprivation and traumatic historical factors, which are less likely to change during the intervention. The contexts can be tracked through data from the initial referral processes and the initial interaction with the service users;

4   changes in the **mechanisms**, that is, in factors in the circumstances of the service users that influence outcomes. Realist evaluators may need to identify the main enabling and disabling mechanisms in relation to the desired outcomes, and to systematically track changes in these mechanisms over time. This process is usually part of an agency's assessment and review procedures, but the information on mechanisms may be made more explicit in the routine recording systems. A set of key mechanisms may be identified for further investigation through the experience of programme workers, research findings to date, analysis of data currently available, and through the interactions with service users.

The above are the four main components of the realistic effectiveness cycle. The data from all four may enable regular analyses with potential explanations of why the intervention procedures worked or not. The model of intervention, if it is going to be effective in a generative sense, has to change in accordance with changes in the complex weaving system of mechanisms and contexts – the theory, the assessment, the intervention, the outcomes – all change in the fluid contexts of reality.

The Centre for Evaluation Studies is undertaking a number of such 'clear box' evaluations at the present time, building on the progress made in the previous studies undertaken by this author with social work and health agaencies (Kazi, 1998a,1998b, 2000a). There are also examples of the beginnings of realist evaluation from colleagues at Umeå University in Sweden, and from University of Tampere and STAKES (National Research and Development Centre for Welfare and Health, Helsinki) in Finland (see Kazi et al., 2000a).

Methodologies for Realist Evaluation

In their search for 'clear box' evaluations, realists tend to be in favour of a wide range of research methods, both qualitative and quantitative, and typically a wider range than that preferred by researchers of either the empirical or interpretivist persuasions (Lawson, 1998; Sayer, 2000). However, the actual choice of research methods depends on the nature of the programme under investigation, as well as the researcher's epistemological preferences even amongst realists. For example, Sayer (2000: 21) classifies the realist research designs as either *intensive* or *extensive*. Intensive research investigates the working of a process in a particular case or small number of cases, as well as the questions 'what produces a change?' and 'what did the agents actually do?'. Intensive research produces causal explanations, though not necessarily representative ones. The typical methods described by Sayer in the intensive research design include the study of individuals in their causal contexts, interactive interviews, ethnography, and qualitative analysis. Sayer's definition of intensive research is therefore consistent with the way it has been applied in the Outlook example outlined in Chapter 4 (see also Spurling, Kazi and Rogan, 2000).

Extensive research designs, on the other hand, address research questions regarding the regularities, patterns and distinguishing features of a population; and the distribution or representation of certain characteristics or processes. Typical methods are described as large-scale surveys or surveys of smaller representative samples, formal questionnaires, standardised interviews, and statistical analysis. According to Sayer, extensive research designs do not produce causal explanations as intensive designs do; rather, they provide descriptive representative generalisations lacking in explanatory depth.

The conventional impulse to prove causation by gathering data on regularities, repeated occurrences, is therefore misguided; at best these might suggest where to look for candidates for causal mechanisms. What causes something to happen has nothing to do with the number of times we have observed it happening. Explanation depends instead on identifying causal mechanisms and how they work, and discovering if they have been activated and under what conditions. (Sayer, 2000: 14)

The reader would notice that Sayer's intensive methods are qualitative and originate from interpretivist approaches; and the extensive methods are quantitative, originating from positivist and post-positivist approaches. Sayer's preference is largely for qualitative methods, at least where the research aim is to address the causal mechanisms.

Lawson's (1998) preferred methods, on the other hand, are largely quantitative. He describes his methodological preferences in this explanatory process as: 'contrastive, interest laden and critical, with a significant empirical component including measurement, collection, tabulation, transformation and graphing of statistics; also detailed case studies, oral reporting, including interviews, biographies, and so on' (1998: 165).

Lawson's preferred approaches include the analysis of patterns or demi-regularities: 'we notice the effects of sets of structures through detecting relatively systematic differences in the outcomes of prima facie comparable types of activities (or perhaps similar outcomes of prima facie different activities) in different space-time locations, and so forth' (1998: 153).

Any patterning or standing out alerts us to the existence of something unknown. For example the realist evaluator can seek out two or more situations where outcomes may have been expected to be related in some manner, and then identify one mechanism in one situation only, to attempt to determine the reasons why, that is, to identify a causal factor. In this way, Lawson explains, his largely quantitative methodological approach can solve the problem of retroduction.

This author's view is that both Sayer and Lawson are right, and the difference lies in their emphasising one or the other part of what are the beginnings of methodologies dedicated to realist evaluation research. Sayer's intensive research can be done with one or a small number of cases, and in this process, outcomes, mechanisms, contexts, and the content of a human service programme can be systematically tracked in the realist effectiveness cycle as described earlier in this chapter. One difference with Sayer, however, is that this author maintains that quantitative methodologies such as single-case evaluation (Kazi, 1998a) should also be included in intensive research, particularly in the systematic tracking of outcomes. The findings from this intensive research with individual cases can be aggregated with the help of group designs, to help identify the demi-regularities as suggested by Lawson. The intensive work may determine what works, for whom and in what contexts in individual cases. The aggregation of this data may enable the investigation of patterns across a group of individual cases. In this way, inferences may be drawn, one mechanism at a time, in order to identify the causal mechanisms and the conditions in which they are triggered to achieve the desired outcomes.

The different positions of both Sayer and Lawson with regard to methodologies in realist research originate from the perspectives identified as empirical practice and interpretivist in Chapter 2, and confirm this author's view that dedicated methods for realist research are not yet developed. Whilst realism is developed as a philosophy of science and as a research perspective, it lags behind in terms of the development of methods specifically designed for retroduction. These methods will emerge as more and more realist evaluations are implemented and published, and this book aims to make the beginnings of a contribution in this regard in the foregoing chapters.

In the quest for methodologies that can be used in realist evaluations, we now turn to an example of turning a 'black box' evaluation 'greyer' through the investigation of patterns in a largely quantitative study as indicated by Lawson. These are the first steps in integrating a realist effectiveness cycle, before any attempt at a 'clear box' evaluation. This is not an example of a realist evaluation following the principles outlined above where the effectiveness cycle is integrated and at least one full cycle is complete; rather, it is about how an evaluator can establish a partnership with practitioners, and *begin* to integrate the realist effectiveness cycle. The other examples in the foregoing chapters are further down the road in integrating this cycle into practice, and therefore this example begins the journey along that road.

Example: Evaluation of Adult Rehabilitation Programmes

The first example is that of the integration of outcome measures into practice, and the use of other data routinely collected by practitioners in their agency recording systems in an attempt to explain the outcomes (Kazi et al., 2002). This example is based on the interim results of a study involving the integration of single-subject design procedures in the daily practices of adult rehabilitation programmes in the Huddersfield area of the Calderdale and Huddersfield NHS (National Health Service) Trust, West Yorkshire in England (Kazi, 1998a), up to the year 2001. The study concentrated on programmes that provide services for people aged over 65 years who suffer acute conditions affecting their ability to live independently. The area has a population of 218,000, with the Trust providing services to over 50,000 new patients of all ages per year. This project is the continuation of a partnership between the Centre for Evaluation Studies within the University of Huddersfield and the Calderdale and Huddersfield NHS Trust. The purpose of the study is to enable practitioners to develop effective, evidence-based interventions with this client group. This study is ongoing, and the data collection is still in progress.

First, work was undertaken with all practitioners to identify the outcome measures and other data collection methods that would be appropriate for all the rehabilitation services for people aged 65 years or above. These broad outcomes enable conclusions of a 'black box' type of evaluation. However, the use of statistical analysis involving other data that is also routinely collected by the agency may help to turn the 'black box' 'greyer' by identifying useful patterns in the data, and revealing some potential mechanism–context–outcome configurations which otherwise may remain hidden (Duguid and Pawson, 1998; Kazi, 1999, 2000a, 2000b; Lawson, 1998). A software package for quantitative data, SPSS (Foster, 2001), was applied to enable the use of inferential statistics including the selected outcomes, as well as the other context and intervention variables for all older people who were receiving these rehabilitation services and who agreed to take part in the research.

Purpose and Methodology

The main objectives of the project are as follows:

1 to develop realistic, evidence-based and effective models of intervention for the rehabilitation of older people;
2 to develop appropriate methods of evaluation of the rehabilitation services in partnership with service providers and service users;
3 to determine the comparative effectiveness of the three main types of rehabilitation services within the Huddersfield area of the Calderdale and Huddersfield NHS Trust.

This study builds on previous projects with Oakes Villa Rehabilitation Centre, Barton Day Centre and Community Rehabilitation and Adult Community Physiotherapy Teams that have been successful in integrating validated, reliable outcome measures within these services. The use of these outcome measures is generating data which can now be used in statistical analysis to identify not only the outcomes that were successful, but also the patient demographic characteristics, medical conditions, the type of services provided and other contextual factors associated with the successful outcomes.

The method included the integration of single-subject designs into the practice of rehabilitation programme teams at Oakes Villa (a residential unit) and Barton (non-residential services both at a day centre and in the community), to systematically track outcomes using standardised measures. Oakes Villa continue to use their own measure, Oakes Villa Activities of Daily Living Scale (Kazi and Firth, 1999) which has been validated recently. The Unit has used this measure for five years on over 400 patients, and this chapter reports on cases in the two years 2000 and 2001. At Barton, a main aim of this research study was to work in partnership with practitioners to integrate outcome measures into their practice, and this has been achieved in the year 2001. Each case in Barton and Oakes Villa is systematically tracked, and the results across the larger numbers of cases are aggregated using statistical analysis that enables comparisons between different types of interventions, client characteristics and contexts.

Interim Findings to Date

Oakes Villa Rehabilitation Service

A feature of this evaluation is that single-subject designs have been integrated into the daily practice of Oakes Villa, an adult rehabilitation unit set up to help older people regain their independent living skills as part of the recovery from acute medical conditions such as strokes. Usually, such evaluations tend to concentrate on effects and pay little attention to the actual content and the context of services (University of Leeds, 1992). For example, studies involving single-case designs are often limited by concentrating on outcome measures, with very little description of interventions (Kazi, 1998a). This study demonstrates that whilst empirical practice approaches provide the foundation, and that whilst it is desirable to maintain a concentration on outcome data, other perspectives can also be drawn upon to provide a more complete evaluation of the effectiveness of a particular service.

Through a series of focus group meetings with the staff, it was found that Oakes Villa's overall aim was to help people achieve a good quality of life, harnessing their own expectations and abilities (Kazi and Firth, 1999, 2000). The emphasis is not on their disabilities, but on what they can do positively. The service users are helped to make informed decisions on what they want to do – whether they want to return home, or live in care. Relatives are also helped to come to terms with the changing realities in their lives following an acute medical condition that led to problems in maintaining independent living. According to the staff team, Oakes Villa is more like a home than a hospital; it provides the users the space to make important decisions about their future, and the staff aim to provide honest answers to the relevant questions and to help the users remain in charge of their own destiny. The user is involved in the decision-making process, from admission through to the review system. The user is not given a quick visit to their home, but helped to assess the home situation, and to come to terms with any disability in the context of the home situation where they may want to return. The main decision in the rehabilitation process is that of the patient – if there is no motivation, then rehabilitation is not possible, and therefore the emphasis is on helping service users to make informed decisions.

The process of rehabilitation begins from day one at Oakes Villa. The clients are assessed on their abilities in relation to the activities of daily living. Their own wishes are an important part of the assessment, which also takes into account the abilities they had prior to the acute condition. However, the service users' perceptions of their ability to live independently are sometimes not objective. During the admission process, goals are set, and the assessment is conducted in a relaxed, informal way. A care plan is drawn up, and all members of staff work to the same plan, and have the same expectations. This consistency is maintained through daily team assessment meetings to record the progress made, based on a full assessment of the client over the previous 24 hours.

Single-subject Designs and Other Outcome Indicators

A fundamental requirement of single-case subject designs is the measurement of the client's target problem (that is, the object of the intervention or treatment) repeatedly over time (Bloom, Fischer and Orme, 1999; Kazi, 1998a). The practitioner is required to select an outcome measure that best reflects changes in the client's condition, and then to apply the same measure over a period of time to enable a systematic tracking of progress. The establishment of a causal link between the programme and client outcomes was not an aim of this particular application.

The Oakes Villa staff developed the Oakes Villa Activities of Daily Living Scale – a seven-point rating scale ranging from dependency to independence – based on adaptation of a number of standardised measures. As the Unit provides short-term interventions, they wanted a measure that could be used daily or at least every few days. The outcome measure used at the Oakes Villa Unit is a seven-point rating scale (at first, the measure was a six-point rating scale as reported in Kazi, 1997a) created by the staff themselves in consultation with the author. It is essentially a rating scale ranging from one to seven as follows:

1 totally dependent, i.e., requiring someone else to undertake the task
2 receiving moderate assistance, i.e., quite a bit of help to do the task
3 receiving slight assistance, i.e., finishing off with partial help
4 receiving enabling assistance, i.e., setting the scene
5 independent with supervision
6 independent with equipment
7 independent

The project's staff enhanced the scale's reliability by providing specific examples to anchor each point of the scale, by agreeing the definitions as precisely as possible within the staff group as a whole, and by measuring on the scale as a collective staff team activity. Each variable (that is, specified client activity) is assessed daily against the scale, and then assigned a score. An inter-observer reliability test was carried out in November 2000 with eight service users rated in each of 13 weekdays by eight members of the team across 26 variables. The reliability was found to be very good, with an alpha of .83.

The data from outcome measurement in the form of a systematic tracking of client progress against pre-identified key variables (for example, variables identified both in the community care assessments and/or the initial assessment at the rehabilitation unit) enabled the application of single-case designs which provided an indication of the progress made by each client. Daily scoring of clients' abilities is an everyday part of the team's work and is therefore not seen as something extra. No one who has joined the team since has queried why it is still done but has accepted it as normal working practice. The measure is also combined with an overall indicator – the destination of discharge from Oakes Villa, that is, whether they go back to independent living or into residential or nursing care. A follow-up assessment is also made six months after discharge from the unit, providing an indication of success in achieving longer-term rehabilitation.

This example is based on the results from 2000 and 2001, and includes 103 out of 110 cases where repeated measures were available. The ADL measure is used against the specified daily living activities for each client, and then the results are aggregated according to the number of activities where improvements were made. A nominal scale is created where the 'improved' category records the number of cases where improvements were made in the majority of activities, 'no change' where there is no change in the majority of activities, and 'deteriorated' where deterioration is observed in the majority of activities. This process used by the practitioners was tested for accuracy with the use of SPSS. First, all the daily ADL scores for each week were added together, providing an overall score, and

Table 3.1   *Change in majority of scored ADLs in Oakes Villa*

Change	Frequency	%
Deteriorated	4	3.9
No change	13	12.6
Improved	86	83.5
Total	103	100

Table 3.2   *Destination of clients at discharge from Oakes Villa*

Destination	Frequency	%
Died	1	0.9
Hospital	7	6.4
Nursing/residential home	10	9.2
Own home	91	83.5
Sub-total	109	100
Not yet discharged	1	
Total	**110**	

then the first weekly overall score was subtracted from the last weekly overall score. It was found that, out of 61 cases included in this procedure, there were inaccuracies in only two cases. Table 3.1 indicates the overall findings from the use of this outcome measure in the two-year period.

The majority of clients (83.5%) improved, and only 3.9% became worse. Table 3.2 confirms this trend, as 83.5% were discharged successfully to their own homes.

To date, no significant associations have been found between the two outcomes – Oakes Villa ADL and the destination at discharge – and the other mechanisms and contexts, such as age, marital status, gender, type of housing, current and previous medical conditions. However, when the Spearman test was used, it was found that there was a significant association $(r = .712, n = 110, p = .000)$ between having a live-in carer and marital status, with 88 out of 110 being a widow or widower and living on their own. At the same time, there was also a significant correlation between gender and marital status, although the measure of association was weaker $(r = .260, n = 110, p = .006)$, as 75 out of 110 were both female and widowed. There was also a significant correlation between receiving home visits by a district (community) nurse and marital status, with more visits directed at those living on their own following discharge $(r = -.318, n = 110, p = .002)$. However, in terms of outcomes, these characteristics did not have an impact; for example, 81% of males and 84.1% of females were discharged to their own homes and 94.7% of males and 81% of females improved on the Oakes Villa ADL measure. Therefore, it can be concluded that Oakes Villa was largely effective across gender, age range, and the different types of medical conditions.

Barton Services

Barton provides rehabilitation services to patients over the age of 16 years, and at January 2000, nearly 25% of the service users were aged 65–75 years, and 21% were aged over 75 years. The services are aimed at all patients who require active physical rehabilitation. All patients are assessed by a multi-disciplinary team and an individual care programme is developed. The programme lasts until the agreed goals are achieved. Home visits or outreach work are provided, as well as attendances at the centre. In January 2000, the number of referrals in one year had reached 9027. In one snapshot week in March 2000, a total of 125 patients were treated by the multi-disciplinary team in over 170 sessions. Examples of medical conditions include hip surgery, pulmonary rehabilitation, falls prevention and Parkinson's Disease. The Barton Rehabilitation team consists of a rehabilitation manager, four nurse coordinators, ten physiotherapists, four occupational therapists, and four rehabilitation assistants, as well as other administrative and ambulance staff. There are also a variety of other professions involved part-time. Barton's philosophy is to: 'provide a holistic service for clients with a physical disability through a multi-disciplinary team approach. Each individual will be assisted through their active participation to regain maximum potential for independent living, thus assuring that their physical and psychological needs are met' (from a publicity poster).

In addition to the day centre staff, the Community Rehabilitation Team is also based at Barton, although it sees people in their own homes and elsewhere as appropriate. It provides long-term monitoring and support for patients suffering from chronic neurological conditions. This team consists of physiotherapists, occupational therapists and technical instructors.

Findings at Barton

As indicated earlier, a number of outcome measures has been successfully integrated into the practice of most professional groupings at Barton. However, at the time of writing, most of the repeated scores are not yet available, and therefore this chapter reports on the interim findings from the use of Dartmouth COOP Chart (DCC) which is used generally for all patients at Barton. The measure is reported to have good reliability (Jenkinson, 1994), and the pictorial charts tend to be user-friendly as a self-report measure. Table 3.3 indicates that a large majority (77.4%) had improved, and only 9.7% had reported deterioration.

As with the analysis of the Oakes Villa data above, there were no significant associations between the DCC outcome and the other potential mechanisms and contexts such as the type of service provided, age, gender, type of housing and type of medical condition. However, the Spearman test indicated significant associations between:

Table 3.3   *Result of DCC scores*

Change	Frequency	%
Deteriorated	3	9.7
No change	4	12.9
Improved	24	77.4
Total	31	100

1 length of treatment and change in DCC (r = .382, n = 31, p = .034). The longer the treatment period, the worse the difference in the DCC repeated scores, indicating that those on shorter treatment programmes achieved better DCC results;

2 having live-in carer and gender (r = .772, n = 31, p = .000). More males had a wife or partner living with them, whereas more females tended to be widows living on their own;

3 having live-in carer and marital status (r = .950, n = 31, p = .000). To confirm the above, more females were widows living on their own, whereas more males lived with their wives/partners;

4 having live-in carer and attendance at Barton Centre (r = .396, n = 31, p = .028). Clients with spouse/partner tended to attend half days, whereas those without a live-in carer attended more whole days;

5 marital status and referral source (r = .707, n = 31, p = .000). More males who were living with their partners/wives tended to be referred by general practitioners (physicians in the community), whereas more females tended to be referred by hospitals and other non-community services. This is also confirmed by a significant correlation between gender and referral source (r = .554, n = 31, p = .001).

These interim findings are only indicative at this stage, given the small number of cases. However, the trend is towards better Dartmouth COOP Chart outcomes, and those who receive shorter programmes are more likely to indicate better results, even though this is not related to type of medical condition. The above associations have identified some relevant demographic characteristics in the patient population and the different types of services required to meet the needs of the diverse groups.

Conclusion for Both Oakes Villa and Barton

An outcome of these studies is that the evaluation approaches, namely single-case evaluation within a realist framework, have been integrated into the daily practices of the rehabilitation services. The integration of evaluation research procedures into practice represents an advance in evidence-based practice approaches, and may help to provide a solution to the problems of (a) the divide between research and practice, and (b) the use of research findings to inform future practice. The partnership between the

Centre for Evaluation Studies and the rehabilitation teams indicates that the divide between practitioners and researchers is being bridged in this study. The practitioners are learning more about the evaluation research approaches relevant to their practice, and the academics are becoming more aware of the needs of practice and of the need to develop appropriate evaluation strategies for practice. The evaluation findings do not stop at the point of indicating effectiveness or otherwise. Rather, these strategies use the empirical findings as a starting point, to dig deeper into the contexts of practice and to identify what type of interventions work with what type of patients and in what type of contexts. This type of evaluation may enable the development and replication of successful models of intervention in adult rehabilitation.

This study illustrates how a 'black box' type of evaluation that focuses on outcomes alone, can be transformed into a 'grey box' evaluation that moves towards an explanatory account of the factors that influence the outcomes, using demographic data that may be routinely recorded in human service agencies. However, in this study, there is no account of mechanisms as yet, and most of the factors entered in the database are in fact contexts, such as gender, age and marital status. The aim is to provide regular analysis with the data that is available at any given time, and to help programmes develop their data collection methods within the realist effectiveness cycle to enable a deeper analysis of the causal factors. These findings have been shared with the practitioners, who are considering the practice implications, and working out ways of extending the account of mechanisms and contexts in the database for deeper analysis in a prospective realist evaluation.

Realist evaluation provides opportunities for human services to effect real changes in the circumstances of service users through a process that attempts to penetrate beneath the surface, that is, not to be satisfied with appearances but to strive for explanations of the initial findings. Houston (2001) suggests that one of the contributions of realism is that, by 'returning our attention to "depth" in social work, it provides a much needed antidote to the criticisms that social work has lost its core concern: the alleviation of human misery' (p. 858).

This example illustrates how a realist perspective encourages the inquirer to use the available data to strive for an analysis of mechanism–context–outcome configurations, that is, potential explanations of why a programme may work with some people and not with others. Some evaluations may begin along that road, as illustrated here, but others are further down the road, as indicated in the next five chapters. The examples of studies in the following chapters help to identify the methodologies that can be applied by realist evaluators, along the road of investigating the causal mechanisms that can account for a programme's effectiveness, and to help develop the programme for the future.

4

An Example of Qualitative Research Methods in Realist Evaluation

This chapter analyses the use of qualitative methods in realist evaluation, based on an application from a realist evaluation project located in a charity working with the drug-using community (Kazi and Spurling, 2000; Spurling, Kazi and Rogan, 2000). The purpose of this chapter is not to report on the findings of this evaluation research project at this stage (the three-year project ended in November 2002), but to examine the inclusive nature of realism with regard to the use of qualitative approaches in research. As in Chapter 3, this is also an example of a study that is at the beginning of the realist effectiveness cycle described in the previous chapter, that is, the key mechanisms are only just being identified. However, unlike the example in Chapter 3 where quantitative methods were used, this study is based on largely qualitative methods.

Funded by the National Lottery Charities Board (now Community Fund) over three years, this project is a partnership between Single Homeless Accommodation Project (SHAP), Outlook Team at Lifeline, and the Centre for Evaluation Studies at the University of Huddersfield. The research project seeks to enable the development of realistic and pragmatic models for the social inclusion of the drug-using community. Rather than concentrate on the problem of drug use itself, the project focuses on the influences and contexts in the lives of people that led to the drug use in the first place. The research project is based at the Outlook team of Lifeline that examines and explores the processes by which drug users may develop and sustain alternative lifestyles. The project aims to contribute to the development and evaluation of intervention models aimed at reducing drug use and facilitating alternatives. The Outlook team focuses on personal programmes or strategies such as the promotion of employment, education and leisure, developed specifically for the needs of drug users to enable them to deal with the influences that led to the use of drugs and to help them to change their lifestyles. The emphasis of the research project is on evaluating intervention with the aim of developing effective social inclusion models with the drug-using community.

The project aims to benefit some of the most disadvantaged, socially-excluded people in the Kirklees local authority region whose circumstances have influenced their decision to misuse drugs, and who, as a consequence, face social exclusion in some of the most extreme forms – including chaotic lifestyles, lack of employment or training, under-achievement in education, some of the worst housing conditions, and being at risk of or engaging in criminal activity. Through the development of realist social inclusion strategies to help improve the quality of life, this research aims to directly benefit individual drug users, their children and families. The project also aims to make a contribution to the voluntary and state agencies working with the drug-using community through the dissemination of the outcomes of the research, including the identification and development of effective models of intervention. SHAP, Lifeline's Outlook team and the wider community of service providers will also benefit in the enhancement of their capacity to develop and to evaluate appropriate models of service provision for the drug-using community.

Spurling, Kazi and Rogan (2000) outline the methods used in this particular realist evaluation. A particular feature of this evaluation is the use of repeated interviews with service users to systematically track the content of services, the outcomes achieved, and the mechanisms and contexts in which these outcomes are produced, largely from the perspectives of the service users. As Spurling outlines:

> The computer package NUD*IST (Non-numerical, Unstructured Data – Indexing, Searching, Theorising) is being used to assist in the analysis of data generated by the in-depth interviews and observation. Each interview has been coded identifying contexts, aims/outcomes and enabling and disabling mechanisms … . At this stage, coding for contexts is done on a relatively superficial level, merely providing the backdrop to the aims and mechanisms. For example, any discussion of drug use is being coded as context, not only when discussed in relation to previous use, or use by family. Whilst the analysis of different contexts will become more sophisticated, at present this allows aims and outcomes to be coded in a very straightforward manner within different contexts. Enabling and disabling mechanisms are identified on a thematic basis, and therefore are also located within different contexts. (Kazi and Spurling, 2000: 12)

These methods originate from the interpretivist perspectives, but they are used in this particular application within a realist framework to identify changes in the content of services, the outcomes achieved, the mechanisms in the service users' circumstances, as well as the contexts in which practice takes place.

An Example of Qualitative Research within a Realist Evaluation

The purpose of this chapter is to examine the inclusive nature of realism with regard to the use of qualitative approaches in research. For this purpose, interviews of the first five Outlook service users who were interviewed more than once in the way described by Spurling were selected for analysis. The data from these interviews was analysed with the help of template analysis undertaken by researcher Dawn Lawson. The description of the process of analysis is based on the notes from the detailed records that the researcher was asked to provide for this purpose.

The aim was to investigate the extent to which it was possible to achieve retroduction using qualitative analysis in researching mechanism–context–outcome configurations (Pawson and Tilley, 1997a). In this process of retroduction, the researcher's perspectives would have a strong influence in how the mechanisms are selected and tested, and it could be argued that different researchers would arrive at rather idiosyncratic conclusions. However, Madill, Jordan and Shirley (2000) found that triangulation in the use of multiple researchers (as well as in the use of multiple research methods) can be used to assess the consistency of the findings. They provide an example of results from two independent analyses of three interviews. It was found that, although the two analysts presented a different number of categories, the two analyses could be integrated within ten common themes, and the differences tended to be at the level of analytic detail. The authors conclude that the thematic similarity between the analyses demonstrated that 'qualitative researchers can produce results which are, at least not wildly idiosyncratic' (2000: 9).

The data analysed for the purposes of this chapter relate to five service users of the Outlook team at Lifeline, an agency that aims to help users come off drug misuse by promoting positive objectives in their lifestyles rather than focusing on the actual drug use. These five service users were interviewed at two points in time, and we not only wanted to know what their situation was, but also how it changed over time. Outcomes are what the user wants to achieve in his/her life – it may include ending drug misuse, but usually it will also include positive changes that the user wants to achieve, such as education, career, and family life. Next, we want to know what are the enabling and disabling mechanisms in the life of the person, that is, what would enable these outcomes to be achieved, and what would disable them. For example, enabling outcomes may include motivation and support from family and friends. Disabling mechanisms could be a drug-misusing peer group's influences, and lack of motivation to change lifestyles. Then there are contexts – these are similar to mechanisms, but take a longer time to change, for example, housing, demographic characteristics, and histories of problems. The content is what Outlook provides, such as an Outlook worker acting as a role model, and the various activities available such as football, computing, women's group, and craft work.

The Process of Template Analysis

The data was analysed using template analysis, as described in Crabtree and Miller (1999) and King (1998). The researcher constructs a list of codes representing themes in the textual data – some of these are defined a priori, but they can also be modified and added to as the researcher reads and interprets the text. The purpose is to seek regularities from the qualitative data (Drisko, 1997, 2000; Tesch, 1990), and therefore the process of analysis is formal and orderly and well specified (for example, the work of Miles and Huberman, 1994). Based on Drisko (2000: 3). The process of template analysis may be described as follows:

1   the template researcher defines codes on an a priori basis (theoretical; current question) or from an initial read of the data;
2   these codes then serve as a template ('bins') for all data analysis;
3   the template may be altered as the analysis continues;
4   text segments that are empirical evidence for template categories are identified;
5   codes assigned to text segments are mere identification 'tags' without conceptual use;
6   template approaches may yield thick descriptions, typologies or taxonomies, often reflected in matrices or charts.

Application of Template Approaches

In this particular application, coding was seen as central: 'coding is analysis – codes are tags or labels for assigning units of meaning to the descriptive or inferential information compiled during a study … for our purposes it is not the words themselves but their meaning that matters (Miles and Huberman, 1994: 56).

Following from the broad instructions provided by this author, a top-down approach was used, with the five main headings of outcomes, enabling mechanisms, disabling mechanisms, contexts and content as the main themes (or higher-order codes), and with sub-themes (or lower-order codes) underneath each. The researcher Dawn Lawson described the process of template analysis as follows:

The first stage in the analysis was an initial reading of the interviews. Annotated notes were made from any information that was relevant to the higher-order codes. The text pertaining to the higher-order quotes was summarised and located under the appropriate code. From this summary, several lower-order codes were identified. In order to examine these in the context of the higher-order codes an initial template was designed. This incorporated the codes assigned to all interviews collectively. There were now two templates, one for the first interviews and another for the second. The lower-order codes were listed as sub-headings under the relevant higher-order code.

At this point all the interviews were re-read and now the actual quotes from the interviews were coded. For each interview the quotes were allocated once again into higher-order codes only. Separate documents were produced under each higher-order code, and the relevant quotes for each interview were added. At this stage the quotes from the interview were re-examined and reassigned to lower-order codes.

It was decided that the quotes obtained from the second reading of the interviews should be re-read and organised to ensure accurate and reliable coding. The information was organised in the same format as previously used. Under each higher-order heading, the quotes from each

Table 4.1   *Schedule of repeated interviews*

Outlook service users	First interview date	Second interview date
Ben	7/8/00	18/10/00
John	11/7/00	8/8/00
Mark	31/1/00	3/3/00
Sarah	6/12/99	19/1/00
Sid	25/11/99	20/1/00

individual interview were analysed. From this last draft of the quotes a collective template including the information from all the interviews was designed. Some lower-order quotes were redefined and assigned to different higher-order codes where it was felt appropriate. For example, enabling support under enabling mechanisms was defined as 2.1, but in this template there were further lower-order codes. An enabling relationship was defined as 2.1.1. This lower-order code was further clarified to include family (2.1.1.1) and friends (2.1.1.2). Finally, the information was reorganised one last time to provide separate templates for each participant interviewed for both interviews. (email communication with author, 6 June 2002)

According to the notes kept by the researcher to describe the process, the analysis began with summaries of the data to provide an overall idea of what could be expected. As the analysis progressed and the level of under-standing of the interviews increased the lower-order codes were redefined, and the individual templates were constructed for each interview. Matrices were selected as a means of displaying the data as they 'essentially involve the crossing of two or more main dimensions or variables (often with sub-variables) to see how they interact' (Miles and Huberman, 1994: 239). The main themes in the analyses consist of the tracking of changes over time in the outcomes, mechanisms, content and contexts with the five service users, with repeated interviews as indicated in Table 4.1. Pseudonyms have been used to protect the identity of the service users.

Findings from Template Analysis

Outcomes   Tables 4.2 and 4.3 consist of outcome matrices based on the templates of the repeated interviews prepared by the researcher. The matrices indicate that, in the relatively short periods between the first and second interviews, the outcomes desired by the service users were fairly consistent. For example, in both interviews Ben's outcome sub-themes included career and education, reducing drug use, and personal/social time. However, some differences can also be observed over time. John had a list of outcomes including career, education, reducing drug use, and personal/social aims in the first interview; however, at the second interview he had narrowed them down to career plans with his desire to be a shopkeeper. Mark emphasised his desire to be physically fit in the first interview, but this outcome was not included in the template for the second interview. Sid, on the other hand, added a few more desired outcomes in the second interview, such as the desire to have a relationship, and career plans. These findings indicate

Table 4.2 *Changes in outcomes matrix: template analysis of first interviews*

Ben	John	Mark	Sarah	Sid
1.1 Reducing/ending drug use	1.1 Career/education plans	1.1 Fitness and physical well being	1.1 Personal/social aims	1.1. Ending/reducing drug use
1.1.1 doesn't like lifestyle	1.1.1 future employment	1.1.1 wants to get physically fit	1.1.1 has been put down by several people and says she had started to believe it herself	1.1.1 has a real desire to stop and leave drugs behind. Wants a clean break from the past
1.1.2 uses prescribed drugs to reduce addiction	1.1.1.1 wants to help people with heroin problems, to put something back into society	1.1.1.1 goes to gym	1.1.1.2 wants to be something better than she is	1.1.2 still thinks about drink, but is doing so less and less
1.2. Career/education plans	1.1.2. Education	1.1.1.2 plays badminton	1.2. Career/education plans	1.1.3 wants to develop the strength he sees in others who have managed to stop drinking
1.2.1 future employment	1.1.2.1 has started an access course	1.1.1.3 goes running and training	1.2.1 education	1.2. Personal/social aims
1.2.1.1 wants to work in the future	1.1.2.2 wants to do a degree	1.1.1.4 plays football	1.2.1.1 wants to be able to read and write	1.2.1 will admit to anyone that he is an alcoholic, but he says it is not easy. Wants to accept what is in the past and behave better in future
1.2.1.2 wants something that has a routine	1.2. Reducing/ending drug use	1.2. Career/education plans	1.3. Reducing/ending drug use	1.2.2 needs to develop greater self-confidence and self-esteem
1.2.1.3 wants to be kept busy	1.2.1 only uses two days prescribed speed, doesn't want it to get in the way of college	1.2.1 education	1.3.1 wants to try to stay clean	1.2.3 needs to accept that he can never drink again
1.2.2 Education	1.3. Consequences of drug use	1.2.1.1 would like to go to university		1.2.4 wants to have a fuller life
1.2.2.1 wants to get more qualifications	1.3.1 feels he has wasted enough time as a user, and doesn't want to waste any more	1.3. Reducing/ending drug use		
1.2.2.2 wants better social life	1.4. Personal/social aims	1.3.1 doesn't want to be a heroin user for the rest of his life		
1.3. Fitness/physical well being	1.4.1 wants to feel accepted somewhere	1.3.2 doesn't want to do any drugs at all, has stopped smoking too		
1.3.1 wants to start getting fit again		1.4. Personal/social aims		
1.4. Personal/social aims		1.4.1 wants to keep going to counselling sessions		
1.4.1 wants variation in life				
1.4.2 wants life more on a level, no manic ups and downs				
1.4.3 wants to meet someone he feels comfortable with				

Table 4.3 *Changes in outcomes matrix: template analysis of second interviews*

Ben	John	Mark	Sarah	Sid
1.1. Career plans	1.1. Career/education plans	1.1. Career/education plans	1.1. Reducing/ending drug use	1.1. Reducing/ending drug use
1.1.1 future employment	1.1.1 career	1.1.1 education	1.1.1 just decided that she doesn't want to live like she was and wants to stop	1.1.1 rule number one for him is not to have a drink even if he wants one
1.1.1.1 wants to work to earn decent money	1.1.1.1 wants to open a small second-hand shop. He believes you can meet people and make money at the same time	1.1.1.1 has decided which universities to go to	1.1.2 doesn't want to go back to square one and start using again	1.1.2 wants to learn to interact with people without using alcohol
1.1.1.2 ideally wants two part-time jobs for variation in life		1.1.1.2 is doing college work at moment, and wants to get on top of that and get it finished	1.2. Career/education plans	1.1.3 the longer he goes without drink the better he feels
1.2. Education			1.2.1 education	1.2. Personal/social aims
1.2.1 wants to learn a little bit about everything, not just one thing		1.2. Reducing/ending drug use	1.2.1.1 wants to learn to read and write	1.2.1 wants to be able to socialise again
		1.2.1 wants people to say he started out bad but has made good	1.2.2. Doesn't want a job yet, but maybe in future if she thought she could do it	1.2.2 wants to question the social circles he moves in
2. Reducing drug use		1.2.2 looks forward to a time when drugs won't play a big part in his life anymore	1.3. Personal/social aims	1.2.3 wants to grow in himself and take responsibility, as he believes he has been stunted by alcohol
2.1 doesn't want to substitute one addiction for another		1.2.3 wants to view his drug use as a chapter in his life that is over with	1.3.1 would feel better in herself if she could read and write	1.2.4 wants a relationship
3. Doesn't want to be bored		1.3. Personal/social aims	1.3.2 would like to do something productive at college, something she felt was worthwhile	1.2.5 wants a two-way friendship
3.1 wants to use time constructively		1.3.1 wants to socialise well at university		
3.2 wants variation in life				1.3. Career/education plans
3.3 wants to improve health				1.3.1 career
				1.3.1.1 wants regular unpaid part-time work
				1.3.1.2 would like some of his writing to be published

changes in the outcomes desired over time, rather than changes in the outcomes themselves, and in the actual study this data will be complemented by the findings from standardised measures (Spurling, Kazi and Rogan, 2000).

Enabling Mechanisms   As indicated in Chapter 3, the concept of mechanisms is bound up with the notion of embeddedness and the stratified nature of realism. Manicas explains: 'because social structure is both constraining and enabling, what one can and cannot do is determined both by existing social resources, and more particularly, by the nature of the social relations defined by the structures and one's place in them' (1998: 321).

The matrices in Tables 4.4 and 4.5 indicate the enabling mechanisms that were identified from each set of interviews, that is, the mechanisms in the circumstances of service users that can enable them to achieve their desired outcomes. These variously included enabling support from family and friends, motivation, and a number of lifestyle changes. For example, Ben's relationships with family and friends were enabling mechanisms that remained so in the period between the first and second interviews. However, circumstances do change in the open system, and therefore whilst education was an enabling mechanism in the first interview, this was replaced by voluntary work in the second interview. In Sid's interviews, the enabling mechanisms identified in the first interview remained, but more were added in the second as his lifestyle changed.

Disabling Mechanisms   Tables 4.6 and 4.7 indicate the disabling mechanisms as identified from the data. Disabling or countervailing mechanisms can be regarded as those that work against the achievement of the service users' desired outcomes. For example, with regard to the desired outcome to reduce drug misuse, disabling mechanisms would include those that influence the service users in promoting the misuse of drugs. The disabling mechanisms identified in the matrices include relationships, peer group pressures, availability of drugs, and motivation, and they remained fairly consistent in the time periods between the first and the second interviews.

Content of Service Provided at Outlook   The content of services include the generating mechanisms of change initiated when the service users are in contact with, or use the facilities provided by, Outlook. These generative mechanisms are introduced to help promote the enabling mechanisms and to neutralise, or to at least reduce the effects, of the disabling mechanisms in enabling service users to achieve their desired outcomes. Tables 4.8 and 4.9 provide the templates regarding the service users' perceptions of the content of Outlook's services. Reducing boredom, offering support and advice, counselling, meeting other people, help with self-esteem, practical help and activities were among the main sub-themes across the five service users, and across the first and second interviews.

Table 4.4 *Changes in enabling mechanisms matrix: template analysis of first interviews*

Ben	John	Mark	Sarah	Sid
2.1. Enabling support	2.1. Motivation to reduce drug use	2.1. Motivation to reduce drug use	2.1. Enabling support	2.1. Enabling support
2.1.1 relationships	2.1.1 reducing contact with drug users	2.1.1 he really dislikes drugs because of the affects they have on people	2.1.1 family	2.1.1 family
2.1.2 parents		2.1.2. doesn't want to do any other drug, not even methadone	2.1.1.1 brother	2.1.2 friends
2.2. Lifestyle changes	2.2. Lifestyle changes	2.1.3 feels physically better now that he has reduced his drug use, which motivates him to continue further		2.2. Lifestyle changes
2.2.1 social	2.2.1 education			2.2.1 has become more involved in local community through voluntary work and joining a choir
2.2.1.1 has started to broaden social circle, getting in touch with friends	2.2.1.1 is committed to doing a college course, so he believes it will limit his opportunity to use drugs	2.2. Lifestyle changes		
2.2.2 Education	2.3. Enabling support	2.2.1 physical		
2.2.2.1 it is nice to have things to keep busy with that are enjoyable, but accepts that at college have to do things that you don't enjoy	2.3.1 relationships	2.2.1.1 has stopped smoking		
2.2.3 physical fitness	2.3.1.1 romantic relationship	2.3. Enabling support		
2.2.3.1 going swimming regularly		2.3.1 his dad encouraged him to use Outlook the first time		
		2.3.2. lives at home with parents who help him, mum looks after money so he is not tempted to buy drugs		

Table 4.5   Changes in enabling mechanisms matrix: template analysis of second interviews

Ben	John	Mark	Sarah	Sid
2.1. Enabling support	2.1. Motivation to reduce drug use	2.1. Enabling support	2.1. Relationships	2.1. Enabling support
2.1.1 relationships	2.1.1 feels better physically now he has reduced his use of drugs	2.1.1 relationships	2.1.1 friends (non-users)	2.1.1 relationships
2.1.1.1 friends	2.1.2 a course of treatment is helping him to reduce drug misuse	2.1.1.1 friends	2.2. Motivation to reduce drug use	2.1.1.1 friends
2.2. Motivation to maintain no drug misuse	2.1.3 feels better in himself for reducing the drug misuse as he feels he has things going for him	2.1.1.2 family	2.2.1 has been off drugs for 4/5 months	2.1.1.2 family
2.2.1 has accepted that it is a slow process of recovery	2.2. Lifestyle changes	2.2. Motivation to reduce drug use		2.2. Motivation to maintain no drug misuse
2.2.2 has more to look forward to	2.2.1 employment	2.2.1 doesn't want to crave drugs, wants to stop using drugs		2.2.1 he doesn't socialise around pubs
2.2.3 feels more in control	2.2.1.1 looking forward to working for himself	2.2.2 has realised what he has missed out on and wants to change things		2.2.2 entered a pub with work and drank tea, nothing alcoholic
2.3. Lifestyle changes	2.2.1.2 it is something to do and sees it as a good time	2.3. Lifestyle changes		2.2.3 the cravings gradually reducing
2.3.1 employment		2.3.1 education		2.2.4 feels he is calmer as a person
2.3.1.1 has undertaken some voluntary work		2.3.1.1 more organised for college		2.2.5 thinks he is on the right track but doesn't want to rush things
		2.3.1.2 getting back into routine of things		2.3. Lifestyle changes
		2.3.2. Physical		2.3.1 employment
		2.3.2.1 is getting fitter, doing more exercise		2.3.1.1 has undertaken voluntary work for the National Trust
				2.3.2. social
				2.3.2.1 joined a choir whilst still drinking and didn't attend often, he is now attending every session
				2.3.2.2 attends meetings when arranged and doesn't miss them
				2.3.3 increasing confidence
				2.3.3.1 after he had stopped drinking his confidence came back slowly
				2.3.3.2 his voluntary work is helping his self-esteem
				2.3.3.3 has asked someone out on a date which he says he never would have done before
				2.3.3.4 says he has to remember not to try to please people by doing things he doesn't want to do

Table 4.6 Changes in disabling mechanisms matrix: template analysis of first interviews

Ben	John	Mark	Sarah	Sid
3.1. Relationships	3.1. Peer group influence	3.1. Peer group influence	3.1. Relationships	3.1. Relationships
3.1.1 family	3.1.1 has a close friend who is also a user	3.1.1 has lived with users and has resorted to misuse	3.1.1 family	3.1.1 friend
3.1.2 parents	3.1.2 this friend was living with him and tempted him back to drugs several times	3.1.2 has 'bumped' into previous friends who are users and has been unable to resist	3.1.1.1 father	3.2. Lack of motivation to reduce drug use
3.2. Peer group influence		3.1.3 his friends really understand him	3.1.1.2 other family 'don't like her'	3.2.1 has tried stopping previously but has relapsed several times
3.2.1 being known as a user and targeted by dealers	3.2 Lack of motivation to reduce drug use		3.1.1.3 husband	
3.2.2 easy availability of drugs without needing money	3.2.1 enjoys the recreational use of drugs	3.2. Lack of motivation to reduce drug use		
3.2.3 can't mix with other users	3.2.2 wants to reduce but not eliminate drugs from his lifestyle	3.2.1 remembers how good it feels to be high		
3.3. Lack of motivation to reduce drug use	3.2.3 doesn't see drug use of much of a problem as going out and getting drunk	3.2.2 tempted to meet up with old friends for a good time		
3.3.1 remembers the good times he has had on drugs		3.2.3 drugs make him feel more extroverted		
3.3.2 problem of relapses		3.2.4 having money he feels is a danger because he could buy drugs		
		3.2.5 he sees drugs as exciting and dangerous 'like bungy jumping'		
		3.2.6 when people let him down he uses it as an excuse to use drugs again		
		3.3. Rejection by society		
		3.3.1 problems with feeling accepted		
		3.3.2 pressure to conform		
		3.4. Relationships		
		3.4.1 family		
		3.4.1.1 father		

Table 4.7 Changes in disabling mechanisms matrix: template analysis of second interviews

Ben	John	Mark	Sarah	Sid
3.1. Disabling support 3.1.1 family 3.1.2 parents 3.2. Peer group influence 3.2.1 must be careful of the people (drug misusers) you mix with	3.1. Lack of motivation to reduce drug use 3.1.1 believes heroin to be great for making you feel good about yourself, gives you a better attitude 3.1.2 doesn't believe smoking drugs is a problem 3.1.3 believes taking drugs helps get nearer the 'truth'	3.1. Lack of motivation to reduce drug use 3.1.1 has relapsed several times 3.1.2 thought he could use a small amount of drugs and then stay clean, but relapsed 3.1.3 disheartened that he still hasn't kicked it 3.1.4 remembers the good times he had when he was on drugs 3.2. Disabling support 3.2.1 relationships 3.2.1.1 family 3.2.1.1.1 parents 3.2.2 Friends 3.2.2.1 wants them to think he is doing well 3.3. Rejection by society 3.3.1 doesn't feel confident when talking to his friends, problems of fitting in 3.3.2 wants to fit in with his family and can't at the moment 3.3.3 wants to be like his friends, successful, fashionable, etc.	3.1. Disabling support 3.1.1 relationships 3.1.1.1 family 3.1.1.1.1 husband 3.1.1.1.2 mother and father 3.1.1.1.3 other family members 3.2. Peer group influence 3.2.1 has friends who are users 3.2.2 unable to resist temptation if friends are using 3.3. Rejection by society 3.3.1 problems of being accepted 3.3.1 people judge and label you	3.1. Lack of motivation to reduce drug abuse 3.1.1 got annoyed over something and then thought of having a drink. He didn't actually do it though 3.2. Disabling support 3.2.1 relationships 3.2.1.1 problems with a fellow alcohol misuser

Table 4.8 *Changes in content matrix: template analysis of first interviews*

Ben	John	Mark	Sarah	Sid
4.1. Reducing boredom	4.1. Support and advice	4.1. Support and advice	4.1. Reducing boredom	4.1. Reducing boredom
4.1.1 meeting people	4.1.1 practical help	4.1.1 help with self-esteem/confidence	4.1.1 something to do	4.1.1 meeting people
4.1.1.1 just having people to talk to, everyday chat	4.1.1.1 encouraged to make more of himself	4.1.1.1 confidence has increased the more he has attended Outlook	4.1.1.1 can do things you wouldn't normally	4.1.1.1 outlook is recreational
4.2. Support and advice	4.1.1.2 encouraged to take up a college course	4.1.1.2 encouraged to accept problems and can then deal with them	4.2. Activities provided	4.1.1.2 somewhere you can have fun
4.2.1 help with self-esteem/confidence	4.1.2 help with self-esteem and confidence	4.2. Reducing boredom	4.2.1 arts and crafts	4.1.1.3 it is difficult to walk in and leave with nothing
4.2.1.1 can talk about difficulties of withdrawal	4.1.2.1 encouraged to come to terms with himself	4.2.1 meeting people		4.1.2 something to do
4.2.2 practical help	4.1.2.2 encouraged to share problems	4.2.1.1 who are sympathetic to his cause		4.1.2.1 believes that it is important to fill your time as boredom can lead you back
4.2.2.1 encouraged to look for college courses	4.1.2.3 has begun to get involved with things more	4.2.1.2 recognising how difficult drug abuse is to overcome, and acknowledging successes		4.2. Support and advice
4.3. Activities provided	4.2. Reducing boredom	4.2.1.3 wants to meet people similar to him		4.2.1 help with self-esteem/confidence
4.3.1 arts and crafts	4.2.1 meeting people	4.3. Counselling		4.2.1.1 helped him to recover his self-worth, feels he is building a few bridges
	4.2.1.1 making friends	4.3.1 helped him to sort problems out		4.2.1.2 rediscovering that he can interact with people, can meet all sorts of people and get along with them
	4.2.1.2 meeting similar people with same problems as you	4.4. Activities provided		4.3. Counselling
	4.2.1.3 being part of a group	4.4.1 football		4.3.1 the counselling service influenced decision to use Outlook
	4.2.2 something to do	4.4.2 DJ workshop		4.4. Activities provided
	4.2.2.1 to kill time especially on a 'grey day'	4.4.3 Outlook magazine		4.4.1 computers
				4.4.2 fitness sessions

Table 4.9 *Changes in content matrix: template analysis of second interviews*

Ben	John	Mark	Sarah	Sid
4.1. Atmosphere of Outlook	4.1. Meeting people	4.1. Future use of Outlook	4.1. Activities provided	4.1. Activities provided
4.1.1 it is relaxed	4.1.1 wants to keep contact with other people attending outlook	4.1.1 can never see himself quitting at the moment	4.1.1 gym	4.1.1 computers
4.1.2 the people are friendly			4.1.2 computers	4.1.2 gym
	4.1.2 meeting people helps you realise you are not the only one with problems	4.1.2 Outlook has become a way of life, part of his routine	4.1.3 DJ workshop	4.1.3 magazine that is produced
4.2. Support and advice	4.1.3 everyone is welcomed		4.2. Future use of Outlook	4.2. Atmosphere of Outlook
4.2.1 someone to talk to		4.2. Individual staff	4.2.1 wants to continue using Outlook	4.2.1 it is recreational which helps to return to normality
		4.2.1 mentions an Outlook worker as being helpful and supportive to him		4.2.2 forum for discussion
		4.3. Support and advice		4.3. Meeting people
		4.3.1 someone to talk to		4.3.1 it gets you out of the house
		4.4. Atmosphere of outlook		4.4. Counselling
		4.4.1 a nice comfortable place		4.4.1 that is the reason he came back to Outlook – for the counselling
				4.5. Future use of Outlook
				4.5.1 will probably be using it for years, but thinks his recovery will be a slow one

The Context of Service Users Mark, Henry and Julnes, define contexts as 'the physical, organisational, cultural and political settings in which programmes and clients are embedded and in particular those setting aspects that influence programme success' (2000: 195). The mechanisms identified in the preceding sections are triggered under certain conditions, and these conditions include the context in which programmes operate and the contexts in the circumstances of the service users. Contexts can and do change, such as housing conditions and employment, but they tend to change slower than the mechanisms.

Tables 4.10 and 4.11 indicate the contexts in the templates across the five service users and over the time period between the first and the second interviews. The contexts include housing, history of family problems, history of abuse, rejection by society, and history of problems with confidence and self-esteem.

Identifying Patterns and Causal Mechanisms from Qualitative Data

These repeated interviews took place within fairly short periods of time, and in the research project at Outlook these interviews are part of the general integration of the realist effectiveness cycle which systematically tracks the mechanism–context–outcome configurations, along with the generative mechanisms produced at Outlook, as part of a three-year longitudinal study (Spurling, Kazi and Rogan, 2000). These five sets of interviews were used in this chapter to investigate the extent to which it was possible to achieve retroduction using qualitative analysis. As indicated in Chapter 3, the aim is to identify the key factor(s) that may be responsible for the outcomes, or at least helped to produce the outcomes. In the process of retroduction, the researcher also has to take into account the fact that all concrete outcomes are the result of a plurality of causes, operating at different strata of reality (Manicas, 1998). Some common mechanism–context–outcome patterns are indicated in the data from the five sets of interviews in terms of some common outcomes, mechanisms and contexts.

The outcomes desired by the service users analysed in the templates included reducing or ending drug use, changing lifestyles, developing education and careers in employment, improving social life, improving physical fitness, building meaningful social relationships, developing self-confidence and self-esteem, and relieving boredom. The enabling mechanisms in the circumstances of these service users included enabling relationships with both family and peers, opportunities for education, motivation, and opportunities for voluntary work and employment. The disabling mechanisms included disabling relationships with family, peer group influences, availability of drugs, rejection by society, motivation, and boredom. Therefore, there is a plurality of causal mechanisms at play, and there is an overlap as well.

Ben	John	Mark	Sarah	Sid
5.1. Housing 5.1.1 living in close proximity to other users and dealers 5.1.2 previously hasn't lived alone which has caused problems	5.1. History of low confidence/ self-esteem 5.1.1 was criticised by father when younger, damaged self-esteem 5.1.2 previously drank to boost his confidence 5.1.3 drugs help with self-esteem because he is nervous when meeting people, which causes him stress 5.2. Housing 5.2.1 now has own flat instead of a bedsit, much happier now 5.3. History of boredom 5.3.1 has done jobs in the past, which have been poorly paid and monotonous, which is why he turned to drugs 5.4. Rejection by society 5.4.1 problems with acceptance 5.4.2 was always embarrassed at school as he was slightly coloured 5.4.3 always called names at school 5.5. Family problems 5.5.1 problems with father 5.5.1.1 was continuously criticised as a child 5.5.1.2 never encouraged to do anything 5.5.2 problems with mother 5.5.2.1 she over-compensated for father's criticism; he wasn't comfortable with that	5.1. Rejection by society 5.1.1 problems with acceptance 5.1.1.1 feels he doesn't fit in, drugs make him feel better 5.1.1.2 drugs are a barrier that protect him from getting hurt 5.2. Family problems 5.2.1 he is grateful to be living at home	5.1. Family problems 5.1.1 suffered abuse as a child, gets flashbacks of the abuse. The feelings which lead her to the abuse come back; it was this which led her to drugs originally 5.1.2 doesn't see family much 5.2. Confidence/self-esteem 5.2.1 doesn't expect a lot of anything	5.1. Housing 5.1.1 lives in a nice area he is happy with, no problems

Table 4.11 *Changes in context matrix: template analysis of second interviews*

Ben	John	Mark	Sarah	Sid
5.1. Housing 5.1.1 moved to a nice place 5.2. Family problems 5.2.1 lack of support 5.3. History of low confidence and self-esteem 5.3.1 feeling of inadequacy	5.1. History of low confidence and self-esteem 5.1.1 poor self-esteem was part of reason for abusing drugs	5.1. History of low confidence and self-esteem 5.1.1 has always felt different 5.2. Family problems 5.2.1 problems with mother 5.2.1.1 historically spends a lot of time in the pub which he is uncomfortable with	5.1. Family problems 5.1.1 doesn't get on with mother 5.1.2 doesn't get on with husband's family 5.1.3 doesn't get on with her own family; they put her down 5.2. Housing 5.2.1 feels isolated because she is living away from her friends	5.1. History of low confidence and self-esteem

For example, 'relieving boredom' is an outcome for engaging in meaningful activities; at the same time, boredom itself is a disabling mechanism in relation to the outcome of reducing drug misuse.

The content of the services provided by Outlook introduce or trigger generating mechanisms in these complex realities of the service users' circumstances. Reducing boredom, offering support and advice, counselling, meeting other people, help with self-esteem, practical help and activities were among the main generative mechanisms initiated by Outlook to help harness the enabling mechanisms and to neutralise the disabling mechanisms identified by the service users. Furthermore, all of these mechanisms were triggered in the contexts of housing problems, history of family problems, history of abuse, rejection by society, and history of problems with confidence and self-esteem. In particular, all five service users have the reduction or ending of drug/alcohol misuse as a common outcome, as well as career and education plans, and mechanisms include relationships with family and friends. They have engaged in social activities and received support at Outlook, and the work of Outlook in four out of the five cases is taking place in the context of histories of low self-esteem and confidence.

The above analysis indicates that the use of in-depth repeated interviews and template analysis have identified the outcomes desired by the service users, and the complex weave of mechanisms and contexts in which these outcomes are produced. As Porter and Ryan (1996) explain, the purpose of realist ethnography 'is not simply to uncover the unique experiences of individuals, but to use examination of those experiences to shed light upon the relationship between individual agency and social structure' (p. 416). However, so far in this analysis, this falls short of retroduction, as it has not been possible to identify the actual changes in the outcomes, or the extent to which they were achieved. Although the potential causal mechanisms have been identified, it has not been possible to identify the degree or magnitude of change in each of the outcomes indicated by the service users. We have an indication of the causal mechanisms in the circumstances of each of the five service users, including the causal mechanisms introduced by Outlook, and also indications of the contexts or conditions in which these causal mechanisms may be triggered. However, although we know the desired outcomes, we do not know the changes in each of these outcomes, and therefore it has not been possible to establish which were the causal mechanisms responsible for change at this stage.

Outcomes can be systematically tracked through repeated interviews and indeed, qualitative strategies can be used in a largely quasi-experimental design. In fact, Cook and Campbell say that qualitative strategies should be used in field experimentation (for example, in a quasi-experimental design) 'to describe and illuminate the context and conditions under which research is conducted' (Cook and Campbell, 1979: 93). The point, however, is that, as elaborated in Chapter 2, interpretivist approaches tend to overlook the systematic tracking of outcomes, just as empirical approaches tend to overlook systematic tracking of content and contexts. Therefore, it can be concluded that, although the qualitative methods used in this chapter help to identify the potential causal mechanisms and the contexts in which they may be triggered, in themselves the methods used in this example have been limited in the determination of the causal mechanisms responsible for changes in outcomes. However, the use of qualitative methods in this way constitutes an important step *towards* a retroductive analysis, as illustrated in another study described in Chapters 6–8. Before leaving the Outlook project, it should be noted that, in the actual three-year study, these qualitative methods are combined with the repeated use of standardised outcome measures, and as both types of data have been collected from repeated interactions with over 50 service users, a retroductive analysis of the findings is more likely than with the five sets of interviews used in this example.

The data from the service users were in the form of in-depth interviews, and therefore facilitated the identification of outcomes, mechanisms, content of services received, and contexts from the perspectives of the service users. The narratives of the users were interpreted through the use of template approaches, to assign meanings to the narratives. The interpretation of how members of society see reality is a crucial part of realist evaluation research. Sayer maintains that the social world 'is socially constructed and includes knowledge itself and it therefore cannot be said to exist independently of at least some knowledge, though it is more likely to be past knowledge than that of contemporary researchers' (Sayer, 2000: 11).

Things exist and act independently of our descriptions; at the same time, human actions are concept-dependent, and human concepts make up a part of the reality of these facts. Therefore, social phenomena are intrinsically meaningful. 'Meaning has to be understood, it cannot be measured or counted, and hence there is always an interpretive or hermeneutic element in social science' (Sayer, 2000: 17).

Therefore realism is only partly naturalist, for although social science can use the same methods as natural science regarding causal explanation, it may also diverge from it in using interpretive understanding. For example, Outhwaite (1998) maintains that common sense is a starting point at uncovering the structures. However, as Archer (1998) points out, not all is revealed to human consciousness and sometimes that is because reality is shaped outside our conscious awareness, and therefore there is no 'warrant for confining social causes to the mental or meanings. It is also what makes for social realism: we do not uncover real social structures by interviewing people in-depth about them' (p. 199). It follows, therefore, that although interpretivist approaches are a necessary part of realist research, realist causal analysis may require more than interpretive meanings or understandings.

> Social science needs to do more than give a description of the social world as seen by its members (ethnography); it needs also to ask whether members have an adequate understanding of their world and, if not, to explain why not. (Manicas, 1998: 315)

Realism 'endorses much of hermeneutics, but realism also insists on non-discursive, material dimensions to social life' (Sayer, 2000: 17–18). Therefore, realist explanatory causal analysis may require more than what any one method can offer; a single method (as used in this example; and as used in the quantitative example in Chapter 3) may identify the mechanisms that require further explanation through a combination of research methods. Despite these limitations, the methods used in this example provide an insight into the way the Outlook programmes are interacting with other factors in the circumstances of service users, and represent the beginnings of the integration of the realist effectiveness cycle.

5
Quantitative Methods: Evaluation of Family Centres

This chapter analyses the use of largely quantitative methods within a realist perspective, based on a study of family centres in the local authority of Kirklees. With regard to the analysis of mechanism–context–outcome configurations as advocated by Pawson and Tilley (1997b) in realist evaluation research, outcomes play an important role. In the 'black box', 'grey box' and 'clear box' classification of evaluation research as described in Chapters 1 and 2, the identification of outcomes and how they are produced remains a foundation in all three types of evaluation. However, in realist evaluations, the purpose is not simply to investigate whether programmes work, but also to provide an explanation of how the outcomes were produced, that is, to confirm or otherwise mechanism–context–outcome theories, and to explain the explanations in a continuous cycle in order to better target and develop the programmes in the future.

One way to systematically track the outcomes of a programme is to apply single-case evaluation, and it is argued that this methodology can be used within a realist evaluation framework (Kazi, 1998a). Once single-case evaluation strategies are integrated into the practice of a programme, the systematic tracking of outcomes required by the realist effectiveness cycle (as described in Chapter 3) can be facilitated in a prospective manner. The tracking of outcomes alone provides a 'black box' evaluation; but a foundation may be created upon which other strategies could be applied to achieve 'grey box' and even 'clear box' evaluations.

In this chapter, the extensive use of single-case evaluation in the work of family centres in the Kirklees Social Services Department (in Yorkshire, England) is described, comprising the intensive evaluation in each case. Next, the data is aggregated in the form of one-group pre-test post-test designs (Nugent, Sieppert and Hudson, 2001; Rubin and Babbie, 2001), and an attempt is made to cross-tabulate the outcomes with some basic contextual characteristics of the service users. In this example, the family centre workers were encouraged to integrate the realist effectiveness cycle into their practice, and they agreed to collect additional data with regard to the type of service provided and the client characteristics to enable this type of analysis. In this way, this study demonstrates both intensive evaluation with each service user, as well as the aggregation of results across the 155 children included in the study. However, the methods used are entirely quantitative, and the data is analysed with the SPSS software (Foster, 1998, 2001). This study is influenced by the use of inferential statistics as described in Duguid and Pawson (1998) and Pawson and Tilley (1997b). Both of these publications describe an extensive study of a university prison education programme in Canada where these methods were used.

As described in Kazi, Manby and Buckley (2001), the family centres are part of the Family Support Unit established in April 1997 by the Children and Families Service of Kirklees Metropolitan Council Social Services Department, following a review of family centres and some residential services and a decision to invest in family support services. Kirklees Social Services Department's Strategic Development Plan for the period 1997–2000 emphasised the development of services that prevent family breakdown and promote the support of individuals and families within their own communities. It also emphasised partnership, both with service users and other agencies, in the provision of social care services.

The Family Support Unit brings together a range of family support services for children in need, both directly managed and in partnership with the voluntary sector and other agencies, across five family centres, now reorganised into four centres. The Brackenhall Family Centre was closed during the evaluation period and the workers employed there were relocated to Southgate Family Centre, from where they continued to provide an outreach service to the communities they served previously. The Unit aims to provide a range of services from those that work with families at the point of acute crisis, to those where support will prevent deterioration and improve the quality of life for children in need. The Family Support Unit's work varies to meet the needs of the family and is done in close partnership with the family. A typical involvement is usually 3–6 months of quite intensive work including some evening and weekend activity.

Referrals to family centres come largely from social workers, health visitors and families themselves. Each family centre provides a range of early intervention and support services to children and their families so that children can continue to live safely within their families, including:

1 assessment of need;
2 support to parents as their child's first educator by provision of early years' education which supports children's development and self-confidence and encourages active learning;
3 work on a range of family difficulties including behaviour management, enhancement of attachments, social isolation and speech development;
4 practical parenting skills;

5   group work with parents and life-long learning opportunities;
6   a child-centred environment for use by others for group work, supervised
     contact, etc.

This study (Kazi, Manby and Buckley, 2001) involved the use of single-case designs in the evaluation of the five family centres that provide facilities for young children and their families, in order to enhance family functioning and appropriate child development. The purpose of the study was to enable more than thirty family centre workers to incorporate single-case design procedures into their daily practice, that is, focussing on outcomes. The project was started in January 1999, and a number of consultation and training meetings took place with the participating staff where appropriate outcome measures were developed. The measures were tested in a pre-pilot stage in April, and then the evaluation programme was piloted with a sample of families during June and July 1999. Test–retest reliability tests also took place with seven cases in June. It was agreed that the outcome measures would be used with all families in a six-month period – September to March 2000 – with the expectation that they would be used in daily practice thereafter.

In this respect, the study could be described as 'black box', using Scriven's (1994) classification, as the emphasis was on the use of outcome measures. However, in keeping with Duguid and Pawson (1998), the study was turned into a 'grey box' type by cross-tabulation of the outcomes against other variables such as type of service provided, type of referral, and demographic characteristics. A further point is that, in keeping with the principles of empowerment evaluation (Fetterman, 2001), the purpose of this evaluation was not just to determine the merit and worth of the family centres' programmes, but also to develop self-determination and capacity-building, particularly amongst the family centre workers, and thereby also within the service users through evaluation in partnership. In the integration of evaluation methods to practice, first a partnership was established between the external evaluators and the practitioners, and second, the practitioners were encouraged not only to seek the service users' permission to apply the evaluation methods, but also to share the findings from the evaluation in a prospective manner. During the period of the evaluation, both the practitioners and the service users were aware of the progress made at each stage, and they were able to use this data to shape the content of the intervention programmes for the near future.

Evaluation Research Methodology

The method is largely a replication of a strategy (based on a partnership between academic researchers and practitioners) which has been successful in encouraging practitioners in other social work settings to use hundreds of single-case designs in their practice (see Kazi, 1998a: 93–5, for an extensive account of this strategy). Through several consultancy and training sessions, the workers were encouraged to focus on the target problems of their clients, and to repeatedly use appropriate outcome measures to systematically track client progress. The nature of the single-case design used then naturally fell into place according to the needs of practice. In all cases, the measurement and intervention took place at the same time, and the first measurement was used as a baseline.

> Single-case evaluation is the use of single-case designs by practitioners to track client progress systematically or to evaluate the effectiveness of their interventions or programmes.
>
> The only fundamental requirement is the measurement of the client's target problem(s) repeatedly over time, using appropriate outcome measure(s) or indicator(s) of progress. Practitioners may use published standardised measures and/or develop their own, provided they attempt to minimise potential errors and thereby maximise reliability. In all cases where outcome measures are used repeatedly, it can be determined whether improvement was made.
>
> In some cases it may be possible to obtain baseline measurement before the intervention commences, and/or after the intervention has ended, enabling comparisons between the baseline, intervention and/or follow-up phases. In such circumstances, it may be possible to establish a tenuous causal link between the intervention and its effects.
>
> Single-case evaluation may be applied to one or more target problems with one client or a group of clients, and it can be used in combination with other methods, perspectives or paradigms to address wider evaluation questions. (Kazi, 2000c: 317)

A fundamental requirement of single-case evaluation is the measurement of the subject's target problem (that is, the object of the intervention or treatment) repeatedly over time (Bloom, Fischer and Orme, 1999; Kazi, 1999a). The practitioner is required to select an outcome measure that best reflects changes in the subject's condition, and then to apply the same measure over a period of time to enable a systematic tracking of progress.

However, when aggregating data across cases, Nugent, Sieppert and Hudson (2001) explain that single-case designs and comparison group designs can be integrated in the evaluation of practice. In this application, comparisons were made between the first and the last scores to determine whether the cases had improved, remained the same, or deteriorated across each of the target problems. In this way, the data across the single cases was aggregated to create a one-group pre-test post-test design for each outcome measure. Drawing on realist evaluation strategies (Kazi, 2000a), cross-tabulations have been made between the outcomes achieved and the clients' demographic characteristics, the nature of the referrals and the type of service received, to provide a more in-depth account of the findings from the 155 cases included in this study. In addition to the integration of outcome measures, the family centre workers agreed to collect this additional data in a prospective evaluation to help investigate the circumstances in which the outcomes were or were not achieved.

Pawson and Tilley (1997b) explain that the interventions of a programme trigger varying causal mechanisms within the varying contexts of practice and thereby generate a range of outcomes. This study began with the specification of the range of outcomes expected across the five family centres, and particularly those outcomes that impacted upon children and their families. The family centre workers described the expected outcomes in terms of the development of the child, the development of the child–parent interaction, and the development of the parents' self-esteem within the parenting role.

The practitioners themselves selected and created the outcome measures, in consultation with the authors of the project report (Kazi, Manby and Buckley, 2001). In this author's experience (Kazi, 1998a), practitioners are likely to integrate single-case designs into their practice only if they feel that the measures are appropriate, and particularly if they have a sense of ownership of the evaluation enterprise. In a number of sessions, three main instruments were constructed: the Observation of Child Rating Scale (OCRS), Parent/Carer-Child Interaction Scale (PCIS), and Parents'/Carers' Self-Esteem Questionnaire (PCSEQ). The OCRS measures development milestones, behaviour and play; the PCIS includes practical care, parental responsibility, management of child's behaviour, communication and play; and the PCSEQ measures the parent/carer's feelings and self-concept as a parent. In addition, the Client Satisfaction Questionnaire (CSQ8, Fischer and Corcoran, 1994) was selected because it has proven reliability, with excellent internal consistency (alphas ranging from .86 to .94), and it is very simple to use. The CSQ8 is used to assess client satisfaction with the services received. It has eight questions, each with a Likert-type scale. The total scores range from a possible 8 (no satisfaction) to 32 (very high levels of satisfaction). The CSQ8 was selected as a measure for parents, and also adapted as a measure for referrers who were mainly health visitors or field social workers. It was agreed that the OCRS, PCIS and PCSEQ would be used monthly. The CSQ8 would be used every two months with parents/carers and with the referring agencies where involved.

The OCRS, PCIS, and PCSEQ were subjected to reliability testing with eight families in June. The participating workers were asked to use the measures one day, and then re-test the following day, as the measures were not designed for daily sensitivity. The extent to which the re-test corresponded with the test from the previous day would provide the reliability data. SPSS was used, and it was found that the reliability of all three scales taken together was .92 which was well within the acceptable range (Rubin and Babbie, 1997, 2001).

Results

As in the other single-case evaluation studies based in this region of England (see Kazi, 1998a), the family centre workers have responded very

Table 5.1 *Distribution of cases and numbers included in the evaluation*

Family Centre	Total number of children on roll during evaluation	Total number of cases evaluated	Number of cases not included	Reasons for non-inclusion
Windybank	18	11	7	Refusal of parents to participate
Brackenhall	19	17	2	Contact visits only with no targeted goals
Southgate	44	25	19	– 9 parents attending baby group only – 10 parents attending for contact visits only with no targeted goals
Westtown	49	38	11	– Children attending play sessions only with no targeted goals – Some parents too severely mentally ill to participate – Contact visits only with no targeted goals
Walpole	69	64	5	Refusal of parents to participate
Total	199	155	44	

positively. During the evaluation, 29 family centre workers used single-case designs with 155 children and their families in all five family centres (Table 5.1). In all of these cases, the outcome measures were used more than once. However, the totals for each of the outcome measures fall short of 155 as not all the outcome measures were used repeatedly in every case.

The parents' permission and co-operation was requested in all cases. Table 5.1 summarises the number of cases included as well as those not included in the six-month evaluation period. Out of a total of 199 cases across the family centres, the evaluation methodology was applied in 155 cases (78%). A total of only 12 parents declined to participate, and the remainder of the 44 were not included in the study mainly due to a lack of targeted goals. With all other participating service users, the workers shared the findings from the evaluation with all parents/carers, including the charts, as in the following case example (see Figure 5.1). These examples were selected by the Family Unit's Coordinator to illustrate the process of evaluation applied intensively in each of the 155 cases.

Dates of measurement	PCSEQ	OCRS	PCIS	Parents' CSQ8
13 September	44	24	14	30
5 October	45	28	19	
9 November	41	30	18	
13 December	46	32	17	
13 January	42	31	16	
15 February	45	35	18	
7 March	44	32	15	31

Notes:

PCSEQ: Parents'/Carers' Self-Esteem Questionnaire   Score range: 8 (low) – 56 (high)
OCRS: Observation of Child Rating Scale   Score range: 11(low) – 44 (high)
PCIS: Parent/Carer–Child Interaction Scale   Score range: 6 (low) – 24 (high)
Parents' CSQ8: Parents' Client Satisfaction
    Questionnaire   Score range: 8 (low) – 32 (high)

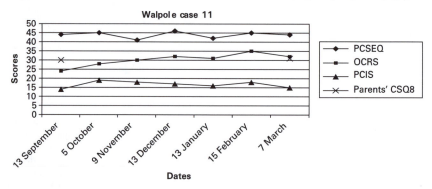

Figure 5.1   *Walpole case 11*

Case Example 1: (Walpole no. 11)

The child was male, of Afro-Caribbean origin, aged 3 years and 4 months at the start of the single-case design. In particular, the intervention included a respite nursery place and an opportunity for the parent to mix socially with other parents, as well as the provision of general support and advice on demand.

Figure 5.1 indicates a fluctuating pattern with regard to the outcomes achieved. Some progress was made with all three measures (higher scores indicate better results), although there was little change in parents' self-esteem and in the parent–child interaction when the last score was compared with the first. Gains in relation to OCRS were more marked. In addition, the CSQ8 was used with the parent in September with a score of 30, and it rose slightly to 31 in March. As the CSQ8 scores range from 4 to 32, the scores reflect very high levels of satisfaction with the family centre's work. There was no formal agency referral and therefore no referrers' CSQ8 questionnaire was completed.

Dates of measurement	PCSEQ	OCRS	PCIS	Parents' CSQ8	Referrer's CSQ8
14 September	47	19	8	21	
18 October		20	9		
10 November	40	23	8		
6 December	40	23	8		
17 January	38	23	9		
14 February	37	23	10		
13 March	43	24	9	23	26

Notes:

PCSEQ: Parents'/Carers' Self-Esteem Questionnaire   Score range: 8 (low) – 56 (high)
OCRS: Observation of Child Rating Scale   Score range: 11 (low) – 44 (high)
PCIS: Parent/Carer–Child Interaction Scale   Score range: 6 (low) – 24 (high)
Parents' CSQ8: Parents' Client Satisfaction Questionnaire   Score range: 8 (low) – 32 (high)
Referrer's CSQ8: Referrer's Client Satisfaction Questionnaire   Score range: 8 (low) – 32 (high)

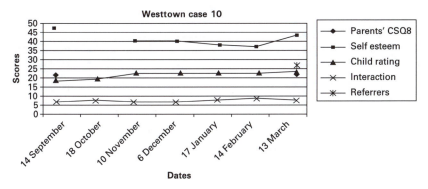

Figure 5.2   *Westtown case 10*

Case Example 2: (Westtown no. 10)

The child was male, white and aged 3 years and 11 months at the start of the single-case design. The referral was made by a social worker, indicating that the mother had learning difficulties and help was required to develop parenting skills. It was also indicated that attendance at the family centre would help the child to interact with other young children. There were also child protection issues in relation to risk of physical and sexual abuse, and neglect. Westtown's intervention included work on parenting skills and appropriate discipline and behaviour management.

Figure 5.2 indicates that the parents' self-esteem dipped markedly and then recovered partially. Parent–child interaction scores were low, improving slightly. Gains were again more marked in relation to the Observation of the Child Rating Scale. The parent's CSQ8 improved slightly, and the referrer's CSQ8 indicated a good level of satisfaction.

Case Example 3: (Southgate no. 20)

The child was white, male and 3 years old at the start of the single-case design. The referral was made by a health visitor because of the mother's

Dates of measurement	PCSEQ	OCRS	PCIS	Parents' CSQ8
24 September	45	40	22	28
22 October	43	38	18	
17 November		41		
28 January	42	37	22	
10 March	43	42	22	

Notes:

PCSEQ: Parents'/Carers' Self-Esteem Questionnaire   Score range: 8 (low) – 56 (high)
OCRS: Observation of Child Rating Scale   Score range: 11 (low) – 44 (high)
PCIS: Parent/Carer–Child Interaction Scale   Score range: 6 (low) – 24 (high)
Parents' CSQ8: Parents' Client Satisfaction Questionnaire   Score range: 8 (low) – 32 (high)

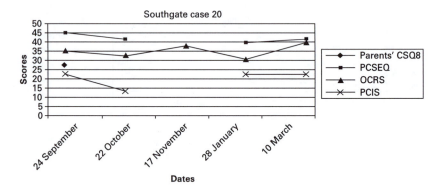

Figure 5.3   *Southgate Case 20*

mental health problems that included panic attacks as well as the need for behaviour management of the child. The intervention at Southgate involved working on behaviour management techniques as well as helping to build the mother's self-esteem.

Figure 5.3 indicates a fairly mixed pattern of change in the outcomes. The parent's self-esteem scores started high and dipped slightly. Parent–child interaction scores were mainly unchanged. Observation of the child scores fluctuated, finishing slightly higher. The parent's CSQ8 score was high, indicating a high level of satisfaction with the family centre's services.

In the first two case illustrations, gains were more marked in the Observation of the Child Rating Scale (OCRS) than for the Parent/Carer–Child Interaction Scale (PCIS), and the Parents'/Carers' Self-Esteem Questionnaire (PCSEQ). This may reflect the fact that family centres had more time for direct work with children, and also that children were more responsive to staff attention and intervention. The PCSEQ self-esteem scores tended to fluctuate, and this may reflect the fact that there was less direct work undertaken with parents. Parent–child interaction scores were low in Case Example 2, where child protection issues were noted on referral. Parents' satisfaction scores and the one referrers' satisfaction score were fairly high or high for all three cases examples, indicating that they were satisfied with the services provided.

Aggregated Findings from all Five Family Centres

The computer software programme SPSS for Windows (Foster, 1998, 2001) was used to analysis the data from the 155 cases. The extent to which progress was made in each case was determined by a comparison between the first scores and the last scores in the six-month period of the evaluation, thereby creating one-group pre-test post-test designs for each outcome measure. The measures were used when the children and parents attended the family centres, and therefore the interventions began at the same time as the measures. However, it can be argued that when the first outcome measures were taken, the interventions were only just coming into effect, and therefore the first scores can be taken as the baseline. Subsequent use of the measures would then indicate whether progress was made or not in each case. Tables 5.2 to 5.26 provide the main outcome data for the evaluation, including cross-tabulations with demographic characteristics, the nature of the referrals and the type of service provided. The figures presented in this chapter are different from those in Kazi, Manby and Buckley (2001), as the database has been updated and some of the missing data identified.

The data from the one-group pre-test post-test designs were aggregated and analysed with the calculation of effect sizes for each outcome measured, as described in Kazis, Anderson and Meenan (1989) and in Rubin and Babbie (2001). The effect size is calculated by taking the difference between the means of the first and last scores, and then dividing by the standard deviation of the first scores. The effect size is then interpreted from the result as follows:

Less than 0.2   =   small
0.2 to 0.5   =   small to moderate
0.5 to 0.8   =   moderate to large
Greater than 0.8 =   large

This process is useful for aggregating the data from several single-case designs or from large numbers of cases, and the effect size for each target problem can be measured to determine the impact of the interventions.

Table 5.2 indicates overall progress in all cases by a comparison of the first and the last scores in all cases across the three outcome measures. The comparison between the first and the last scores indicates that as the interventions progressed over several months, there were improvements for the OCRS score and the PCIS score. Sixty-eight percent of the cases improved using the OCRS scores, and only 24% became worse. More parents

Table 5.2 *Comparisons between the first and the last scores, and effect sizes*

Change in outcomes	PCSEQ: no. of cases	PCSEQ: as % of cases (n = 117)	OCRS: no. of cases	OCRS: as % of cases (n = 126)	PCIS: no. of cases	PCIS: as % of cases (n = 117)
No change	11	10.0	10	8.0	23	19.0
Improved	52	47.3	85	68.0	52	43.0
Deteriorated	47	42.7	30	24.0	46	38.0
Total	110	100	125	100	121	100

Statistics	PCSEQ: last scores	PCSEQ: first scores	OCRS: last scores	OCRS: first scores	PCIS: last scores	PCIS: first scores
Mean scores	39.89	39.44	30.37	26.95	16.48	15.99
Std. deviation	8.17	7.63	5.94	5.68	4.62	3.95

Effect sizes	PCSEQ	OCRS	PCIS
Effect sizes	0.06	0.58	0.13

improved their self-esteem (47.3%), although a significant proportion (42.7%) became worse. As this was the only self-report measure of the three outcome measures, deterioration may indicate more openness and recognition of problems by parents. However, the pattern was almost similar for the PCIS scores, indicating improvements in 43% and deterioration in 38%. These findings are confirmed with the effect size indicating moderate to large effect for OCRS, but only a small effect for each of the other two. Further confirmation was indicated when the Wilcoxon Signed Ranks Test was used (Argyrous, 2000; Foster, 2001). The improvements in the OCRS scores were found to be statistically significant ($Z = -5.901, n = 125, p = .000$); whereas changes in the PCSEQ and PCIS scores were not significant.

Statistical Analysis of Patterns

So far, Table 5.2 provides a quick overview with regard to the performance of the entire group of service users against the selected outcomes. There is no account of why the outcomes were achieved with some children and parents and not with others. As in Duguid and Pawson (1998: 476), 'by discovering which groups performed relatively well within the programme and which groups remained untouched by it or even regressed under it, we begin the journey of understanding it'. The data in this study is not as extensive as in Duguid and Pawson's study, and the variables selected are fewer; however, the number of variables are not decisive – they merely enable a somewhat deeper examination of the programme 'black box', to 'discern shades of grey' (p. 480). We shall now attempt to begin this journey with regard to developing an understanding of the family centres' practice, specifically with regard to the three types of outcomes, PCSEQ, OCRS and PCIS.

Table 5.3   *Parents' self-esteem (PCSEQ) outcomes cross-tabulated by age of child (in years)*

Age	No change	%	Improved	%	Deteriorated	%	Total	%
1	0	0	9	60.0	6	40.0	15	100
2	3	10.3	14	48.3	12	41.4	29	100
3	7	14.0	23	46.0	20	40.0	50	100
4	1	6.3	6	37.5	9	56.3	16	100
Total	11	10.0	52	47.3	47	42.7	110	100

Table 5.4   *Parents' self-esteem (PCSEQ) outcomes cross-tabulated by gender of child*

Gender	No change	%	Improved	%	Deteriorated	%	Total	%
Male	8	15.5	29	42.6	31	45.6	68	100
Female	3	15.2	23	54.8	16	38.1	42	100
Total	11	10.0	52	47.3	47	42.7	110	100

Cross-tabulations of Parents' Self-esteem (PCSEQ) Outcomes

Age is an important factor in work with children. Table 5.3 provides a cross-tabulation of the parents' self-esteem (PCSEQ) outcomes when compared to the first and last scores, and the child's age. This cross-tabulation indicates that the parents' self-esteem improved in more cases than it deteriorated for parents with children aged 1–3 years at the family centres. A reverse trend was apparent for parents of children aged 4 attending the centres. Although these differences were small and not statistically significant, these findings may provide an indication of the contextual differences in the way the family centres' programmes trigger changes in the parents' self-esteem. It may be that the programme is more intensive with the younger children, and there is greater contact with the parents who may tend to stay for a while when bringing their babies and toddlers to the family centre, than with the parents of the children aged four years. This is an example of how the sub-group methodology can peer deeper into the 'black box', and discover a mechanism which otherwise would have remained hidden. However, this explanation requires further explanation (as in Lawson, 1998), to identify the patterns in the mechanisms triggered under the contextual conditions that include the age of the child.

Table 5.4 provides a cross-tabulation of the parents' self-esteem (PCSEQ) outcomes, in terms of the comparison between the first and the last scores, against the gender of the child. This outcome measure was used repeatedly with 110 parents, and of these 68 were parents of boys and 42 were parents of girls. Although the differences were not statistically significant, the table shows that the self-esteem of slightly more parents with boys at the centre deteriorated than improved; whereas the self-esteem of more parents with girls improved then deteriorated. As for the gender of the parents, Table 5.5

Table 5.5 *Parents' self-esteem (PCSEQ) outcomes cross-tabulated by gender of the parent(s) working with the family centres*

Gender	No Change	%	Improved	%	Deteriorated	%	Total	%
Male Parent only			4	66.7	2	33.3	6	100
Female Parent only	3	6.1	24	49.0	22	44.9	49	100
Both male and female parents	8	14.5	24	43.6	23	41.8	55	100
Total	11	10.0	52	47.3	47	42.7	110	100

Table 5.6 *Parents' self-esteem (PCSEQ) outcomes cross-tabulated by the racial origin of the child*

Reason	No change	%	Improved	%	Deteriorated	%	Total	%
1	7	8.1	41	47.7	38	44.2	86	100
2	1	33.3			2	66.7	3	100
3			3	42.9	4	57.1	7	100
4	1	50.0	1	50.0			2	100
5			3	100			3	100
6	2	33.3	2	33.3	2	33.3	6	100
7			2	66.7	1	33.3	3	100
Total	11	10.0	52	47.3	47	42.7	110	100
White	7	8.1	41	47.7	38	44.2	86	100
Non-white	4	16.7	11	45.8	9	37.5	24	100

Notes: 1 = UK white; 2 = Mixed race; 3 = Asian; 4 = Black-Caribbean; 5 = Black-African; 6 = Mixed parentage/black background; 7 = Black other; Non-white = total non-white.

indicates that a substantial proportion of the cases where PCSEQ was used repeatedly included contact with both the female and male parents. With one exception, all the family centres' workers were themselves also female. Table 5.5 indicates that more parents improved their self-esteem than those that became worse across all three groups; but this difference was marginal in the group that included both female and male parents. However, these differences were too small and not statistically significant. Therefore with regard to the gender of the child as well as the gender of the parents, gender was not an important contextual factor with regard to the family centres' ability to improve the self-esteem of parents.

Table 5. 6 indicates that the vast majority of children were white (86 out of 110, or 78.1%), and within this group more parents improved their self-esteem than those whose self-esteem became worse. The findings were similar in the non-white group as a whole; however, within the non-white group there appear to be mixed outcomes. The parents' self-esteem did not improve in the mixed-race category, and more deteriorated than improved

Table 5.7 *Parents' self-esteem (PCSEQ) outcomes cross-tabulated by profession of the referrer*

Referrer	No change	%	Improved	%	Deteriorated	%	Total	%
1	1	2.8	18	50.0	17	47.2	36	100
2			1	100			1	100
3	3	9.4	16	50.0	13	40.6	32	100
4	7	17.1	17	41.5	17	41.5	43	100
Total	11	10.0	52	47.3	47	42.7	110	100

Notes: 1 = Heath visitor/community nurse; 2 = Child psychologist; 3 = Social worker/community care officer; 4 = Self-referral.

in the Asian category. On the other hand, all three improved in the Black-African category. These differences are not explained by the age of the child, as the distribution of age was fairly even across these groups. Although the differences were not statistically significant and the numbers of the individual non-white user groups are too small for drawing any firm conclusions, it appears that the contextual factors with regard to race do provide some conditions in which the role of family centres as generative mechanisms in improving parents' self-esteem are not triggered in the same way for non-white as they are for white parents. There may be disabling mechanisms associated with greater levels of social deprivation and/or discrimination with the specific categories of racial groups, or with cultural norms that are not taken into account in the family relationships. These potential explanations would require further investigation for confirmation.

Table 5.7 indicates that, where PCSEQ was used repeatedly, 36 cases were referred by health professionals, 32 by social services professionals and 43 were self-referred. More cases improved than deteriorated across all categories, with the exception of self-referring parents where the figures were evenly divided. However, none of these differences were statistically significant. Nevertheless, this pattern may indicate that there were causal mechanisms that led to parents referring themselves in the first place, and these causal mechanisms also made them more aware of the problems associated with their parenting. However, further investigation is required to identify the particular mechanisms in order to explain why the parents were almost evenly split between the groups that improved or deteriorated. In percentage terms improvements were a little greater for those referred by other professionals, but again there is a substantial group that deteriorated.

Table 5.8 indicates the results of the parents' self-esteem (PCSEQ) outcomes when cross-tabulated by the reason for referral. The total is less because of missing data, that is, the cases where this outcome measure was used but where the reason for referral was not specified (23 cases) have been excluded. Table 5.8 indicates that a much higher percentage of parents improved their self-esteem than deteriorated, for those referred because of the need for assessment of parenting skills. In fact, there was a significant

Table 5.8 *Parents' self-esteem (PCSEQ) outcomes cross-tabulated by the reason for referral*

Reason	No change	%	Improved	%	Deteriorated	%	Total	%
1	3	14.3	9	42.9	9	42.9	21	100
2					1	100	1	100
3	1	4.3	16	69.6	6	26.1	23	100
4	1	7.7	6	46.2	6	46.2	13	100
5			3	75.0	1	25.0	4	100
6	4	16.0	8	32.0	13	52.0	25	100
Total	9	10.3	42	48.3	36	41.4	87	100

Notes: 1 = Behaviour management; 2 = Special needs child; 3 = Assessment of parenting skills; 4 = Special needs of parents/carers; 5 = Failure to thrive/Child Protection Register; 6 = Respite for parents.

correlation between those referred for assessment of parenting skills and improvement in PCSEQ scores (gamma $r = 0.539$, $n = 87$, $p = 0.015$) with a large effect size. This may be because there was a greater need for parents to be directly in contact with the family centres for this category, and here a substantial part of the intervention was directed at the parents rather than the children. The percentages of those who improved and those who became worse are the same for those referred because of behaviour management. More parents referred because of the need for respite deteriorated than those who improved within this referral category. This outcome may have been because the family centres were providing respite to parents rather than working directly with parents to improve their self-esteem. With regard to the outcome of parents' self-esteem, the 'reasons for referral' cross-tabulation provides a generally mixed finding for all categories. The patterns observed here raise more questions then answers, and therefore further investigation is required to identify the mechanism–context–outcome configurations associated with these types of problems.

Table 5.9 provides the cross-tabulation of parents' self-esteem outcomes (PCSEQ) against the type of service provided by the family centres. Supporting the child's development and educational needs was the service provided in nearly half the cases (52 out of 110). More parents, where this was the service provided, improved their self-esteem than experienced a deterioration. Where the service provided focused on family support or peer support, a larger proportion of parents experienced an improvement rather than a deterioration in their self-esteem. This trend was reversed where the service provided focused on attachment issues. Improvement and deterioration were equal where the service provided focused on parenting skills or group work directly with parents. These findings suggest that the family centres' interventions are more likely to have a beneficial impact on parents' self-esteem where the interventions are concentrated on the child's development. This may be because the causal mechanisms associated with

Table 5.9 *Parents' self-esteem (PCSEQ) outcomes cross-tabulated by type of service provided at the family centres*

Service	No change	%	Improved	%	Deteriorated	%	Total	%
1	2	13.3	4	26.7	9	60.0	15	100
2	6	11.5	26	50.0	20	38.5	52	100
3	3	15.8	10	52.6	6	31.6	19	100
4			8	50.0	8	50.0	16	100
5			4	50	4	50	8	100
Total	11	10.0	52	47.3	47	42.7	110	100

Notes: 1 = Attachment (parent/child relationships); 2 = Supporting child's development and educational needs; 3 = Support for family/peer support; 4 = Parenting skills; 5 = Group work with parents.

Table 5.10 *Observation of Child Rating Scale (OCRS) outcomes cross-tabulated by age (in years)*

Age	No change	%	Improved	%	Deteriorated	%	Total	%
1	1	6.3	11	68.8	4	25.0	16	100
2	3	8.3	26	72.2	7	19.4	36	100
3	4	7.5	36	67.9	13	24.5	53	100
4	2	10.0	12	60.0	6	30.0	20	100
Total	10	8.0	85	68.0	30	24.0	125	100

parents' self-esteem levels may be centred on the development of their child. However, all of these differences in outcome were not statistically significant, and again due to the mixed nature of the findings, more investigation is required to identify the causal mechanisms across all categories.

Cross-tabulations of Observation of Child Rating Scale (OCRS) Outcomes

Table 5.10 indicates that, when the Observation of Child Rating Scale (OCRS) outcomes are cross-tabulated by age, improvement exceeds deterioration in high proportions across all age ranges. As noted above, statistically significant positive outcomes have been achieved with regard to OCRS outcomes, and Table 5.10 indicates that these improvements were largely consistent across the age ranges. Table 5.11 includes 74 boys and 51 girls with whom the outcome measure OCRS was used repeatedly. The ratio of improvement to deterioration was slightly better for boys than for the girls, however, improvements clearly exceeded deterioration for both boys and girls. Unlike the cross-tabulation between age of child and parents' self-esteem above, these findings indicate that the causal mechanisms were triggered across all age and gender groups to generate the improvements in the OCRS outcomes.

Table 5.12 indicates that, as far as the OCRS outcomes were concerned, the improvements were consistent across all three groups of parents; and it

Table 5.11   *Observation of Child Rating Scale (OCRS) outcomes cross-tabulated by gender of the child*

Gender	No change	%	Improved	%	Deteriorated	%	Total	%
Male	4	5.4	53	71.6	17	23.0	74	100
Female	6	11.8	32	62.7	13	25.5	51	100
Total	10	8.0	85	68.0	30	24.0	125	100

Table 5.12   *Observation of Child Rating Scale (OCRS) outcomes cross-tabulated by gender of the parent(s) working with the family centres*

Gender	No change	%	Improved	%	Deteriorated	%	Total	%
Male Parent only	1	16.7	4	66.7	1	16.7	6	100
Female Parent only	4	7.1	37	66.1	15	26.8	56	100
Both male and female parents	5	7.9	44	69.8	14	22.2	63	100
Total	10	8.0	85	68.0	30	24.0	125	100

was found that there were no statistically significant differences in the outcomes across the gender of parent(s) groups. As with regard to the parents' self-esteem, the contextual conditions with regard to parents' gender did not play a major role in triggering disabling mechanisms against the achievement of the outcomes.

Table 5.13 indicates that the OCRS outcomes were consistently greater in the numbers of cases that improved than those that deteriorated across all racial origin groups. When the ethnic categories were broadened into white and non-white groups, it was found that 69.1% of white children improved, as against 64.5% of non-white children, indicating a marginal difference. Unlike parents' self-esteem, the disabling mechanisms and contextual conditions associated with racial origin and discrimination did not affect the OCRS outcomes in most cases.

Table 5.14 shows more children improved than deteriorated from all categories of referral groups on the Observation of Child Rating Scale (OCRS). The ratio of improvement to deterioration was the highest for the largest group of self-referred family centre users with whom OCRS was repeatedly applied. When compared with findings with regard to parents' self-esteem, the mechanism of parents' motivation in the contextual conditions of self-referral may be generating more positive outcomes in this group than in the other groups referred by professionals. However, the differences between the referral groups were not statistically significant.

Table 5.15 shows that improvement exceeded deterioration in high proportions on the Observation of Child Rating Scale (OCRS) when cross-tabulated against all six referral categories. The reason for referral was not

Table 5.13   *Observation of Child Rating Scale (OCRS) outcomes cross-tabulated by the racial origin of the child*

Reason	No change	%	Improved	%	Deteriorated	%	Total	%
1	7	7.4	65	69.1	22	23.4	94	100
2			3	75.0	1	25.0	4	100
3	3	30.0	4	40.0	3	30.0	10	100
4			3	100			3	100
5			3	75.0	1	25.0	4	100
6			6	85.7	1	14.3	7	100
7			2	66.7	1	33.3	3	100
Total	11	8.7	87	69.0	28	22.2	125	100

Notes: 1 = UK white; 2 = Mixed race; 3 = Asian; 4 = Black-Caribbean; 5 = Black-African; 6 = Mixed parentage/black background; 7 = Black other.

Table 5.14   *Observation of Child Rating Scale (OCRS) outcomes cross-tabulated by source of referral*

Referrer	No change	%	Improved	%	Deteriorated	%	Total	%
1	3	7.3	25	61.0	13	31.7	41	100
2			1	100			1	100
3	4	11.4	22	62.9	9	25.7	35	100
4	3	6.3	37	77.1	8	16.7	48	100
Total	10	8.0	85	68.0	30	24.0	125	100

Notes: 1 = Heath visitor/community nurse; 2 = Child psychologist; 3 = Social worker/ community care officer; 4 = Self-referral.

Table 5.15   *Observation of Child Rating Scale (OCRS) outcomes cross-tabulated by reasons for referral*

Reason	No change	%	Improved	%	Deteriorated	%	Total	%
1			17	68.0	8	32	25	100
2			1	100			1	100
3	4	16.7	14	58.3	6	25.0	24	100
4	1	6.7	10	66.7	4	26.7	15	100
5	1	16.7	3	50	2	33.3	6	100
6	2	7.7	19	73.1	5	19.2	26	100
Total	8	8.2	64	66.0	25	25.8	97	100

Notes: 1 = Behaviour management; 2 = Special needs child; 3 = Assessment of parenting skills; 4 = Special needs of parents/carers; 5 = Failure to thrive/Child Protection Register; 6 = Respite for parents.

specified in 28 of the users where OCRS was applied repeatedly, and therefore the 28 cases where this data were missing have been excluded from Table 5.15. With the remaining 97 cases, the ratio of improvement against deterioration for all referral categories was very good. Apart from the one case in reason 2, the OCRS ratings showed the highest ratio of improvement to deterioration where respite for parents was the reason for referral.

Table 5.16 *Type of service provided and OCRS outcomes*

Service	No change	%	Improved	%	Deteriorated	%	Total	%
1			10	62.5	6	37.5	16	100
2	4	6.6	42	68.9	15	24.6	61	100
3	3	14.3	15	71.4	3	14.3	21	100
4	2	10.5	11	57.9	6	31.6	19	100
5	1	12.5	7	87.5			8	100
Total	10	8.0	85	68.0	30	24.0	125	100

Notes: 1 = Attachment (parent/child relationships); 2 = Supporting child's development and educational needs; 3 = Support for family/peer support; 4 = Parenting skills; 5 = Group work with parents.

Although the differences between the referral groups in Table 5.15 were not statistically significant, the provision of respite to parents generated slightly more positive OCRS outcomes than in the other reasons for referral groups. The potential mechanisms may be in relation to family tensions in the home, and the way children behave outside of those environments. This potential explanation, too, needs further empirical investigation.

Table 5.16 shows the Observation of Child Rating Scale (OCRS) outcomes cross-tabulated by the type of service provided by the family centres. Results were positive across all types of service, including attachment (parent/child relationships). Improvement considerably exceeded deterioration for all the categories, and the differences between the groups were not statistically significant. The highest number of improvements were where 'supporting the child's development and educational needs' was the type of service provided, and this may be because of the more structured models of intervention acting as generating mechanisms directly with children. The highest proportion of those improved were in the 'group work with parents' category, indicating that group work with parents was more effective than individual work on parenting skills, with regard to the OCRS outcomes.

Cross-tabulations and Parent/Carer–Child Interaction Scale (PCIS) Outcomes

With regard to Parent/Carer–Child Interaction Scale (PCIS scores), Table 5.17 indicates that improvements clearly exceeded deterioration in all age groups, with the exception of children aged 4 years or more, indicating that there were more problems in parent–child interaction with older children (as also indicated earlier by the poorer parents' self-esteem results for this age group). Table 5.18 indicates that progress was made with both boys and girls in improving the PCIS scores, but that the improvements were proportionally greater with boys. Table 5.19 indicates that, with regard to the PCIS outcomes, the improvements were largely consistent across all three groups of parents, and therefore there were generally no significant differences in the outcomes when cross-tabulated by gender of parent. The biggest

Table 5.17 *Parent-child interaction (PCIS) outcomes cross-tabulated by age of child (in years)*

Age	No change	%	Improved	%	Deteriorated	%	Total	%
1	3	20.0	7	46.7	5	33.3	15	100
2	8	22.9	14	40.0	13	37.1	35	100
3	6	11.8	25	49.0	20	39.2	51	100
4	6	30.0	6	30.0	8	40.0	20	100
Total	23	19.0	52	43.0	46	38.0	121	100

Table 5.18 *Parent–child interaction (PCIS) outcomes cross-tabulated by gender*

Gender	No change	%	Improved	%	Deteriorated	%	Total	%
Male	7	9.7	35	48.6	30	41.7	72	100
Female	16	32.7	17	34.7	16	32.7	49	100
Total	23	19.0	52	43.0	46	38.0	121	100

Table 5.19 *Parent–child interaction (PCIS) outcomes cross-tabulated by gender of the parent(s) working with the family centres*

Gender	No change	%	Improved	%	Deteriorated	%	Total	%
Male Parent only	3	50.0	2	33.3	1	16.7	6	100
Female Parent only	12	22.2	21	38.9	21	38.9	54	100
Both male and female parents	8	13.1	29	47.5	24	39.3	61	100
Total	23	19.0	52	43.0	46	38.0	121	100

improvements were achieved where there were both male and female parents, but these differences were not statistically significant. Therefore, as with OCRS scores, the gender of the child and the gender of the parents, in themselves, did not constitute either favourable or unfavourable contextual conditions in the triggering of generative mechanisms with regard to the PCIS outcomes.

Table 5.20 indicates that the proportion that improved in the PCIS outcomes was greater than those that deteriorated amongst UK whites – the biggest group by racial origin. The pattern is the opposite for almost all of the other smaller groups. When the racial groups were divided into two groups, 48.4% of whites improved, as against 25% of non-whites. It was also found that there was a significant correlation between 'white or not' and 'PCIS outcomes improved or not' (gamma $r = 0.475$, $n = 121$, $p = 0.020$), with a medium to large effect size. It appears that the contextual factors with regard to race do provide some conditions in which the role of family centres as generative mechanisms in improving PCIS outcomes are not triggered in the

Table 5.20 *Parent–child interaction (PCIS) outcomes cross-tabulated by the racial origin of the child*

Reason	No change	%	Improved	%	Deteriorated	%	Total	%
1	16	17.2	45	48.4	32	34.4	93	100
2			1	33.3	2	66.7	3	100
3	4	44.4	3	33.3	2	22.2	9	100
4			1	33.3	2	66.7	3	100
5			1	25.0	3	75.0	4	100
6	1	16.7			5	83.3	6	100
7	2	66.7	1	33.3			3	100
Total	23	19.0	52	43.0	46	38.0	121	100
White	16	17.2	45	48.4	32	34.4	93	100
Non-white	7	25.0	7	25.0	14	50.0	28	100

Notes: 1 = UK white; 2 = Mixed race; 3 = Asian; 4 = Black-Caribbean; 5 = Black-African; 6 = Mixed parentage/black background; 7 = Black other.

same way for non-white as they are for white parents. As we found with parents' self-esteem scores, there may be disabling mechanisms associated with greater levels of social deprivation and discrimination, or with cultural norms that are not taken into account in the family relationships. However, the mechanism–context configurations associated with racial origin do not influence the OCRS outcomes in the same way, as those outcomes relate to the development of the child rather than in relation to the parent. This suggests that these disabling mechanisms are more likely to exist in relation to non-white parents rather than in relation to non-white children. These potential explanations would also require further investigation for confirmation.

Table 5.21 provides the cross tabulation between PCIS scores and the sources of referral. The numbers of cases that improved clearly exceeded those that deteriorated in the self-referred group, whereas in all the other groups more deteriorated than improved. It was also found that there was a significant correlation between 'source of referral' and 'change in PCIS scores' (gamma $r = 0.254$, $n = 121$, $p = 0.033$), but with a small to medium effect size. These findings are similar with regard to the OCRS outcomes in the same self-referred group, although with regard to OCRS the differences were not statistically significant. Therefore, the mechanism of parents' motivation in the contextual conditions of self-referral may be generating more positive outcomes in this group than in the other groups referred by professionals in relation to both PCIS and OCRS outcomes.

The reasons for referral were not specified in 26 cases where PCIS was used repeatedly, and these cases with the missing data are excluded from the cross-tabulation in Table 5.22. Table 5.22 shows that improvement exceeded deterioration only for the 'respite' group. This group also had the highest proportion of those self-referred (16 or 61.5% of the 'respite' group were self-referred). This pattern is similar to that for OCRS outcomes, but

Table 5.21   *Parent–child interaction (PCIS) outcomes cross-tabulated by sources of referral*

Referrer	No change	%	Improved	%	Deteriorated	%	Total	%
1	6	15.0	14	35.0	20	50.0	40	100
2			1	100			1	100
3	6	17.1	14	40.0	15	42.9	35	100
4	11	24.4	23	51.1	11	24.4	45	100
Total	23	19.0	52	43.0	46	38.0	121	100

Notes: 1 = Heath visitor/community nurse; 2 = Child psychologist; 3 = Social worker/ community care officer; 4 = Self-referral.

Table 5.22   *Parent–Child interaction (PCIS) outcomes cross-tabulated by reasons for referral*

Reason	No change	%	Improved	%	Deteriorated	%	Total	%
1	3	12.5	9	37.5	12	50.0	24	100
2			1	100			1	100
3	5	20.8	7	29.2	12	50.0	24	100
4	5	33.3	5	33.3	5	33.3	15	100
5	1	20.0	1	20.0	3	60.0	5	100
6	6	23.1	13	50.0	7	26.9	26	100
Total	20	21.1	36	37.9	39	41.1	95	100

Notes: 1 = Behaviour management; 2 = Special needs child; 3 = Assessment of parenting skills; 4 = Special needs of parents/carers; 5 = Failure to thrive/Child Protection Register; 6 = Respite for parents.

Table 5.23   *Parent–child interaction (PCIS) outcomes cross-tabulated by type of services provided by the family centres*

Service	No change	%	Improved	%	Deteriorated	%	Total	%
1	4	25.0	7	43.8	5	31.3	16	100
2	11	19.0	26	44.8	21	36.2	58	100
3	2	10.0	9	45.0	9	45.0	20	100
4	4	21.1	7	36.8	8	42.1	19	100
5	1	12.5	5	62.5	1	12.5	8	100
Total	23	19.0	52	43.0	46	38.0	121	100

Notes: 1 = Attachment (parent/child relationships); 2 = Supporting child's development and educational needs; 3 = Support for family/peer support; 4 = Parenting skills; 5 = Group work with parents.

again the differences between the 'reasons for referral' groups were not statistically significant.

Table 5.23 shows that more cases showed improvement than deterioration in Parent/Carer–Child Interaction (PCIS) for all types of service, with the exception of parenting skills and support for family/peer group. Although more deteriorated than improved for 'parenting skills', the ratio of improvements to deterioration was the best for 'group work with parents', indicating that group work with parents was more effective with regard to PCIS

Table 5.24   *Parents'/carers' CSQ8 scores*

Repeated CSQ8 measures	No. of responses	Range	Mean	Median
CSQ8-1	134	14–32	28.46	29.00
CSQ8-2	59	21–32	29.24	30.00
CSQ8-3	8	26–32	31.50	31.50
Total responses	201	14–32	28.76	29.00

outcomes (and OCRS outcomes as observed earlier) than the individual work on parenting skills. It was also found that six out of the eight children of parents involved in the group work were aged one year; five included both male and female parents; seven were white, and six were self-referred. However, these numbers are too small to enable the drawing of firm conclusions. Furthermore, with regard to all the type of service groups, it was found that the differences in relation to the PCIS scores were not statistically significant. Due to the mixed nature of the findings, more investigation is required to identify the causal mechanisms across all categories.

Parents'/Carers' Satisfaction with The Family Centres

Table 5.24 indicates the responses of parents to the Client Satisfaction Questionnaire (CSQ8) surveys. 134 out of the 155 parents surveyed at least once (CSQ8-1 in Table 5.24); and then, out of these 115 parents, smaller numbers responded to the repeated surveys (CSQ8-2 and CSQ8-3). There were smaller numbers in the repeated surveys because the majority of the parents felt that their first response was still valid. As the CSQ8 scores range from 4 (no satisfaction) to 32 (maximum satisfaction), all the means are 28.00 or higher, and therefore Table 5.24 indicates very high levels of satisfaction from the parents surveyed across the family centres.

The cross-tabulation of the 134 parents surveyed at least once with their racial origin (Table 5.25) indicates small differences across the racial groups, with high satisfaction scores across all groups. It was also found that the mean scores were almost evenly spread across the parents' gender groups, the child's gender and age groups, and the groups according to sources of referral. However, with regard to the repeated CSQ8 scores, it was also found that female single-parent families reported worsened satisfaction rates (55.6%) than two-parent families (21.9%).

There was a significant correlation between female single-parent families and a deterioration in the CSQ8 satisfaction rates (gamma $r = 0.634$, $n = 59$, $p = 0.005$) with a large effect size. With regard to source of referral groups and repeated CSQ8 scores, it was found that only 27.8% in the group referred by health visitors/community nurses had improved their satisfaction rates, as opposed to 61% in the rest of the referral groups. There was also a significant inverse correlation between being referred by health

Table 5.25   *Parents'/carers' CSQ8-1 scores cross-tabulated by racial origin*

CSQ8 first measure	No. of responses	Range	Mean	Median
UK white	101	14–32	28.46	29.00
Mixed race	5	24–32	29.00	29.00
Asian	8	23–31	26.50	25.50
Black-Caribbean	3	24–30	28.00	30.00
Black-African	4	28–32	29.75	29.50
Mixed parentage/ black background	10	22–32	28.80	30.50
Black other	3	29–32	30.67	31.00
Total	134	14–32	28.46	29.00
White	101	14–32	28.46	29.00
Non-white	33	22–32	28.48	29.00

Table 5.26   *Parents'/carers' CSQ8-1 scores cross-tabulated by reasons for referral*

CSQ8 first measure	No. of responses	Range	Mean	Median
Behaviour management	26	14–32	26.65	27.50
Special needs child	2	24–30	27.00	27.00
Assessment of parenting skills	27	24–32	29.44	29.00
Special needs of parents/carers	12	21–32	28.00	28.00
Failure to thrive/Child Protection Register	5	22–32	28.80	31.00
Respite for parents/carers	30	24–32	29.10	30.00
Total	102	14–32	28.46	29.00

visitor/community nurse and improvement in CSQ8 scores (gamma $r = 0.605$, $n = 59$, $p = 0.014$) with a large effect size. In fact, the largest proportion (21 or 41.2%) in the group referred by health visitor/community nurse was referred for the reason of behaviour management.

When cross-tabulated by reasons for referral (Table 5.26), the behaviour management group of parents recorded a slightly lower mean score when compared to the other reasons for referral groups, suggesting that the problems of behaviour led to lower parents' satisfaction scores.

Similarly, with regard to type of service provided (Table 5.27), those receiving the 'attachment' type of services recorded a lower mean of satisfaction than other groups. However, those receiving 'group work' reported the highest mean scores – a finding which is consistent with the improvements observed in the OCRS and PCIS scores for this group. It was also found that there was a statistically significant correlation between 'type of service provided–group work with parents' and 'CSQ8 scores improved' (gamma $r = 0.750$, $n = 59$, $p = 0.040$) with a large effect size.

Table 5.27   *Parents'/carers' CSQ8-1 scores cross-tabulated by type of service provided*

CSQ8 first measure	No. of responses	Range	Mean	Median
Attachment (parent/ child relationships)	17	14–32	27.65	30.00
Supporting child's development and educational needs	66	23–32	28.47	29.00
Support for family/ peer support	26	22–32	28.85	29.00
Parenting skills	18	19–32	28.50	29.50
Group work with parents	7	14–32	28.86	28.00
Total	134	14–32	28.46	29.00

Referrers' Satisfaction

Altogether, 37 referrers completed an adapted version of CSQ8 to indicate their level of satisfaction with all five family centres' work with regard to 70 children in the first survey (RCSQ8-1 in Table 5.28). Of these 70 responses, only 10 were repeated, with most of the others declining to complete the survey again on the grounds that their views had not changed following the first survey. The referrers consisted of health visitors, community nurses, child psychologists, social workers and community care officers. The range of 15 to 32, and the mean of 24.89 in the first survey of referrers ($n = 70$), indicate fairly high levels of satisfaction, but a little lower than that of the parents/carers indicated above. With regard to those referrers who responded to the repeated survey, the mean was 25.60, indicating a slightly higher rate of satisfaction.

When cross-tabulated by age, it was found that the referrers' CSQ8 mean score was lower for children aged 1 than for the other age groups, but the differences were not statistically significant. However, the mean score was also higher for females than for males, and there was a significant correlation between the child's gender and the range of referrers' CSQ8 scores (gamma $r = 0.500$, $n = 70$, $p = 0.022$), with a large effect size (where the range was defined as less satisfied if lower than the median of 26.00; or more satisfied if equal to or greater than 26.00). With regard to the parents' gender, it was found that the mean score for single parent males (27.80) was higher than for the single-parent females (24.68) and both male and female parents (24.65). It was also found that there was a significant correlation between male only single parents and range of referrers' CSQ8 scores (Spearman $r = 0.270$, $n = 70$, $p = 0.024$) with a small to medium effect size. No patterns could be observed with regard to the sources of referral.

By ethnic origin, it was found that white children generally had a lower mean score than non-white children (Table 5.29), indicating that, although

Table 5.28   *Referrers' CSQ8 scores*

Repeated referrers' CSQ8 measures	No. of responses	Range	Mean	Median
RCSQ8-1	70	15–32	24.89	26.00
RCSQ8-2	10	22–32	25.60	23.50
Total responses	80	15–32	24.98	26.00

Table 5.29   *Referrers' CSQ8-1 scores cross-tabulated by racial origin*

RCSQ8 first measure	No. of responses	Range	Mean	Median
UK white	53	15–31	24.19	25.00
Mixed race	3	27–32	28.67	27.00
Asian	6	20–32	27.50	29.00
Black-Caribbean	1		24.00	24.00
Black-African	2	26–28	27.00	27.00
Mixed parentage/ black background	5	24–29	26.20	26.00
Total	70	15–32	24.89	26.00
White	53	15–31	24.19	25.00
Non-white	177	20–32	27.06	27.00

the referring professionals were generally satisfied with the services provided by the family centres to the clients they had referred, they tended to be more satisfied with the services provided to the non-white clients. This trend was also confirmed with the finding that there was a statistical association between the referrers' satisfaction and whether the child's racial origin was white or not (gamma $r = 0.432$, $n = 70$, $p = 0.006$), with a moderate to large effect size.

With regard to reason for referral groups, Table 5.30 indicates that, as with the clients' satisfaction rates, the lowest referrers' mean satisfaction was with the behaviour management group. However, unlike the clients' satisfaction rates which were highest for the 'respite for parents/carers' group, the referrers' highest mean satisfaction score was for the 'failure to thrive/Child Protection Register' group where the problems may be more complex.

Table 5.31 indicates the RCSQ8 mean scores by type of service. As with the parents' satisfaction rates, attachment received the lowest mean score, and the differences were very small between the rest of the groups.

Developments Following the Evaluation

The Family Centres' Steering Group met on 19 April 2000 after the initial evaluation period had been completed, and confirmed the intention that the evaluation should continue after a pause for the evaluation report to be

Table 5.30   *Referrers' CSQ8-1 scores cross-tabulated by reasons for referral*

RCSQ8 first measure	No. of responses	Range	Mean	Median
Behaviour management	16	16–31	23.31	23.50
Special needs child	2	23–27	25.00	25.00
Assessment of parenting skills	18	15–32	25.06	26.00
Special needs of parents/carers	13	20–32	26.77	26.00
Failure to thrive/Child Protection Register	4	26–29	27.50	27.50
Respite for parents/carers	9	18–29	23.78	24.00
Total	62	15–32	24.94	26.00

Table 5.31   *Referrers' CSQ8-1 scores cross-tabulated by type of service provided*

RCSQ8 first measure	No. of responses	Range	Mean	Median
Attachment (parent/child relationships)	8	18–31	22.88	19.50
Supporting child's development and educational needs	27	16–32	25.00	25.00
Support for family/peer support	15	18–30	24.87	25.00
Parenting skills	17	15–32	25.65	26.00
Group work with parents	3	18–29	25.00	28.00
Total	70	15–32	24.89	26.00

completed. The meeting noted difficulties experienced by family centres in sustaining the workload in connection with the full range of evaluation measures and reviewed each of the measures in detail. An agreement in principle was reached that the primary scales, that is, the Observation of Child Rating Scale (OCRS), Parent/Carer–Child Interaction Scale (PCIS), and Parents'/Carers' Self-Esteem Questionnaire (PCSEQ) should be simplified with the intention of including all relevant questions on one evaluation form. There was also agreement that 1–10 scales should replace the four-point scales, and that the time period for observations in future should be one day, rather than the shorter periods used during the evaluation. The revised scales were tested again using the test–retest method with six families, and the test–retest reliability was found to be .87, a figure slightly lower than the results of the previous test but still high (Rubin and Babbie, 2001).

Discussion and Conclusions

The data for all 155 clients (comprising 78% of all possible cases in the six-month period) suggest that the family centre workers have been very successful in integrating single-case evaluation into their practice, and developing partnerships with parents in carrying out the evaluation process. All the family centres participated in this major evaluation as practitioner researchers, creating and testing new outcome measures, and applying the evaluation research methods into their practice despite the pressures of their normal duties. They used single-case procedures (Kazi, 1998a) with each of the 155 cases, using at least one outcome measure per case, and systematically tracked the outcomes and shared the findings with the parents.

The data from the use of outcome measures were aggregated using a one-group pre-test post-test design (Nugent, Sieppert and Hudson, 2001; Rubin and Babbie, 2001), by drawing comparisons between the first and the last scores in each outcome measure for each case in the six-month period. These comparisons indicate a mixed response with regard to the parents' self-esteem and the interaction between the parent and the child, although those who improved were slightly greater in number than those who became worse. However, the measure based on observations within the family centre itself, that is, outcomes in relation to the children themselves, indicate statistically significant improvements in the majority of the cases (68%), although a small minority (24%) became worse.

These findings are corroborated by high levels of satisfaction indicated by parents/carers, and lower but good levels of satisfaction indicated by the referring professionals. It can be concluded from the above data analysis that the progress made with parents in the six-month period was slower than that with children with whom the family centres were working more directly and for a longer period within each week, but that the family centres were largely effective across the outcome measures used. At this stage, these are the conclusions of a 'black box' type of evaluation.

Mechanism–context–outcome Configurations or Patterns

However, to merely conclude that the family centres were effective with the majority of the children and parents across the three outcome measures and the satisfaction surveys does not tell us why the programmes of intervention worked with some users and not with others, or in other words, what interventions worked, with what kind of service users and under what conditions. Descriptive statistics were used to address these questions to some extent, revealing some potential mechanism–context–outcome patterns which otherwise may have remained hidden.

The realist evaluator will aim to determine what works, for whom and in what contexts as far as possible with the data that is available at any given moment of time, and then return to the evaluation of practice to explain the findings further. In order to discern the patterns in the data presented so far, we now turn to two other statistical methods, namely odds ratios and relative risk (Gomm, Needham and Bullman, 2000; Hennekens, Buring and Mayrent, 1987). Odds ratios and relative risk calculations were carried out in two-by-two tables where the Pearson Chi–square (or Fisher's exact test where a cell was less than five) was found to be significant, as follows:

For a two-by-two table,

	+	−
+	a	b
−	c	d

Odds ratio = ad/bc, that is, a ratio of the odds a:b/c:d. Odds ratios equate to increases in odds, that is, 1.5 is a 50% increase in the odds of an event happening.

Relative risk = (a/(a+b))/(c/(c+d)). Relative risks equate to increase in risk, that is, 1.5 is a 50% increase in the risk of an event happening.

In addition, confidence limits were calculated to determine the significance levels of both the odds ratios and relative risk equating to $p < 0.05$. In Table 5.32, only the odds ratios that were found to be significant at the 95% confidence levels (that is, $p < 0.05$) have been included.

It was found, for example, that parents referred for assessment of parenting skills had an odds of 3:1 for improvement in the PCSEQ scores, and that the relative risk or likelihood of improving on the PCSEQ scores was 71% for every parent referred for this reason. It follows, therefore, that the family centres' intervention interacts with the parenting assessment 'reason for referral' group better than with any other, in achieving the positive self-esteem outcomes.

If the ethnic origin of the child was white, the odds ratio for improving on the PCIS scores was nearly 3:1, and the relative risk or likelihood was 154%. It follows, therefore, that the family centres' interventions are less likely to be successful in developing parent–child interaction with non-white ethnic minorities. One of the reasons could be, that whereas the highest proportion of whites were self-referred, for non-whites the biggest proportion were in the group referred by social workers/community care officers. As for reason for referral, whereas the highest proportion of whites were in the 'assessment of parenting skills' category, that for non-whites was 'respite for parents'. Non-whites were also under-represented in the parents' group work that was associated with favourable outcomes. Although there were no significant differences in the Observation of Child

Table 5.32   *Patterns through odds ratios and relative risk*

Variables	Odds ratio	Confidence limits	Relative risk	Confidence limits
Referred for assessment of parenting skills or not * PCSEQ scores improved	3.34	1.09–10.53	1.71	1.15–2.56
White or not * PCIS scores improved	2.81	1.01–8.12	2.54	0.99–3.80
Self-referred or not * PCIS scores deteriorated	0.38	0.15–0.92	0.53	0.30–0.94
Referred by health visitor/ community nurse * CSQ8 repeated scores–improved	0.25	0.06–0.94	0.46	0.21–1.00
Single-parent females only * CSQ8 repeated scores–deteriorated	4.46	1.26–16.35	2.54	1.22–5.30
Type of service group work with parents * CSQ8 repeated scores–improved	7.00	0.74–333.22	1.86	1.22–2.83
Child's gender * Range of RCSQ8 scores (more satisfied if = or > median 26; less satisfied if < 26)	0.33	0.11–1.00	0.60	0.38–0.95
Single-parent males only * Range of RCSQ8 scores (more satisfied if = or > median 26; less satisfied if < 26)		undefined	2.10	1.63–2.70
PCIS scores improved * OCRS scores improved	2.87	1.15–7.27	1.36	1.07–1.72

Rating Scale (OCRS) scores between the white and non-white groups, the odds of improving the OCRS score were nearly 3:1 if the PCIS scores had also improved, and the likelihood of improving the OCRS scores was 36% more favourable for those with an improving PCIS score, suggesting that the pattern of outcomes generally was somewhat less favourable for non-whites than it was for whites.

It appears that the contextual factors with regard to race do provide some conditions in which the role of family centres as generative mechanisms in improving both the parents' self-esteem and parent–child interaction outcomes are not triggered in the same way for non-white as they are for white parents. There may be countervailing mechanisms associated with greater levels of social deprivation and discrimination with the specific categories of racial groups, or with cultural norms that are not taken into account in the family relationships. However, the referring professionals indicated a higher satisfaction rate for the family centres' work with non-whites than with whites, perhaps reflecting the positive OCRS scores actually achieved with the children. The potential mechanism–context configurations associated with racial origin do not influence the OCRS outcomes in the same way, as those outcomes relate to the development of the child rather than in relation to the parent. This suggests that these disabling mechanisms are more likely to exist in relation to non-white parents rather than in relation to non-white children. These potential explanations would also require further investigation for confirmation.

If a client was self-referred, the odds of the parent–child interaction becoming worse would decrease by 62%, and the likelihood of worsening on the PCIS scores would decrease by 47%. Therefore, the interventions are such that they work better with self-referred clients (with regard to this particular outcome) than other client groups referred by professionals. The mechanism of parents' motivation in the contextual conditions of self-referral may be generating proportionally more positive outcomes in this group than in the other groups referred by professionals. As Duguid and Pawson (1998) found in their analysis, 'it is not programmes that work but their capacity to offer resources that allow participants the choice of making them work' (p. 492).

If a client is referred by the health visitor/community nurse, the odds of client satisfaction improving with the repeated use of the Client Satisfaction Questionnaire (CSQ8) are decreased by 75%, and the likelihood of not improving is increased by 54%. One explanation for this is that a major reason for referral by this source is behaviour management, and the satisfaction rates for clients in this group tend to be lower than for other groups.

For female single parents, the odds of worsening satisfaction rates with the repeated use of CSQ8 are 4:1, and the likelihood of a reduction in satisfaction rates is 54%. One explanation could be that a higher proportion of female single parents were referred by the health visitor/community nurse when compared to the other groups of parents.

Where the type of service is group work with parents, the odds of the repeated CSQ8 scores improving are 7:1, and there is an 86% likelihood of improving the satisfaction rates. This may be because the OCRS scores and PCIS scores are both good for this group. This may be due to causal mechanisms triggered in the socialisation of parents, or in the way the intervention acts as a generative mechanism in the process of group work.

For female children, the odds of receiving a higher rating of satisfaction from a survey of referring professionals was increased by 67%, and the likelihood of receiving such a higher rating is 40%. The referring professionals tended to be more satisfied with the family centres' work with girls, whereas the other outcomes indicate that there were no significant differences between the gender groups.

In a survey of referring professionals' satisfaction, the odds of receiving a high satisfaction rating for male single parents were not defined, as the 'less satisfied' cell was empty; but the likelihood of receiving a higher satisfaction rate for the family centres' work with male single parents was 63%. This may reflect the higher scores achieved on both the OCRS and the PCSEQ outcomes by this group when compared with the other groups of parents.

Limitations in the Identification of Mechanisms

This study is an example of how an outcome study largely located within the empirical practice perspective (as described in Chapter 2) can be turned from a 'black box' to a 'grey box' study, with some additional analyses of the data. However, this study goes further than the example in Chapter 3, as the type of intervention and other factors were also systematically tracked along with outcomes, and were not dependent upon the routine record-keeping practices of the agency. The family centre workers agreed to create new records for the purposes of this evaluation, enabling the detailed 'grey box' analysis as described above. We have not only systematically tracked several outcomes, but also provided some explanations with regard to the circumstances of the service users that were associated with improved outcomes, and others where the outcomes were less successful. This analysis is used by the agency to make decisions about the targeting of services, such as whether to concentrate on service users that are referred by professionals, or on the parents who self-refer, and whether to concentrate on the provision of group work services that were found to be more effective rather than individual work with parents. However, a limitation of this study was that mechanisms were not identified and systematically tracked alongside the outcomes from the outset. Although this study is further along the realist effectiveness cycle than the example in Chapter 3, the potential mechanisms are not yet clearly defined. For example, we have found that parent-based outcomes were less likely to be achieved with ethnic minorities, although the child-based outcomes were more likely to be achieved regardless of the ethnic origin; but the mechanisms that were responsible for these differences between the racial groups have not yet been identified.

This study indicates that an evaluation based on quantitative methods can be transformed into a 'grey box' study with some additional data about the types of intervention, referral sources, reasons for referral, and some contextual data which can be tracked along with the use of standardised outcome measures. However, a limitation is that the meetings with family centre workers concentrated almost entirely on the outcome measures, and no qualitative methods were used to identify potential key mechanisms that may influence the outcomes. As in the concluding discussion in Chapter 4, this study also indicates that, although a single method may be used in realist evaluation, the capacity to identify the causal mechanisms with rigour may be limited, and may require the introduction of additional methods to achieve this aim. The patterns observed here provide only potential explanations and therefore further investigation is required to identify the mechanisms associated with these types of problems. The development of these hypotheses may be facilitated with a combination of quantitative and qualitative approaches, as demonstrated in the following chapters.

6

A Realist Evaluation of Practice:
the NSPCC's Shield Project
and Intensive Analysis

The main purpose of this and the next two chapters is to demonstrate the integration of realist evaluation strategies into practice, and the realist retroductive explanatory process. At present, there are no published examples of this process, and therefore this evaluation may be among the first to achieve a retroduction of this kind. This chapter is based on the results from the integration of the realist effectiveness cycle into the daily practice of the Shield Project (Kazi and Ward, 2001; Kazi, Ward and Hudson, 2002), a collaborative venture involving the National Society for the Prevention of Cruelty to Children (NSPCC) and Kirklees Social Services Department in West Yorkshire. The evaluation is still ongoing, and therefore only the findings from the first two years are included in this chapter. At this stage, the aim is not only to provide an explanation of the project's effectiveness, but also to illustrate how realist evaluation concepts and methodologies can be applied and developed in practice. As the reader may have observed from the previous chapters in this book, various authors have described the realist paradigm, and explained the process of retroduction – the process of identifying the causal mechanisms responsible for the observed programme outcomes. However, to date, none of these authors have actually demonstrated how this can be done, the only exceptions being hypothetical or retrospective illustrative accounts in Pawson and Tilley (1997a, 1997b), Sayer (2000) and Robson (2002). The reader is entitled to wonder if such a retroduction is actually possible and, if it is possible, why has it not been done to date? In addressing these issues through demonstrating the process of retroduction in a real social work agency, this chapter aims to provide more than food for thought for the reader.

The realist evaluation enterprise is about penetrating beneath the observable processes and outcomes of a programme, explaining how the causal mechanisms which generate social problems are countered by a programme's alternative causal mechanisms, identifying the contexts of practice within which programme mechanisms can be successfully fired, explaining the mechanism–context–outcome configuration patterns, and the changing nature of stratified reality. However, there is no published study where all of these rules of Pawson and Tilley (1997b) have been implemented, and indeed, there are no examples of dedicated methods which can achieve all of them. The methods that are typically applied even in realist evaluations at the present time originate from either the empirical practice or inter-pretivist approaches. In this chapter, we turn to a project where realist evaluation approaches (in the form of the realist effectiveness cycle as explained in Chapter 3) have been integrated into the project's daily prac-tice, informing the reviews and the planning of the intervention case work with all service users.

Pawson and Tilley (1997b) provide an example of a CCTV initiative to reduce crime in a car park (and this example is also one of the two cited in Sayer, 2000), where they attempt to identify the mechanisms, and the contexts in which they were triggered. However, they appear to apply this analysis retrospectively, after the outcome data was collected, in order to make sense of it. Indeed, as Lawson also points out:

> The usual starting point for research into the nature of social mechanisms will invariably be conditions where the effect of mechanisms have in some way already been detailed. We start from situations where, fortuitously, relatively stable tendencies are revealed. In this sense, social scientific explanation is inherently backward looking. (1998: 162)

This is typically so in most external evaluations – reports are published, providing explanations or descriptions of past practice, with the hope that they would influence future practice. However, where evaluation strategies are integrated into the daily practice of human service agencies, practitioners can use evaluation data collected from past practice to directly inform future practice (see Chapters 3 and 5). Indeed, where realist evaluation strategies are integrated into the practice of agencies, the rules, as described by Pawson and Tilley above, can be applied in the practice of human service agencies.

The Shield Project: Aims, Models of Assessment Intervention and of Treatment Work

The project consists of a team of social workers who provide assessment and treatment facilities for children and young people who sexually harm others. For just over two years, this team, in partnership with this author, have been developing an evaluation strategy based on the integration of the realist evaluation paradigm into practice. The method is largely a replication of a strategy that has been successful in encouraging practitioners in other social work settings to use hundreds of single-subject designs in their practice (Kazi, 1998a). However, in this replication of the strategy, the methods applied go beyond those required for empirical practice evaluations.

The evaluation of the Shield Project is one of the examples of social work, health and other related practitioners in England working in partnership with the Centre for Evaluation Studies at the University of Huddersfield (Kazi, 1996, 2000b). The main purpose of this partnership is the development of evaluation strategies that can be incorporated into practice in order to demonstrate not only the effectiveness of practice, but also contribute directly to the development of models of intervention (Kazi, 1998a, 2000a). These strategies range from those that can systematically track the outcomes of practice at a minimum, to others that can also address the wider dimensions of practice such as the systematic tracking of the content of interventions, as well as the contexts in which practice takes place.

In this particular application, single-case designs (as described in Chapter 5) are used together with other methods within the realist evaluation paradigm to systematically track the content of interventions, outcomes, mechanisms and contexts in relation to each case (as described in Kazi, 1999, 2000a; and in Chapter 3). The social workers selected several standardised measures from Fischer and Corcoran (1994); some measures are for general use with all clients, and others are for measuring target problems particular for each client. In the cases where standardised measures were applied repeatedly, single-case designs (Bloom, Fischer and Orme, 1999) have been used across several target problems. Qualitative methods have been used to systematically track the changes in the circumstances of the clients, as well as changes in the content of interventions. There are also three process outcomes which are applicable in all cases, that is, whether the child/young person was engaged in the assessment work or not, whether either parent was engaged or not, and whether the assessment was completed or not. The evaluation procedures were applied to investigate not only what interventions work, but also for whom they work and in what contexts, thereby contributing to the development of realist evidence-based practice. The workers selected realist evaluation procedures to enable them to identify and develop effective assessment models that work in particular contexts.

The content of the Shield Project's Assessment Work

The content of the Shield Project's assessment and therapeutic intervention work was systematically tracked during the evaluation period through team meetings (including at least one every three months which was also attended by the evaluator), and the descriptions of the project and its work written by team member Ann Ward and team manager Gerry Hudson (for example, in Kazi and Ward, 2001). In particular two focus-group meetings were held with the team in a period of six months, facilitated by the evaluator, focusing on the content of the Shield team's work.

Kitzinger and Barbour (1999: 4) describe focus groups as 'group discussions exploring a specific set of issues. The group is "focused" in that it involves some kind of collective activity .... Crucially, focus groups are distinguished from the broader category of group interviews by the explicit use of group interaction to generate data'.

With regard to recording and transcribing the data from focus groups, the authors suggest that the 'most basic level of recording focus-group discussions depends on note taking and the use of a flip chart to construct, with group participants, a summary of the meeting' (p. 15). Flip charts were used in both focus groups specifically focusing on the content of Shield's work, and a transcript of the first focus-group meeting was distributed prior to the holding of the second meeting. The focus-group meetings investigated both the assessment work and the therapeutic work, but as the evaluation at this stage is concentrating on the assessment work, the contents of the therapeutic interventions are not described here (readers can refer to Kazi and Ward, 2001, for more details of the therapeutic interventions).

The aims of the service are described by the Shield Project as:

1   to prevent children and young people from being sexually harmed by other children and young people;
2   to promote the physical, social and emotional well-being of children and young people who sexually harm others;
3   to develop a multi-agency plan to address the complex needs of young people who sexually harm others and to reduce the risk of reoffending.

The workers described their project's assessment work as follows:

All assessment work is co-worked by two workers with the aim of completing a full and holistic assessment, and is undertaken prior to any longer-term therapeutic intervention. The main aim of the assessment is to identify the context in which the behaviours take place, the attitude of the young person and their family to the behaviour and any strengths or difficulties that would either reduce or heighten the risk of the behaviour reoccurring. The assessment aims to be holistic by exploring all aspects of the young person's life and not just the sexually harmful behaviour, such as affective triggers, self-efficacy, and relationships (Ryan, 1999). The assessment needs to identify the level of risk and make recommendations for managing or reducing the level of risk in the future.

The assessment process includes exploration of relevant issues, gathering of information, and hypothesising potential causal mechanisms. The assessment is influenced by theoretical models such as solution-focused and cognitive approaches, and the theoretical perspectives of the individual workers. As a team, the Shield Project has an eclectic approach to theoretical models in relation to understanding sexual behaviour. Learning from the work of Finkelhor (1984) who proposed a comprehensive approach rather than adherence to a particular school of thought, the team is not influenced exclusively by any one model, and draws upon several theoretical approaches, for example, the sexual abuse cycle (Lane, 1997), which is based on a repetitive and compulsive sequence of cognition and behaviour prior to, during, and after the acts of sexual abuse; attachment theory where sexual aggression is seen as symptomatic of deficits in early or later attachment; and Finkelhor's (1984) four pre-conditions model which includes motivation, overcoming internal and external inhibitors, and overcoming or undermining the victim's resistance.

In the early stages, the involvement of the Shield workers may be through the provision of advice or consultation to the local authority social worker. If it is agreed that a full assessment is required, then project workers would meet with the parents/carers and social worker in order to discuss the role of the project, discuss the content of the assessment and gain the family's agreement for undertaking the assessment work.

The parents may be reluctant, embarrassed and even feel threatened, but an atmosphere would be fostered where an open and honest discussion could take place. A work agreement would then be drawn up between the parent/carer and project workers. Parents/carers are encouraged to contribute to this agreement by identifying significant people they feel should be consulted as part of the process, or identifying key areas they would like to be included in the assessment. As part of this meeting with the parents, support for the child/young person will be identified, and agreement will be reached with parents with regard to expectations of the work from both sides. Parents/carers are made aware of the sexually explicit language that will be used when talking to their child. At this point, it is also agreed how information would be fed back to the parent, as work with the child is likely to take place away from home.

A separate child-centred agreement is drawn up with the young person. This would be discussed at the first meeting. Parents/carers are encouraged to attend the first session with their child in order to make introductions, reassure their child that they are supporting them in engaging in the work and give the child permission to talk freely to project workers. Once all the introductory visits are made, the child will be seen separately from his/her parents/carers.

In the sessions with the child/young person and/or the parents/carers, the emphasis will be on a positive approach rather than a judgmental one, and the clients will be encouraged to tell their own stories to build up a realist picture for the assessment process. Every effort is made to keep people engaged and motivated in the work with Shield. With regard to work around the alleged offences, it is not the aim during assessment to challenge too greatly the level of denial. This is a baseline assessment that marks the level of responsibility they are able to accept for their sexually harmful behaviour at this moment in time. This will enable the assessment to identify areas of future work and the potential for change.

It is expected that there will be some level of denial from most of the young people that the project works with, and that their parents may also deny there is a problem. The assessment would focus on identifying work that would be useful to the young person in accepting responsibility for their own behaviour and existing structures that would support them in doing this. Recommendations will be made about future therapeutic intervention or change work and include comments on the likelihood of the young person being able to make use of this.

The assessment will also identify enabling and disabling mechanisms or factors which would support (or not) the young person in changing their behaviour. These would include parental attitudes, support available and other strengths or stresses the family has. Recommendations would be made about any possible work with parents that could address the issues identified. (Kazi and Ward, 2001: 4–6)

Application of the Realist Effectiveness Cycle

From the outset there has been an intention to evaluate the work provided by the project. The realist paradigm has underpinned the establishment of systems used by the project and this has influenced the way in which data are collected and recorded. A three-month pilot was undertaken to 'test out' the proposed systems for information-gathering between October and December 1999. Informed by the pilot, the methods used to identify and track the processes and outcomes of intervention were developed by the project workers in partnership with the author.

The realist approach does not rely upon the measurement of outcomes alone, but also seeks to identify the context in which the work took place, the content of the interventions and the enabling and disabling mechanisms affecting the outcome. It is accepted that these mechanisms or tendencies will not be static (as explained later in this chapter) and so changes over time are also tracked. A method of systematically recording these factors has been incorporated into the existing recording systems used by the team. The methods used in data collection and tracking (as described by Ann Ward and the other Shield team members) are:

Tracking of Contexts   Contexts to the work are identified at the beginning of any piece of work in the initial plan. Subsequent changes in contexts are recorded in summaries of the sessions undertaken with each case. This includes information from other sources, such as the local authority social worker. This qualitative data is then the subject of review and analysis.

Tracking of Mechanisms   Enabling and disabling mechanisms are identified in the initial plan of work. Mechanisms affecting the work in later individual sessions are recorded on the agency's session plan and summary forms. A common language used to record this data has been identified (that is, in the recording form SP5) and the data is only recorded following discussion in joint supervision sessions. Again, this qualitative data is subsequently reviewed and analysed as a team activity.

Tracking of Content   The content of the planned intervention(s) is included in the initial plan and work agreement. The agency's session recording forms (SP3/4) then provide a vehicle for recording both the plan for the content of each session and the actual content of the session. In order to standardise and facilitate this recording process, a menu of possible content/subject areas has been included in the SP3/4. Periodic review meetings provide the opportunity to review and analyse the content of the work undertaken.

Tracking of Outcomes   Process outcomes are recorded at the end of a piece of work, such as attendance. The conclusions and recommendations contained in the agency's assessment report on a young person comprise the outcomes of the assessment and the final review meeting identifies the outcomes of any intervention(s), for example, any change in the young person's attitudes or the level of risk he or she presents. The results of quantitative measures used (see case examples later in this chapter) are recorded on EXCEL and on SPSS.

Thus, wherever possible, the recording systems already in use by the team have been adapted to record the above information, for the purposes of both quantitative and qualitative analysis. These recording forms include: (a) initial plan; (b) work agreement; (c) SP3/4 – the session plans/summaries; (d) review meetings; (e) supervision notes.

As indicated in the above quotations from the Shield workers (pp. 98–9), the application of the evaluation strategy has been developed by the practitioners in partnership with the author, and the gathering of data as described is now incorporated into all activities of the team. This partnership has enabled the team to understand the theoretical basis for the evaluation and to use this understanding to develop systems that are applicable to daily practice. The team has devised the methods of data collection; the application of the evaluation strategy is therefore owned and valued by the team and fully incorporated into their daily practice.

Intensive Research Combining Quantitative and Qualitative Analysis

The realist evaluation framework for the evaluation of practice requires the systematic tracking of outcomes, mechanisms, contexts, and the content of the interventions in each case, in order to achieve an analysis of what works, for whom and in what contexts, as described in Chapter 3. For each case there is a qualitative analysis of the data, based on individual session records, supervision notes, plans, reviews and reports, as described below, and there is also quantitative data from the use of single-case evaluation. Cross-tabulation of outcomes and content of interventions in this particular application involves the use of single-case designs, as described in Chapter 5. Single-case evaluation involves the use of single-case designs by practitioners to track client progress systematically, or to evaluate the effectiveness of their interventions or programmes. A fundamental requirement is the measurement of the client's target problem(s) repeatedly over time, using appropriate outcome measure(s) or indicator(s) of progress. Several standardised measures were selected by the Shield staff team from Fischer and Corcoran (1994), and a measure for victim empathy was also created but abandoned as it was not very useful for practice. As the measures selected were of American origin, a few minor changes in wording were made in some of the other measures, to make the language more specific to local requirements. These changes may have an affect on the reported alphas indicated in the original descriptions of the measures. Further reliability tests were planned but not implemented because of the small numbers of cases where the measures have been used to date. The measures used were:

1 The Self-Concept Scale for Children (SC) is designed to measure the self-concept of children. The SC consists of 22 descriptive adjectives measuring children's feelings about themselves, with scores ranging from 22 to 110. Test–retest reliability is reported to range from .73 to .91, indicating good stability. The higher the score, the more positive the behaviour.

2 The Behaviour Rating Index for Children (BRIC) measures children's behaviour problems. The BRIC is a 13-item questionnaire designed for

use by people engaging with the children, such as parents, teachers, children themselves, and significant others. The BRIC is scored on a five-point Likert-type scale, with a potential range of scores from zero to 100. Higher scores indicate more severe behavioural problems. The reported internal consistency for the BRIC is good, with alphas ranging from .80 to .86 for adults and .60 to .70 for children. Test–retest reliability ranges from .71 to .89, but only .50 for children.

3   The Aggression Inventory (AI) is designed to measure behavioural characteristics or traits in adults. It is a 30-item instrument, with each item rated on a five-point scale. After summing the scores for each subscale and dividing by the number of items, the scores range from one to five, with higher scores indicating more aggression. Internal consistency alphas reportedly range from .65 to .82. However, in this application the AI was adapted for use with children and the scoring system was changed to the actual scores for each sub-scale plus an overall total score. A reliability test was carried out with five children, with retests taking place within one week. It was found that test–retest reliability was .85 for the overall score, indicating excellent stability, although the number of respondents was very small.

4   The Hare Self-Esteem Scale (HSS) is used to measure self-esteem in school-aged children. It is a 30-item instrument, with three sub-scales that are area specific – peer, school and home. The sum of all units is viewed as an overall measure of self-esteem. Higher scores indicate higher self-esteem. Test–retest reliability is reported to be .74 for the general scale. In this application the number of items was reduced to 21 and the Likert-type scale was increased from four to five scale points.

5   The Child's Attitude Toward Father (CAF) and Mother (CAM) are 25-item instruments designed to measure problems children have with their parents, from the child's perspective. The range of scores is zero to 100, with higher scores indicating greater magnitude or severity of problems. The CAF has a mean alpha of .95 and the CAM .95, indicating high levels of internal consistency.

6   The Adolescent Coping Orientation for Problem Experiences (A-COPE) is used to measure adolescent coping behaviours. It is a 54-item instrument designed to measure behaviours adolescents find helpful in managing problems or difficult situations. Higher scores indicate better coping behaviours. The A-COPE is a slightly modified version of the Young Adult-COPE with an overall alpha of .82 and test–retest reliability of .83. In this application, the number of items was reduced from 54 to 26.

7   The Victim Empathy measure was created by the project staff to monitor changes in the level of victim empathy and remorse. It is a 25-item instrument with a nominal yes/no against each item. The measure has only been used with three of the Shield Project's service users. Project workers found that, to use the measure appropriately, the subject must

be able to identify a 'victim', and therefore in most circumstances the measure has not been very useful. At the time of writing, this measure is no longer in use. Due to the small number of cases, no reliability tests were carried out.

Qualitative Data

The purpose is to identify the mechanisms and contexts at the beginning of the work and any changes that take place during the work. The method of recording used by the team supports this process by ensuring information about mechanisms, contexts and content is recorded clearly and is easily accessible. At the time of writing, the qualitative analysis included 17 cases, and two of these are included as examples in this chapter. The qualitative research strategies are based on action-oriented approaches (Drisko, 2000; Rodwell, 1998; Taylor and White, 2000), as the aim is to develop the assessment model to meet the needs of each child/young person, and the feedback from the data informs this process.

The source of all data is the interaction between the client and significant others with the project workers, as well as the cyclical connection between reflection and action. This interaction and reflection is then recorded and categorised within the realist perspective to systematically track outcomes, mechanisms, contexts and the content of the work. Taylor and White (2000) argue that health and social welfare workers cannot reproduce material-situated reality, and what they do is in fact order reality by supporting some versions (such as narratives of users and significant others) and burying others. 'However, by reflecting on the process of choice and judgement and thinking about ways in which forms may be redesigned to show more of our "working", we may develop a different and more critical approach to the data contained within them' (2000: 158). In this project, the forms have been designed from the outset using the language of realist evaluation, as described above.

Different researchers have different ways of processing and analysing data, depending on the researcher's own perspectives and interests. In this particular application, the qualitative data is summarised in the course of focus-group meetings (Kitzinger and Barbour, 1999) within the team, where the team as a whole discuss and review each case, including case recordings, and write an account of the contexts, mechanisms and the content of the work at each review. Reliability of the qualitative data is enhanced by the fact that all sessions are co-worked by two workers introducing at least two perspectives, and the team focus-group meetings add a further collective perspective of the team in reinterpreting the data. However, the limitations arising from the team's collective interests and perspectives mean that the problems of reliability still have to be taken into account. Although the sources of all qualitative data with regard to the identification of causal mechanisms are the young persons, their families and significant others, these data are mediated by the team in the process of recording and analysis. As Lawson (1998) explains, the identification of the particular phenomena to be explained, as well as the particular set of causal factors pursued, 'always depends upon the position, perspective and understanding of the viewer involved' (p. 172). Nevertheless, the particular interests of the viewer do not usually shape these factors. 'Causal mechanisms that are productive of actual phenomena exist at their own level of being, independently for the most part, of any investigation' (p. 173). The use of repeated staff meetings for qualitative review of the data enable a clearer picture of reality at each stage of work with the clients, helping to deal with this limitation.

The qualitative analysis is then combined with single-case analysis, to enable an explanation of the effectiveness of Shield's work in each case, particularly in explaining how the causal mechanisms are triggered in the contexts of the clients, and how the causal mechanisms that influence the social problems and behaviour are countered by the alternative causal mechanisms introduced by the Shield Project's models of intervention. Therefore, by studying the individual in his/her own causal contexts, the evaluation strategy for each case meets the requirements of intensive research as described by Sayer (2000); but a quantitative element in the form of single-case evaluation is also added to systematically track changes in the outcomes produced in those contexts, as indicated in the two case examples.

Case Example 1: Client K

Client K is a 15-year old male subject of a two-year supervision order for sexual offences with girls both within and outside his family. He has committed a number of serious sexual offences.

The single-case evaluation charts for K (Figures 6.1, 6.2 and 6.3) indicate that self-concept has risen; his general attitude has improved and he is more amenable and mature about the sessions. BRIC scores have clearly improved, and victim empathy has also increased slightly. No further allegations have been made against him. In September, carers reported more positive behaviour in the children's home, leading to an increase in his freedom and reduction in his supervision. The Shield Project has engaged with K's mother to carry out attachment repair, and she has agreed to have minimal contact. In October, K's mother had made no definite arrangements for contact and was very reluctant to visit her son, however, telephone contact continued. Further reductions were made in the level of supervision.

In the qualitative analysis of context and mechanisms, the causal mechanism that appears to shine through is the damaged relationship with both separated parents – the effect of the mother's letter on K's motivation and

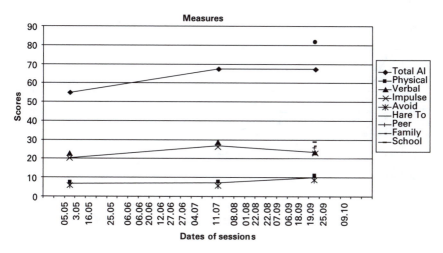

Figure 6.1   *K's outcome measures*

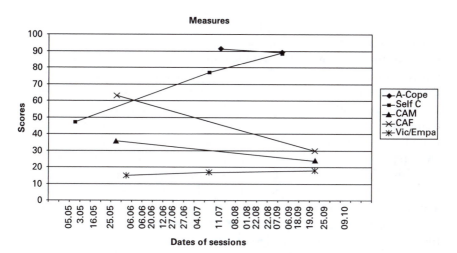

Figure 6.2   *K's outcome measures*

behaviour is an indication of this. This causal mechanism is triggered in the context of the parents' acrimonious separation, and the previous history of sexual abuse against both K and his mother. The causal mechanisms that are enabling improved K's behaviour, that is, those which are countering or neutralising the disabling mechanisms include the nature of the care place-ment, school, and the mother's willingness to engage in the work with the Shield Project. The generative causal mechanisms introduced by the Shield

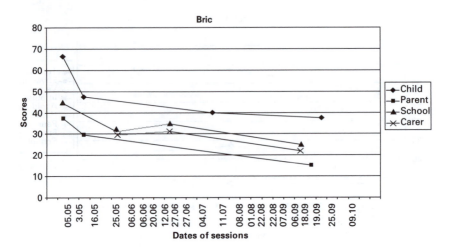

Figure 6.3   *K's outcome measures*

Project include the issues of family background and the current situation, discussing the actual offence, processing previous trauma and attachment repair, cognitive approaches to managing behaviour, assessing and developing motivation to change, and trauma outcome process with K, and holding separate sessions with his mother. Indications are that the improvements in the outcomes may have been caused by the Shield Project's introduction of causal mechanisms that connected with the other enabling causal mechanisms, and these causal mechanisms were triggered in the contexts of the parents' acrimonious separation and the history of sexual abuse. These enabling causal mechanisms, as well as the generative mechanisms introduced by Shield, were able to neutralise the disabling causal mechanism, although this battle is by no means over, and the main disabling causal mechanism of K's relationship with his parents still shines through occasionally.

In the course of applying the realist effectiveness cycle, both the qualitative and the quantitative analysis were used prospectively to shape and target the content of the Shield Project's intervention with K. In particular, the identification of the disabling causal mechanisms helped to introduce alternative causal mechanisms which reinforced the other enabling causal mechanisms, in the course of Shield's work. In this way, by integrating realist evaluation strategies, the Shield project team were able to improve the services provided to both K and his mother.

Case Example 2: Client H

H is a 13-year-old girl who is alleged to have indecently assaulted her 3-year-old brother. The single-case evaluation chart (Figure 6.4) indicates that

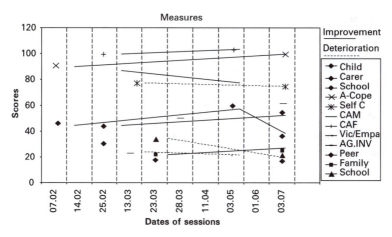

Figure 6.4   *H's outcome measures*

some progress was made in only four out of the 12 outcome measures used with H. H's BRIC became worse, and then improved, with the difference between the first (45) and the last (40) scores indicating an improvement. H's CAM improved from 87 to 78; family HSS improved slightly from 22.5 to 26, and the A-COPE improved from 90 to 100. Therefore, the only improvements made were in H's perception of her own behaviour, her attitude towards her mother, self-esteem within the family, and her coping inventory. In their records, the workers reported that improvements had also been achieved in H's understanding of the incident, and thereby in her ability to engage in the work. They also reported that no further allegations of sexually inappropriate behaviour had been made, or concerns expressed by significant others regarding H's sexual behaviour. However, it had not been possible to explore H's feelings regarding her mother's rejection of her.

The workers also reported that H's general difficult behaviour was ongoing and in fact getting worse. The outcomes from the other measures (Figure 6.4) corroborate this view. The school BRIC deteriorated from 32.5 to 50, the carer's BRIC from 45 to 52.5, SC from 78 to 75, CAF from 100 to 104, Victim Empathy from 23 to 21, AI from 50 to 62, peer HSS from 20 to 19, and school HSS from 35 to 20. Therefore, there was deterioration in each of the school's and carer's perceptions of H's behaviour, H's self-concept, H's attitude to her father, victim empathy, aggression inventory, peer self-esteem, and school self-esteem.

The potential disabling mechanisms influencing H's behaviour that are shining through are her mother's rejection of H, and H's rejection of her father and his recourse to legal action regarding contact. These mechanisms are triggered in the contexts of H being in foster care, the history of physical and sexual abuse against H, her father's remarriage, and H's recollection of domestic abuse when her parents were together, as well as H's poor history with regard to both school and peers. Also within these structures, enabling mechanisms are emerging, such as the ability of foster carers to cope with H's behaviour, H's good relations with social services, and H accepting the initial allegations and thereby engaging better with the work. Shield has introduced alternative mechanisms to neutralise the disabling mechanisms, such as engaging with H regarding her family background as well as the current situation, and her understanding of her behaviours. However, on the whole, the disabling mechanisms are shining through more than the enabling mechanisms, thereby explaining the mixed response in the outcomes at the surface.

These two case examples illustrate the process of intensive realist research applied in each case by the practitioner–researchers at Shield in partnership with the author as the external evaluator. These case examples indicate how we can penetrate beneath the observable inputs and outputs of the programme in each case, in order to explain how the potential causal mechanisms that generate the social problems, general behaviours and harmful sexual behaviours are countered with alternative causal mechanisms that enable the clients to change in a positive direction. This intensive research also indicates how the alternative mechanisms introduced by the Shield Project's interventions interact with the other existing mechanisms, and the contexts or conditions in which all of these mechanisms are triggered. This intensive evaluation research also enables the explanation of mechanism–context–outcome configurations over specific time–space locations in each case, and in the circumstances in which these mechanisms and contexts are continually changing. The application of the realist effectiveness cycle in each case enables the practitioners not only to explain these configurations retrospectively at the time of the reviews, but also to better target and develop the models of intervention in order to be more effective in the future with each client. The Shield Project's individual work with their clients, and the way it is evaluated and developed, also exemplify realist evidence-based practice in action.

Aggregation of Data Across Cases

The cases of K and H above indicate how the data from each case is analysed as part of intensive practitioner research; the next stage of the evaluation is to aggregate the data from all cases to establish 'what works, for whom and in what contexts'. As described in Chapter 3, these analyses indicate not only what works, but also why it works or not in the various circumstances of practice, that is, in the changing nature of stratified reality.

This aggregation is an application in practice of Lawson's (1998) realist strategy of detecting patterns in outcomes, and the conditions in which the multiple mechanisms are triggered, in the process of investigating the causal mechanisms.

The computer software package SPSS is being used to analyse the quantitative data for this realist evaluation; to date, there are 49 cases in the database. Only those cases where there is sufficient information on the contexts and mechanisms are included, and therefore the database excludes others where only advice and consultancy are offered but without the required information for a realist evaluation.

In this particular application of realist evaluation, first the realist effectiveness cycle has to be applied in all cases, as explained above. Therefore, the development of extensive research in this report presupposes the use of intensive research in each case, utilising both qualitative and quantitative data analysis. If, and only if, this condition is satisfied, then the data can be aggregated across all the cases which are the subject of intensive research. Therefore, the extensive data analysis presented in the next two chapters is derived from the intensive research in each case, as described above. The measures are identified through the use of single-case evaluation that enables the systematic tracking of the planned outcomes. At the same time, the potential causal mechanisms that lie underneath these outcomes at the surface are identified, as well as the contexts in which they are triggered. Through intensive research in each case, it is possible to identify some causal mechanisms that were common in more than one case, as well as the contexts, in order to identify the patterns across all cases. In this way, the beginnings of the realist evaluation are made for an entire project or human service programme. The aggregated qualitative and quantitative analyses are presented in the next chapter.

7

The Shield Project: Extensive Analysis in Realist Evaluation

In this chapter, we present the extensive analysis of both qualitative and quantitative data in a realist evaluation that is seeking to identify the causal mechanisms and the contexts in which they are fired. Pawson and Tilley (1997b) identify a list of mechanisms that they suggest may be influencing the success of a CCTV initiative to reduce crime in a car park, but they also add that their list is speculative, and that they have not been able to draw upon research in this field as it is rather limited. The identification of potential causal mechanisms is an important part of realist evaluation, and for this purpose realists use abstraction, in a movement from the empirical to the concrete to test theories about the potential mechanisms. Robson (2002: 37) suggests that, in this process, 'it is not a difficult task for practitioners with a well-developed intimate knowledge of the situation (and for researchers with whom they have shared this knowledge) to come up with a set of proposals for the mechanisms and contexts likely to be relevant'. Robson also suggests that, in Pawson and Tilley's example, it may be possible to draw upon other studies of similar situations such as shopping malls to help identify the relevant contexts and mechanisms. In this particular study, the Shield workers did draw upon their knowledge of the clients' situations, and tested this knowledge in their intensive research with each case. Taking up Robson's advice, they also used the findings from the existing body of research in the western world which identifies factors that are reported to be common amongst children/young people who sexually harm others.

These are the sources that we will examine in detail in this chapter. We begin with the process of qualitative analysis used to identify the mechanisms, then we consider the findings from research, and then finally, we begin to identify the extent of outcomes achieved, and the extent of the evidence indicating the presence of the relevant mechanisms and contexts, as well as some process outcomes with regard to the assessment work carried out with the service users. Then, in the next chapter, we begin to investigate the patterns that help to determine what works, for whom and in what contexts in assessment work with this client group.

As outlined in the previous chapter, in each case identified for assessment work, the Shield team will hold repeated focus-group meetings to identify the outcomes achieved so far, the contexts, enabling mechanisms, disabling mechanisms, and the content of the work. The data from each meeting takes the form of a written record for each case under the following themes:

1 **Outcomes** are agreed with the service users, and standardised measures are applied, as indicated in Chapter 6. The outcomes include impact outcomes, such as changes in behaviour, as well as process outcomes, for example, whether the assessment was completed or not.
2 **Contexts** are defined as structures in the circumstances of people that take a longer time to change (when compared to mechanisms below), such as housing, employment; as well as historical circumstances in which practice takes place, for example, whether the parents are sepa-rated or not, whether there is a history of domestic violence, sexual abuse and other trauma. The contexts provide the conditions in which causal mechanisms are triggered to produce the outcomes.
3 **Mechanisms** are factors in the circumstances of the service users that influence the agreed outcomes. They are either **enabling**, that is, help-ing to achieve the outcomes; or **disabling**, that is, working against the achievement of the outcomes. The **content** could be seen as generating mechanisms, that is, additional factors in the clients' circumstances introduced by the interventions and/or actions of the Shield Project social workers, with the intention of generating change.

After each focus-group meeting, the data analysis takes the form of a qual-itative case study, with evidence outlined against each of the broad themes at each meeting pertaining to each case. This information is systematically tracked over time, and the records are changed if the focus group agrees that changes have occurred in the client's circumstances, that is, with regard to outcomes, mechanisms, contexts and the content of the work. These records are collated together and displayed in the form of a data display and matrices as described in Miles and Huberman (1994). A display is a 'visual format that presents information systematically, so that the user can draw valid conclusions and take needed action' (p. 91). The full data set is pre-sented, but it takes the form of a condensed, distilled presentation drawn from the full range of data sets utilised to date, displayed in matrices. A matrix is essentially 'the crossing of two lists, set up as rows and columns' (p. 93) for each case, and when aggregating data across cases, matrices 'essentially involve the crossing of two or more main dimensions or vari-ables (often with subvariables) to see how they interact' (p. 239). Matrices enable the noting of patterns and themes across cases. In this application, a matrix is drawn up for each case, and the data across cases is aggregated as in the Appendix which outlines the matrix for all 17 cases to date where this form of repeated focus groups and qualitative data analysis have been used by the Shield team. The Appendix also includes two columns which are drawn from the quantitative data analysis outlined in the foregoing, namely whether the requirements of the assessment model were met or not, and whether the assessment was completed or not. As the qualitative information is condensed, for each case it includes only the main contexts and mechanisms identified by the workers, and not all, as can be observed in the individual case discussions in relation to the cases K and H.

Sexually Harmful Behaviours and Research Findings

Juvenile sexual offenders are defined as individuals aged 18 or younger who commit a sexual offence against a victim of any age (Johnson and Knight, 2000). As noted earlier, the Shield Project works with cases that are not subject to the criminal process, and therefore the cases in the Appendix indicate a range of sexual behaviours. Research on young people who sexually harm others indicates a lack of clear definitions regarding what is normal sexual behaviour during adolescence (Burke, 2001). For example, in a survey of practitioners, Masson (1997/8) found that 57% of respondents were concerned about the lack of clarity regarding what is normal and abnormal sexual behaviour at different stages of development. However, there is a need for some working definition regarding these behaviours. 'While all children and adolescents engage in a variety of sexual behaviours, some of these are considered inappropriate by adults and come to clinical attention .... A limited subset of these behaviours entails molestation or coercion of other children' (Lightfoot and Evans, 2000: 1185). Therefore, the literature on young people who sexually harm others tends to focus on coercive behaviour. For example, Vizard, Monck and Misch (1995: 732) describe deviant sexual behaviour as the 'use of coercion or force, sexualised interactions which are age-inappropriate for the partner, and partners who are not peers'. Therefore, in the Appendix all but two of the behaviours (with the exception of R and M) involve coercive behaviours. With regard to the other two behaviours, they are also a cause for concern and there is a suspicion in research to date that such behaviours could be precursors to adult sexual offending (Vizard, Monck and Misch, 1995).

To put the incidents in the national and international context, the focus tends to be on coercive behaviours identified as sexual offences. According to Beckett (2001), there are 30 programmes similar to Shield in the United Kingdom and Ireland. In Great Britain, according to Home Office figures of 1998 as reported in Beckett (2001), there were 33,200 recorded sexual offences, and 6,400 perpetrators were found guilty; about a third of these perpetrators were aged under 21 years. About a third of the recorded allegations identified the perpetrators as aged 17 or less. In the USA, crime reports and surveys indicate that adolescents are responsible for 20–30% of all rapes, 30–50% of all reported cases of child abuse, and 40% of reported sexual offences (Burton, 2000; Hunter, Hazelwood and Slesinger, 2000; Veneziano, Veneziano and LeGrand, 2000; Worling and Curwen, 2000). In New Zealand, juvenile sex offending constitutes 11% of the total annual rate of sexual offending for the past nine years (Lightfoot and Evans, 2000). Research indicates, therefore, that sexual harmful behaviour by children and young people is a matter of concern in the western world, and a number of studies have been carried out identifying the characteristics of the offenders.

The Identification of Contexts and Mechanisms

The Appendix indicates a variety of contexts and mechanisms across the 17 cases. The sources of the information included the referral sources, the case files at the local authority social services, and the Shield workers' interaction with the child/young person, the parents and/or significant others, and from multi-disciplinary sources, such as school teachers. In addition, the Shield workers were also influenced by research findings from North America, Europe and Australasia.

Research from across the western world indicates that children/young people who sexually harm others are a heterogeneous group, and that there are a wide range of reported circumstances, including a wide range of behavioural patterns, background histories and treatment needs (Burke, 2001; Johnson and Knight, 2000; Pithers and Gray, 1997; Veneziano, Veneziano and LeGrand, 2000; Zolondek et al., 2001). At the same time, research also indicates that there are a number of factors that appear to be common across large numbers of cases. For example, in a number of North American studies, disruptive or dysfunctional family-of-origin experiences appear to exist commonly in the childhood backgrounds of adolescent and adult sexual offenders, including familial chaos, marital discord, parental separation, parental rejection, lack of age-appropriate social competence, loneliness and social isolation, cognitive distortions, truancy, learning difficulties, and a history of sexual abuse/victimisation (Aljazireh,1993; Gal and Hoge, 1999; Marshall, 1993; Pithers et al., 1989; Schram, Milloy and Rowe, 1991; Smallbone and Dadds, 2000, 2001).

In their study of 70 male juvenile sex offenders aged 13–21 years in Australia, Kenny, Keogh and Seidler (2001) found that poor social skills and learning problems were related to recidivism. In their theoretical model, the authors include historical factors such as physical and emotional abuse or neglect, marital discord, separation or divorce, domestic violence, parental criminology or psychopathology or both, parent/sibling offending, unemployment and mobility as distal precursors. In New Zealand, Lightfoot and Evans (2000) carried out a study to understand the variables contributing to sexual offending. They included 20 young people who had engaged in coercive sexual behaviour and a matched group of clinic-referred young people with conduct disorders. The sexually abusive group were more likely to have experienced physical abuse (60% as against 35%) and verbal/emotional abuse (60% as against 42%) than the clinical group. Confirmed sexual abuse remained at 15% for both groups, although suspected sexual abuse was 80% in the sexually abusive group as against 35% in the clinical group. Twice as many sexually abusive young people (65%) were found to have experienced multiple disruption to attachment than in the clinical group (32%).

In a study of 107 adolescent offenders in Germany, Hummel et al. (2000) found that 19.6% claimed to have been the victims of sexual abuse mostly during their childhood, and as a proportion of those who later committed sexual offences against children ($n = 36$), the percentage was 44%. Higher proportions of the adolescents with a history of sexual abuse also reported a history of discontinuity of care, school problems and social isolation from peers.

Factors Used as a Typology for Prediction

These factors are often used in an attempt to establish a typology of young people who may sexually harm others. For example, in a retrospective study of juvenile sexual offenders, Johnson and Knight (2000) found that physical abuse, sexual abuse, alcohol abuse, peer aggression and school disruption were direct or indirect predictors of sexual coercion. In a study in Sweden of 56 young sexual offenders aged 15–20 years, Langstrom, Grann and Lindblad (2000) identified a preliminary typology which included low socio-economic status, parental divorce, separation from either biological parent, non-supportive/abusive family, social skills deficiency, special educational needs, previous contact with social services, and substance abuse.

It is clear from the literature that one of the purposes for identifying the factors commonly associated with young people who sexually harm others is to identify risk factors, and not necessarily to establish what interventions work with what sorts of young people. For example, a number of studies have attempted to identify typologies for the purpose of predicting risk of engaging in sexually harmful behaviours. A study by Malamuth et al. (1991) indicated an association between early home experiences of domestic violence and the perpetration of violence against women. In a retrospective study of juvenile sexual offenders, Johnson and Knight (2000) found that physical abuse, sexual abuse, alcohol abuse, peer aggression and school disruption were direct or indirect predictors of sexual coercion. Rasmussen, Burton and Christopherson (1992) argued that prior traumatisation was one of a number of precursors to sexual perpetration, with other predisposing factors including social inadequacy, lack of intimacy and impulsiveness.

Widom (1995; also cited in Gray et al., 1999, and Morrison, 2000) calculated odds ratios which indicated that sexually abused children were 4.7 times (and physically abused children 4.1 times) more likely than non-abused children to be arrested as an adult for a sex crime, suggesting that the etiologically significant factor in the emergence of abusive sexuality is exposure to trauma, not sexual abuse per se (Gray et al., 1999).

However, research also indicates caution with regard to using these factors as predictors of risk. For example, although a history of sexual abuse is prominent in the literature, not all those children/young people who are sexually abused become perpetrators (Kenny, Keogh and Seidler, 2001). 'Attempts at establishing a profile of a typical offender appear to be elusive, as there is little explanation as to why most adolescent boys – who have low self-esteem, poor social skills, and family instability – do not offend' (Burke, 2001: 224). Although social isolation, low self-esteem, dysfunctional families, poor academic achievement, and previous victimisation are frequently attributed to this group, the results are empirically inconclusive and contradictory (Vizard, Monck and Misch, 1995). A recent meta-analysis does not find a relationship between prior sexual victimisation and later recidivism (Hanson and Bussiere, 1998).

Dearth of Evaluation Studies

A review of the literature regarding research on young people who sexually harm others also indicates that more studies have been done to identify the factors leading to these behaviours, and that there is very little evaluation of the interventions used with these groups of young people. For example, Ryan (2000) notes that there are more than 300 programmes in the USA treating adolescents who sexually harm others. At the same time, Worling and Curwen (2000) report that, since 1975, there have been only 10 published reports of criminal recidivism following specialised treatment in the USA and Canada. Johnson and Knight (2000) also confirm that there have been few empirical studies on juvenile sexual offenders when compared with adult sex offenders. Many of the studies that do exist focus on offender and offence characteristics, whilst ignoring the possible covariation with other variables. In a British survey of practitioners, Masson (1997/8) found that 67% of respondents were concerned about the dearth of evaluation studies.

In this particular study, these research findings are not used to predict risk of sexual harm in the future; rather, they are used to help in the evaluation of the Shield Project. In particular, these findings are used to help identify the contexts and mechanisms of the Shield Project's clients, and to identify where the Shield model of assessment is more effective and in what circumstances it is less effective.

Findings from the Qualitative Analysis

The Appendix indicates findings that appear to be consistent with those of the above literature review. The group of 17 cases are heterogeneous, indicating a variety of mechanisms and contexts. However, there are some mechanisms that appear to be more common, such as the relationship between parents, support from parents, peer relationships, the young person's ability to engage in the work, and the multi-disciplinary relationship between the professionals. Some common contexts include: separation of parents; separation from parents; learning disabilities; histories of domestic violence, sexual abuse, physical abuse and neglect; histories of school problems and peer relations, and histories of social services involvement, mental health problems and drug/alcohol misuse. Many of these findings are also consistent with those found in the above literature review.

A safeguard was that these contexts or mechanisms were not identified from suspicion alone (for example, in Lightfoot and Evans, 2000, the reported level of sexual abuse victimisation was 15%, and the level of suspected victimisation was 80%), but through other sources, such as disclosures or entries in social services' records. However, with regard to limitations, a major problem is that histories of sexual abuse and physical abuse are often based on self-report, and often not verified through other means. Therefore, respondents can over- or under-report their histories of abuse (Murphy et al., 2001). Also, retrospective self-reports of childhood experiences (such as whether the clients' mothers were themselves victims of sexual abuse) are open to a number of possible biases (Widom, 1988), for example, reinterpreting past memories in the context of present experiences.

A realist evaluation may develop beyond the study of single cases and towards the identification of patterns across cases. Miles and Huberman (1994) suggest that the use of matrices enables the identification of such patterns from qualitative data analysis. However, in this application (the Appendix) the practitioners tended to use the focus group and qualitative review methods with cases where they had been able to interact with the child and either parent, and therefore in most cases they had met the requirements of the assessment model, and also completed the assessment. There were only two cases out of 17 where the requirements were not met, and only three where the assessment had not been completed, and therefore it was not possible to identify patterns or mechanism–context–outcome configurations in relation to these two outcomes.

Quantitative Data Analysis and Patterns Across Cases

At this stage, we have outlined the main findings in relation to the outcomes, mechanisms, contexts, and the content of the intervention, in relation to the 17 cases where the qualitative methods were used to date. The quantitative analysis is carried out alongside this qualitative analysis through the use of the SPSS software package for quantitative data. At the time of writing, the project evaluation has completed the first phase of just over two years, and this analysis is based on a database of a 100% sample of 49 clients where case files where kept and data on mechanisms and contexts were available. Cases where Shield workers provided advice only to referrers and where case recordings were at best minimal were excluded.

Inferential statistics or sub-group analysis (Duguid and Pawson, 1998) may be used to identify useful patterns in the data, thereby revealing some potential mechanism–context–outcome configurations. As indicated in Chapter 3, Lawson (1998) defines demi-regularities as 'patterns of regularities of sorts, regularities that are recognisable as such despite being something rather less than strict' (p. 162). The reasons why these regularities are not strict are, first, because the environment in which the mechanisms operate may not be homogeneous and there may be a large number of countervailing factors and, second, the mechanisms themselves are likely to be unstable over time and space.

Although demi-regularities (or patterns) are less than strict, and less than universal, the countervailing mechanisms may be such that the primary mechanisms often dominate. Therefore, at any specific time–space location, there may be systematic and identifiable mechanisms in play which realist evaluation strategies may uncover. As the patterns are uncovered in the course of the application of the realist effectiveness cycle, the realities are also likely to be uncovered to the extent that any relevant mechanism overlooked in the early stages of the work may be discovered over time.

First, we need to know which outcomes were achieved or not. Then, these findings are analysed with all the rest of the variables with regard to the contexts and mechanisms. For those that improved (as well as for those who are in the no change or deteriorated category) with each measure, we need to know what the contexts were, what the mechanisms were and whether these mechanisms were enabling or disabling, how these mechanisms changed over time, and what the components of the content of interventions were that were used.

The Systematic Tracking of Outcomes

As outlined in Chapter 6, a number of standardised measures were selected and/or developed for use by the Shield Project workers. However, these outcome measures were to be used in specific cases where there were specific target problems that could be measured, and the selection of cases and the appropriate outcome measures were left at the discretion of each worker. In the first two-year period of this evaluation, it was found that some of these outcome measures were not used at all, and others were at best used in only several cases. In the event, the data were not sufficient to enable the use of inferential statistics to identify patterns across the cases. Therefore, at best, where single-case designs were used (for example, in the illustrations of cases K and H previously), the data are aggregated in the form of one-group pre-test post-test designs (Rubin and Babbie, 2001) by comparing the difference between the first and the last scores for each group of measures used.

The data from the one-group pre-test post-test designs were aggregated and analysed with the calculation of effect sizes for each outcome measured, as described in Chapter 5. The effect size is calculated by taking the difference between the means of the first and last scores, and then dividing by the standard deviation of the first scores. This process is useful for aggregating the data from several single-case designs or from 8 large numbers of cases, and the effect size for each target problem can be measured to determine the impact of the interventions.

Changes in the Child Behaviour Rating Index for Children (BRIC) Scores

Table 7.1 indicates the effect size with regard to the Child Behaviour Rating Index for Children (BRIC) scores which measures children's behaviour problems and which can be used from the perspectives of the child and others. In this table, the BRIC is used from the perspective of the child/young person. Higher scores indicate more severe behavioural problems. This measure was used more often than any of the other standardised measures, in seven cases; of these, there were improvements in six, and the seventh became worse. The mean scores were 44.5 for the first scores and 27.1 for the last scores, indicating a considerable change. The effect size was –0.94, indicating a large effect size, as the lower the score the better.

Table 7.2 indicates the effect sizes of changes in the parent, school, and carer BRIC scores, again comparing the first and the last scores. These measures were used less frequently than the child BRIC, and the effect size was also less. The parent BRIC effect size was moderate to large, at –0.69, indicating that on the whole the child/young person was right in indicating improvements in their behaviours, although the parents in these five cases felt that the improvements were slightly less than what was indicated in Table 7.1. The school BRIC, on the other hand, indicated an even larger effect size, at –2.38, suggesting that in fact the behaviours of the three young people had improved a great deal. In the four cases where the carer BRIC was used (that is, where the child/young person was not living at home), the carers indicated a moderate effect size of –0.67 which was almost the same as that indicated by the parents. On the whole, these effect sizes indicate that considerable improvements were achieved in the behaviours of the several young people in the course of the Shield Project's work.

Table 7.1   *Shield child BRIC outcome and effect size*

Cases	First scores	Last scores	Change
K	67.50	27.50	Improved
A	32.50	30.00	Improved
H	45.00	40.00	Improved
M	70.00	15.00	Improved
X	27.50	40.00	Deteriorated
Q	42.50	15.00	Improved
Z	25.00	22.50	Improved

Statistics	Child BRIC first score (where repeated only)	Child BRIC last scores	Change: effect size
Valid N	7	7	
Median	42.5	27.5	
Mean	44.3	27.1	
Std. deviation	18.2	10.5	
Effect size			–0.94

Table 7.2   *The effect sizes of changes in the parent, school and carer BRIC scores Parent BRIC effect size*

Statistics	Parent BRIC first score (where repeated only)	Parent BRIC last scores	Change: effect size
Valid N	5	5	
Missing (not used or not repeated)	44	44	
Mean	36.8600	22.5000	
Std. deviation	20.8008	7.7055	
Effect size			–0.69

School BRIC effect size

Statistics	School BRIC first score (where repeated only)	School BRIC last scores	Change: effect size
Valid N	3	3	
Missing (not used or not repeated)	46	46	
Mean	51.6667	36.6667	
Std. deviation	6.2915	19.0941	
Effect size			–2.38

Carer BRIC effect size

Statistics	Carer BRIC first score (where repeated only)	Carer BRIC last scores	Change: effect size
Valid N	4	4	
Missing (not used or not repeated)	45	45	
Mean	36.2500	31.2500	
Std. deviation	7.5000	18.5405	
Effect size			–0.67

Table 7.3   *Self-concept effect size*

Statistics	Self-concept first score (where repeated only)	Self-concept last scores	Change: effect size
Valid N	3	3	
Missing (not used or not repeated)	46	46	
Mean	70.3333	82.6667	
Std. deviation	20.5994	7.5056	
Effect size			0.60

Table 7.4   *The effect of changes in CAM and CAF scores*

CAM effect size

Statistics	CAM first score (where repeated only)	CAM last scores	Change: effect size
Valid N	5	5	
Missing (not used or not repeated)	44	44	
Mean	51.0600	52.2000	
Std. deviation	20.5577	21.2415	
Effect size			0.06

CAF effect size

Statistics	CAF first score (where repeated only)	CAF last scores	Change: effect size
Valid N	5	5	
Missing (not used or not repeated)	44	44	
Mean	53.6000	62.8000	
Std. deviation	29.0568	45.3564	
Effect size			0.32

Changes in the Self-Concept Scale for Children Scores

The Self-Concept Scale for Children (SC) is designed to measure the self-concept of children, and the higher the score the more positive the self-concept. Table 7.3 indicates that a moderate to large effect size was achieved in the three cases where this measure was used repeatedly.

Changes in the Child's Attitude Toward Father (CAF) and Mother (CAM) Scores

The Child's Attitude Toward Father (CAF) and Mother (CAM) are designed to measure problems children have with their parents, from the child's perspective. Higher scores indicate a greater magnitude or severity of problems. The effect size on CAM scores was almost negligible at 0.06, but a small to moderate effect size was achieved in the CAF scores during the Shield Project's work with these five cases.

Table 7.5   *Results of AI reliability tests and the effect size*

Aggression Inventory Reliability Test coefficients

Reliability tests	Physical	Verbal	Impulsive	Avoidance	Total AI
First test	83.4	89.7	90.8	82.4	84.9
Second test	90.5	100.0	87.2	70.0	96.0

Aggression Inventory effect size

Statistics	AI first score (where repeated only)	AI last scores	Change: effect size
Valid N	5	5	
Missing (not used or not repeated)	44	44	
Mean	59.8000	63.6000	
Std. deviation	11.8617	6.6558	
Effect size			0.32

Changes in the Aggression Inventory Scores

The Aggression Inventory (AI) is designed to measure behavioural characteristics or traits in adults. However, in this application the AI was adapted for use with children and the scoring system was changed to the actual scores for each sub-scale plus an overall total score. Higher scores indicate more aggression. Test–retest reliability tests were undertaken on two occasions. The first test was carried out with five children, repeated within one week. The alpha of all 10 responses was .76. The results of the test–retest reliability are indicated in Table 7.5, ranging from 82.4 to 90.8, with a good reliability of the overall scale of 84.9. The scale was modified from a three-point scale to a five-point scale, and then the instrument was tested again, this time with two children within one week. The test–retest reliability ranged from 70.0 to 100.0 for the sub-scales, and again with an excellent reliability of 96.0 for the overall scale. A limitation is that the numbers of respondents in the tests were very small, and the internal consistency could not be tested as the measure was actually used in only five cases.

In the five cases where the AI was used, the effect size was negative, as the higher the score the worse the aggression. In fact, the group deteriorated in their aggression levels, indicating a negative effect size ranging from small to moderate. An explanation of the Shield workers was that although verbal aggression was getting worse, physical aggression had improved in the five cases.

Changes in Hare Self-Esteem Scores

The Hare Self-Esteem Scale (HSS) is used to measure self-esteem in school-aged children. It has three sub-scales that are area specific – peer,

Table 7.6   *Effect size of change in Hare Self-Esteem scores*

Hare Self-Esteem Peer effect size

Statistics	HSS Peer first score (where repeated only)	HSS Peer last scores	Change: effect size
Valid N	5	5	
Missing (not used or not repeated)	44	44	
Mean	39.4000	38.8000	
Std. deviation	24.5214	24.8234	
Effect size			−0.02

Hare Self-Esteem Family effect size

Statistics	HSS Family first score (where repeated only)	HSS Family last scores	Change: effect size
Valid N	5	5	
Missing (not used or not repeated)	44	44	
Mean	24.9000	28.0000	
Std. deviation	6.9318	8.2462	
Effect size			0.45

Hare Self Esteem School effect size

Statistics	HSS School first score (where repeated only)	HSS School last scores	Change: effect size
Valid N	5	5	
Missing (not used or not repeated)	44	44	
Mean	26.2000	24.2000	
Std. deviation	6.3008	3.7014	
Effect size			−0.32

school and home (or family). Higher scores indicate higher self-esteem. As indicated earlier, research studies have indicated that low self-esteem, problems in school, problems in social skills and problems in peer relationships are among the factors that are often reported in children and young people who sexually harm others. Table 7.6 indicates that the effect size of changes in the Peer Hare Self-Esteem scale was slightly in the negative, suggesting that problems in peer self-esteem worsened slightly in the five cases where this measure was used. However, with regard to family self-esteem, the effect size was 0.45, indicating a positive change of small to moderate effect size in the group of five cases. On the other hand, the school self-esteem became worse at −0.32, indicating a small to moderate worsening effect size. However, as the HSS was adapted from the original, the reported reliability does not apply, and due to the small number of cases where it was used, it was not possible to undertake additional reliability tests.

Table 7.7   *Effect size of changes in A-COPE scores*

Statistics	A-COPE first score (where repeated only)	A-COPE last scores	Change: effect size
Valid N	4	4	
Missing (not used or not repeated)	45	45	
Mean	84.0000	95.2500	
Std. deviation	22.3308	4.8563	
Effect size			0.50

Changes in Adolescent Coping Orientation for Problem Experiences (A-COPE) Scores

The Adolescent Coping Orientation for Problem Experiences (A-COPE) is used to measure adolescent coping behaviours. Higher scores indicate better coping behaviours. Table 7.7 indicates that the effect size in the group of four cases was 0.50, that is, moderate to large during the Shield Project team's work with these cases.

Overall Findings from Standardised Outcome Measures

The numbers of cases where these outcome measures were used were small, with the highest number of seven cases where the Child Behaviour Rating Index for Children (BRIC) was used. It was found that improvements were made in the behaviours of six of the seven children/young people, and that the effect size was large. In the smaller numbers of cases where the BRIC was also used with parents, the school teachers and the carers, the effect size ranged from moderate to large among both the parents and the carers, and large among the school teachers, providing additional evidence of progress made in the behaviours of these children during Shield's work with them. The three cases where the Self-Concept Scale for Children (SC) was used indicated an effect size ranging from moderate to large. As for the Child's Attitude Toward Father (CAF) and Mother (CAM), the effect size on the CAM scores was almost negligible, but a small to moderate effect size was achieved in the CAF scores during the Shield Project's work with the five cases. There were also improvements in Family Hare Self-Esteem scores, indicating a small to moderate effect size in the five cases where this measure was used. The effect size for the four cases where the Adolescent Coping Orientation for Problem Experiences (A-COPE) was used, indicated improvements in all four cases ranging from a moderate to large effect size. Overall, these effect sizes indicate modest improvements across a range of outcomes where standardised measures were used repeatedly.

Table 7.8   *General case outcome: whether assessment was completed or not*

Assessment – case outcome (n = 44, excluding five ongoing cases)	Frequency	%
Not completed, inappropriate referral	6	13.6
Assessment inappropriate, consultation offered but not used	2	4.5
Assessment inappropriate, consultation offered and accepted	7	15.9
Assessment not completed, offer declined	9	20.5
Assessment completed	20	45.5
Total	44	100.0

However, some outcomes actually became worse during the work of Shield, namely the HSS Peer Self-Esteem scale which was slightly in the negative in the five cases, and the HSS School Self-Esteem scale which indicated a deterioration ranging from small to moderate effect size. In the five cases where the Aggression Inventory was used, the effect size was also small to moderate in the negative, suggesting that aggression had actually worsened.

Overall, there were improvements in the majority (seven) of outcomes where standardised measures were used, almost no change in one, and a deterioration in three outcomes. However, because of the small numbers of cases where these measures were used (ranging from three to seven), it is not possible to use statistical analyses to identify patterns in relation to these outcomes.

Other General Outcome Indicators

There were some outcome indicators which were generally applicable to the 49 cases in the database, namely whether the assessment was completed or not, the engagement of the child in the Shield's assessment work, and the engagement of the parents. Table 7.8 indicates the results with regard to the 'assessment completed' general outcome, excluding five cases that were currently in progress. It was found that assessment was completed in 20 cases, comprising 45.5% of the total of 44. However, the remainder of the cases also included some consultation type of cases where the information on contexts and mechanisms was available, but an assessment was not planned. Nevertheless, it may be possible to determine the causal mechanisms that lead to the completion of an assessment, and the contexts in which they are triggered.

Table 7.9 indicates the second general outcome indicator – whether the child/young person was engaged or not. In a fairly large number of cases, engagement with the child/young person was not planned, such as in the consultation cases. However, when all of the cases are taken together, it was found that the Shield project engaged with 13 (or 28.3%) of the

Table 7.9   *Engagement of the child/young person in the programme*

Engagement of child/young person in programme (n = 46, excluding cases not yet seen)	Frequency	%
Not at all, e.g., not part of the planned intervention	22	47.8
Met, but declined to participate	2	4.3
Unwilling participation	9	19.6
Good participation	8	17.4
Excellent participation	5	10.9
Total	46	100.0

Child engaged or not	Frequency	%
No	33	71.7
Yes	13	28.3
Total	46	100.0

Table 7.10   *Engagement of either parent in the programme*

Engagement of either parent in programme (n = 46, excluding cases not yet seen)	Frequency	%
Not at all, e.g., not part of the planned intervention	14	30.4
Met, but declined to participate	6	13.0
Unwilling participation	11	23.9
Good participation	11	23.9
Excellent participation	4	8.7
Total	46	100.0

Parent engaged or not	Frequency	%
No	31	67.4
Yes	15	32.6
Total	46	100.0

children/young people. It should be recognised that work with the client was not anticipated in a number of cases included here; nevertheless, it may be possible to determine the type of cases where the Shield Project is likely to engage the child/young person in assessment work.

Similarly, Table 7.10 indicates that the Shield Project engaged with at least one parent in 15 (32.6%) of the cases. Again, a number of cases are included where meetings with parents were not required; nevertheless, it may be possible to determine in what type of cases the Shield Project is likely to engage with the parents as part of its assessment work.

Content Variables

With regard to the content variables of the Shield Project's assessment work, the assessment model was divided into four components: (a) family background; (b) current situation; (c) actual offence (or sexually harmful behaviours); (d) changing/understanding behaviours.

Table 7.11   *Assessment sessions held with the child/young person*

N = 49 cases	Total no. of sessions with the child/YP	No. of sessions including family background	No. of sessions including current situation	No. of sessions including actual offence	No. of sessions including changing/ understanding
Totals	163	69	86	47	71
Mean	3.33	1.41	1.76	.96	1.45
Minimum	0	0	0	0	0
Maximum	12	5	7	5	8

Table 7.12   *Assessment sessions held with either parent*

N = 49 cases	Total no. of sessions with either parent	No. of sessions including family background	No. of sessions including current situation	No. of sessions including actual offence	No. of sessions including changing/ understanding
Totals	106	60	67	40	45
Mean	2.16	1.22	1.37	.82	.92
Minimum	0	0	0	0	0
Maximum	10	7	7	4	8

For the assessment model requirements to be met, all of these four components would be addressed with both the child/young person and at least one parent. As described in Chapter 6, the case recording system included a form for each session that would indicate which of these components were addressed in the content of the assessment work sessions. The evaluator conducted regular secondary analyses of the case records to establish how many sessions were held with the child/young person and with either or both parents and/or significant others, and the components of the assessment model that were present in each session. In this way, it was also possible to record the first and the last contact with the clients during the assessment work, thereby calculating not only the number of sessions held, but also the duration of time during the assessment work. In addition, as part of the integration of the evaluation process into practice, the practitioners were required to indicate the number of multi-disciplinary meetings held, and generally whether the requirements of the assessment model were met, or not, in each case.

Tables 7.11 and 7.12 indicate the number of sessions held in the course of the assessment work with the child/young person, and with either parent. Altogether, 163 sessions were held with the children/young persons, and 106 with the parents. The mean (or average) for the child/young person was 3.33 sessions, and for the parent 2.16. The maximum number of sessions per child/young person was 12 and with the parent 10.

Table 7.13   *Number of days in assessment work and multi-disciplinary meetings held*

N = 49 cases	No. of days between first and last contact	No. of multi-disciplinary meetings held
Totals	2918	77
Mean	59.55	1.71
Minimum	0	0
Maximum	233	7

Table 7.14   *The extent to which the requirements of the assessment model were met*

N = 45	Frequency	%
None of the requirements were implemented	9	20.0
Only a few of the requirements were implemented	10	22.2
Most of the requirements were implemented	8	17.8
All of the requirements were implemented	18	40.0

N = 45	Frequency	%
Requirements of the model met	19	42.2
Requirements of the model not met	26	57.8

The discussion of the current situation was the most common component in all sessions, and the discussion of the actual offence was the least common, reflecting the Shield assessment model of seeking to engage the child/young person and the parent in all circumstances. Table 7.13 indicates that the total number of days between the first and the last contact with clients was 2918, and on average 59.55 days. The maximum number of days in one case was 233. In fact, it was found that the average number of days in cases where the assessment was not completed was 16.63 days, and in the cases where it was completed, 123.40 days. Table 7.13 also indicates that, altogether, 77 multi-disciplinary meetings were held, on the average of 1.71 per case, with seven as the maximum number per case.

Table 7.14 indicates the extent to which the requirements of the model were implemented, from the perspective of the workers. It appears that none of the requirements were implemented in 20% of the cases, and all of the requirements were met in 40% of the cases. This information was then dichotomised, including 'none' and 'only a few' as 'not met', and 'most' and 'all' as 'met'. The result was that the requirements of the model were met in 42.2% of the cases, and not met in the remaining 57.8%.

Systematic Tracking of Contexts

Contexts are defined as structures in the circumstances of people that take a longer time to change (when compared to mechanisms below), and historical events that still have an impact on the client. As indicated earlier, contexts provide the conditions in which causal mechanisms are triggered and the programme outcomes are produced.

With regard to demographic characteristics of the 49 cases in the database up to March 2002, there were 42 males and seven females. The ethnic origin was classified as white British for 46 cases, and as Asian or Afro-Caribbean for the remaining three. The age of the sample ranged from 7 to 19 years, with a mean (average) age of 12.76 years. Both the median and the mode were 13 years. Zolondek et al. (2001) found that the modal age reported in studies of juvenile sex offenders tended to be between 14 and 15 years, with some evidence that about a quarter of these had engaged in sexually abusive behaviours before the age of 12 years. In their own national study of juvenile sexual offenders in the USA, the average age of onset of the behaviours ranged from 9.7 to 12, which is comparable with the findings from the Shield sample.

Table 7.15 indicates the contexts found in the circumstances of the sample of 49 cases in this study. These contexts were identified as the relevant ones from research in the western world about young people who sexually harm others (as indicated earlier in this chapter), from the contexts that emerged consistently in the qualitative analysis of cases (see Appendix), and from the experience of the Shield team workers. The sources of information included the referral form, secondary analysis of local authority social services' records, and information obtained through interaction with the children/young people and their families and with significant others (such as multi-disciplinary sources).

The findings from Table 7.15 are consistent with those from research as outlined earlier in this chapter. In particular, the contexts are similar to those found in the study from Sweden. Langstrom, Grann and Lindblad (2000) identified a preliminary typology which included parental divorce, separation from either biological parent, non-supportive/abusive family, social skills deficiency, special educational needs, previous contact with social services, and substance abuse. In the Shield database, 83.7% had separated parents; 30.6% did not live with either parent; 73.5% had a history of school problems; 73.5% had a history of poor peer relationships; 44.9% had a learning disability; 61.2% had a history of social services' involvement; and 26.5% had a history of alcohol/drug misuse within their families.

With regard to prior history of abuse and neglect, the findings appear to be consistent with those from research reviews, as reported earlier in this chapter. Children with sexual behaviour problems typically have sexual victimisation histories, and rates for children under 12 range from 65–100%; for sexually aggressive adolescents the rates are 50–65% (Burton, 2000). In the Shield sample, which included children/young people across both of these age ranges, the rate of sexual abuse was found to be generally lower, at 46.9%. This figure is also lower than in Burton (2000) who notes that roughly 30% of boys who act out sexually have no history of sexual

Table 7.15   *Contexts in the circumstances of the children/young people (n = 49)*

Contexts	Frequency	% (*n* = 49)
Learning disability	22	44.9
Living in foster or residential care	15	30.6
Parents separated	41	83.7
History of domestic violence	31	63.3
History of mother being sexually abused	12	24.5
History of child/young person being sexually abused	23	46.9
History of child/young person being physically abused	30	61.2
History of school problems	36	73.5
History of social services' involvement	30	61.2
History of poor peer relationships	36	73.5
History of emotional neglect	30	61.2
History of mental health problems	21	42.9
History of alcohol/drug misuse	13	26.5

victimisation. However, this figure is consistent with a study in Germany. In a sample of 107 adolescent offenders, Hummel et al. (2000) found that 44% of those who committed sexual offences also claimed to have been the victims of sexual abuse, mostly during their childhood. Adolescents with a history of sexual abuse also reported a history of discontinuity of care, school problems and social isolation from peers. With regard to 24.5% of mothers reportedly being themselves victims of sexual abuse, this finding is consistent with that of Pithers et al. (1998) but rather lower, which may reflect the limitations with regard to under- and over-reporting of such data, as indicated earlier in this chapter.

In particular, in a national sample of adolescent sexual offenders under-going treatment in the USA, from a database developed by the National Adolescent Perpetrator Network (Ryan et al., 1996), previous history of abuse included physical abuse (42%), sexual abuse (39%), neglect (26%), and domestic violence (63%). Although the histories appear to be similar in Table 7.15 (for example, 63% for domestic violence), the differences in the other percentages can be explained with two riders. First, the Shield sample is not a representative national sample of similar children and young people across the United Kingdom; second, most studies tend to concentrate on male juvenile sexual offenders who have been through the criminal justice system, whereas the Shield sample includes largely those who are not subject of such proceedings, as well as those who exhibit behaviours that are a cause for concern but do not directly harm others (see Appendix for a sample of behaviours).

Systematic Tracking of Mechanisms

Mechanisms are factors in the circumstances of the service users that influence the desired outcomes, as indicated in Table 7.16. They are either

Table 7.16 *Mechanisms and changes in the mechanisms (n = 49)*

Mechanism	Positive (enabling)	Negative (disabling)	Improved	Deteriorated
Support network regarding education	31 (67.4%)	15 (32.6%)	11 (25.6%)	8 (18.6%)
Ability to make and maintain supportive peer relationships	17 (37.0%)	29 (63.0%)	4 (9.3%)	6 (14.0%)
Support from parent(s)	24 (54.5%)	20 (45.5%)	8 (20.0%)	7 (17.5%)
Parents' relationship and agreement on support for child	17 (40.5%)	25 (59.5%)	3 (7.1%)	3 (7.1%)
Child/young person's ability to engage in the work	18 (40.9%)	26 (59.1%)	6 (13.6%)	8 (18.1%)
Multi-disciplinary relationship with other professionals	31 (61.3%)	18 (36.7%)	9 (18.4%)	6 (12.2%)

enabling (helping to achieve the outcomes), or disabling (working against the achievement of the outcomes). These mechanisms have been selected from the qualitative review of 17 cases (see Appendix), from the research findings as outlined earlier, and from the experience of the Shield workers. In the team meetings where the evaluator was also present, the Shield workers selected the mechanisms that they thought were most relevant across all of their cases (such as in Kazi and Ward, 2001). Each of the mechanisms is identified as either an enabling (positive) or a disabling (negative) mechanism in relation to the outcomes as outlined earlier (assessment completed, the child/young person engaged in the assessment work, and either parent also engaged in the assessment work). As Pawson and Tilley (1997b) explain in their Rule 8, the nature of stratified reality is such that new mechanisms and new contexts emerge at any time–space location during the course of practice, and therefore as more cases are evaluated intensively, other mechanisms or contexts may be added to the database. Towards the end of 2001, for example, the Shield workers added a new mechanism, namely multi-disciplinary relationship with other professionals, as they felt this could influence the outcomes. They also added new contexts, namely, history of emotional neglect, history of mental health problems, and history of alcohol/drug misuse within the family (see Table 7.15).

Furthermore, as Lawson (1998) explains, some mechanisms may shine through, and others may act as countervailing mechanisms to neutralise or to stop them from shining through. 'I see no a priori reason to suppose that any relatively enduring, transfactually acting, social mechanism need be particularly constant in the way it operates over time and space; nor am I aware of any evidence which indicates that any are' (p. 162). Concrete phenomena are produced by numerous countervailing tendencies, and their explanation entails drawing upon antecedently established knowledge of these mechanisms and structures that are responsible for them.

In the systematic tracking of mechanisms, therefore, the practitioner– researcher has to be aware that mechanisms, or tendencies, would change over time, even in the same space within the open system, that is, even when contexts or conditions in which these mechanisms are fired are rela- tively stable. In the configuration of a combination of countervailing mech- anisms, it is not sufficient simply to identify a mechanism, but to indicate how an identified mechanism has changed over time. For example, if during one time period, the 'support network regarding education' is seen as a disabling mechanism in the achievement of the engagement of the child in the assessment work, in the passage of time it may become less disabling, and may even be transformed into an enabling mechanism, if relationships within the school change, or if the child is able to settle in the school over time. Therefore, it cannot be assumed that this relatively enduring mecha- nism (the support network regarding education) will remain constant.

In order to systematically track changes in the mechanism, therefore, at the stage of review during the intensive evaluation of a case, the practi- tioners would not only identify the mechanisms, but also determine how the previously identified mechanisms had changed. In Table 7.16, each mechanism is identified as either enabling (positive), or disabling (nega- tive), and against each mechanism (whether enabling or not) the practitioner–researcher also identifies the change in each of these mecha- nisms as either 'improved' (that is, moving in the direction of enabling), 'deteriorated' (that is, moving in the direction of disabling) or 'remained the same' (that is, moved neither in a disabling nor enabling direction) in the period of the analysis. This latter judgement is made on the basis of the available empirical referents (such as the nature of relationships with school teachers) at any one point in time, and may change again over the passage of time. A further point here is that the change patterns in the potential causal mechanisms require prospective systematic tracking, as at any one point in time the actualisation of the mechanism–context– outcome configurations are likely to be different from other points in time, as argued earlier. Therefore, if these configurations are retrospectively analysed, there is a danger that the researcher will be influenced by the latest configurations, and such analysis may not reflect the actual patterns of change in the causal mechanisms over time.

Mechanisms are the underlying structures or factors in the circumstances of the clients that change and have an impact on the outcomes for each client. In Table 7.16, the support network regarding education was consid- ered to be an enabling mechanism in 67.4% of the cases, but it was dis- abling in nearly a third of the cases. Improvements in this mechanism were observed in 25.6% of the 49 cases, but further deterioration was noted in 18.6%. By contrast, ability to make and maintain supportive peer relationships was considered to be disabling in the majority of cases (63%), and the observed changes in either direction were also much less. Support from the parent(s) was seen as enabling in just over half of the cases, and further improvements were indicated in a fifth of the cases. The parents' relationship and agreement on support for the child was considered to be disabling in the majority (59.5%); the proportion that did change in either direction was lowest when compared to the other mechanisms, indicating that this may be a more intractable problem which changes only in a small number of cases during the period of the assessment work. The child's ability to engage in the work was also considered to be a disabling mechanism in the majority of cases (59.1%), and in 18.1% this mechanism moved in a worsening direction during the assessment work. On the other hand, multi-disciplinary relationship with other professionals was enabling in the majority (61.3%), and actually improved in 18.4% of the 49 cases. However, this mechanism was disabling in 36.7% of the cases, and actually became worse in 12.2%.

Enabling the Identification of Patterns

The data that have been presented so far in this chapter indicate that the Shield team as a whole has worked successfully to integrate the realist evaluation approach into their daily practice, to the extent that right from the referral stage, the workers examine the contexts and mechanisms for each case, and systematically track the outcomes, as well as changes in the mechanisms and contexts. This data is used to develop the models of intervention with each client as part of a realist effectiveness cycle, and this data is analysed using both intensive and extensive, and both quantitative and qualitative, research strategies as described above. These strategies enable the identification and systematic tracking of patterns in the mechanisms, contexts and outcomes with each client, as well as across all clients, in order to provide an explanation of what works, for whom and in what contexts. Whether such an evaluation can be achieved will be demonstrated in the next chapter.

Appendix 7.1 *Matrix of qualitative review templates against requirements of the model met and assessment completed*

Key: M = mother; F = father; engaged = engaged in work with Shield; req yes = requirements of assessment model met; ass completed = assessment completed; SSD = Social Services Department.

Client and sexually harmful behaviours	Context	Enabling	Disabling	Changes noted	Req yes	Ass completed
W Sexual intercourse with sister	Hist sex abuse SSD involvement Single M Poor school attendance	W engaged W relationship with M M's partner positive W's relationship with F positive	Multi-disciplinary relationship Difficult sibling relationship Poor boundaries in household		yes	yes
F Indecent assault against adult Further allegations	Lives with M and F Paedophile activity in area Poor school attendance Other crimes	F engaged M engaged and supportive	Poor boundaries in household Poor concentration ability Inappropriate peers Low self-esteem Multi-disciplinary relationship		yes	yes
G Indecent assault on peer-aged girls	Lives with M and step-F No contact with F	G engaged M engaged and supportive	On Sex Offender Register Difficulties in school where offences took place		yes	yes
J Indecent assault on 5–6-year-old boys	Family left home due to vigilantes F history of alcohol problems No previous SSD J learning disability	M engaged and supportive Good attendance and relations in school Good SSD support	J Poor social skills No peers or social network		yes	yes
Z Indecent assault on two younger step-sisters	Lives with single M No contact with step-F since incident	Admits offences Both parents supportive of work and engaged	Worsening behaviour in school	No further concerns re behaviour in school	yes	yes

(Continued)

Appendix 7.1 *Continued*

Client and sexually harmful behaviours	Context	Enabling	Disabling	Changes noted	Req yes	Ass completed
	M mental health problems No previous SSD Good school relations	Good cooperation between parents Multi-disciplinary relationship Appropriate peer relationships	Parents' expectations too high	M custodial sentence for DSS fraud Multi-disciplinary relationship less effective		
K Supervision order for sexual offences against girls	Residential home Acrimonious separation of parents K and M victims of sexual abuse Behaviour problems in school Isolation from peers	K engaged M and partner engaged well Better performance in school Multi-disciplinary relationship	Damaged relationship with both parents M not in contact with K K avoids difficult issues	Forming appropriate girlfriend relationship Worsening behaviour in residential home K more able to express feelings K's relations with M worsened and affected motivation	yes	yes
D Indecent assult on 8-year-old girl	Lives with single M Moved from refuge re domestic violence M history of sexual abuse SSD history	M engaged and supportive	D denies allegations Low self-image as had to leave refuge because of his behaviour		yes	no
E Sexually aggressive and touching	Short-term foster care Placement with aunt broken down E has history of sexual and physical abuse	Multi-disciplinary relationship Good placement No problems in school	Moving from good foster care placement Poor social skills Poor peer relations Poor relationship boundaries		Not known	no
P Sexual abuse of sister	Residential care Domestic violence	P shows motivation and commitment	M will not engage Multi-disciplinary relationship	ADHD medication stopped; grown in confidence and social skills	no	yes

(Continued)

Appendix 7.1 *Continued*

Client and sexually harmful behaviours	Context	Enabling	Disabling	Changes noted	Req yes	Ass completed
	P has short attention span ADHD medication		Irregular school attendance Blurred boundaries Chaotic lifestyle	Bullied at residential placement Drinking and drug use		
A Attempted intercourse with 7-year-old girl	Crowded living, shared living with separated M and F Acrimonious separation Learning difficulty Poor peer relations and social skills	Family very supportive Multi-disciplinary relationship	Lack of supervision by M Unresolved emotional trauma	Started college Developing peer relations and social skills M's supervision improved	yes	yes
L Long term history of sexualised behaviour	Lives with single M Domestic violence L sexually abused L has limited concentration span	L engaged M engaged and supportive	Shares bedroom with younger sibling Poor boundaries Poor parental supervision	M moves, sleeping arrangements changed, improved boundaries L accommodated, well-settled in long-term residential care	yes	yes
H Teenaged girl, indecently assaulted 3-year-old brother	Foster care after incident Domestic violence Parents separated No contact with M after incident H refusing contact with father	H engaged and accepts responsibility Multi-disciplinary relationship Good foster placement Improved performance in school	Rejection by M Does not want contact with F but he is using legal means	Difficult behaviour at foster home Moved to long-term foster home Worsening behaviour in school Renewed contact with F F's relations with SSD better	yes	yes
Q Indecently assaulted three younger females	Foster care Domestic violence Neglect	Q engaged	Not accepting responsibility	Has age-appropriate girlfriend who is now pregnant	yes	yes

(Continued)

Appendix 7.1 *Continued*

Client and sexually harmful behaviours	Context	Enabling	Disabling	Changes noted	Req yes	Ass completed
R Sexual suggestions to girls and masturbating in class	Permanently excluded from previous school Living with both parents Domestic violence	M engaged and supportive School supportive	Control of temper/ violence Poor boundaries Substance misuse Use of interpreter with M Difficult relations between parents and school F refuses to meet with workers R denies allegations	Inappropriate behaviour stopped	yes	yes
V Indecent assault on 2-year-old female relative	Living with both parents Neglect Domestic violence Witnessed sexual abuse of sister Learning difficulties Poor peer relationships Poor attendance at school	Parents engaged well	Parents and V deny allegations Police enquiries took a long time, delayed work Multi-disciplinary relationship		yes	yes
N Indecent assaults on 5-year-old sister and young female cousin	Lives with single M M has mental health problems N has contact with F No previous SSD	M engaged and sought help Both parents supportive	N has difficult relationship with siblings Multi-disciplinary relationship	N has re-offended against sister	yes	yes
M Sexualised language and masturbating in front of others	Lives with single M Learning disability	Multi-disciplinary relationship	Boundaries at home		no	no

8

Patterns of What Works, For Whom and in What Contexts

It has been demonstrated in the previous chapters how the realist effectiveness cycle can be integrated into practice and how the systematic tracking of changes in outcomes, mechanisms, the content of programmes, and the contexts can be achieved through both intensive single-case evaluation and extensive group analysis and through the use of both qualitative and quantitative strategies. Having achieved this integration, the next step is to apply and to develop the methodologies and strategies to investigate patterns in the relationships between the outcomes and mechanisms, and the contexts in which they are produced. At any specific time–space location, there may be systematic and identifiable mechanisms in play which realist evaluation strategies can uncover. However, the question is, what are the approaches that enable realist evaluators to uncover these patterns?

Within the realist paradigm (Chapter 3), the aim is to identify the causal factor responsible for the programme outcomes that can be observed. The goal is to 'posit a mechanism which if it existed could account for the phenomena singled out for explanation' (Lawson, 1998: 156). The integration of the realist effectiveness cycle into practice, and the combination of both intensive and extensive research in the study described so far, may have the potential to enable the causal mechanisms to be identified in the process of realist evaluation.

The intensive research (as described with the case examples in Chapter 6) enables the identification of patterns in the particular set of causal factors identified over time with each case. The aggregation of this data and the use of inferential statistics may help to identify the patterns across a group of cases. However, this analysis does not remain static, as the mechanisms and contexts of the clients, as well as the alternative mechanisms introduced by the project in individual cases, change over time. The realist concept of emergence (Chapter 3) suggests that mechanisms can transform themselves, and that new ones may also take their place. Therefore, the extent to which these causal mechanisms are identified and tracked accurately will also change over time. The analysis presented here, therefore, may change as the numbers of cases are increased, and as the investigation of the clients' realities is developed in this prospective evaluation. A prospective realist evaluation that utilises both quantitative and qualitative methods may enable a more thorough investigation of the mechanism–context–outcome configurations over time. As described in Chapter 3, realist evaluation seeks to provide an explanation of an explanation, in an ongoing cycle, that is, why and how certain mechanisms have or have not emerged, where they have emerged, and why they have been 'reproduced or transformed in particular ways' (Lawson, 1998: 162).

Investigating the Mechanism–Context–Outcome Configurations

Having aggregated the data from the outcomes, programme content, mechanisms and contexts as in the previous chapter, the next step is to establish the relationships between them. Miles and Huberman (1994) suggest that these patterns can be identified through the use of matrices in qualitative analysis, and if the analysis (presented in the Appendix 7.1 at the end of the last chapter) can be done in all cases (and not almost entirely with cases where assessment was completed as in Appendix 7.1), it may be possible to identify the mechanisms and contexts associated with the cases where the assessment was completed, and to determine if they were different in the cases where the assessment was not completed. However, to go beyond this, that is, to determine the extent to which the relationships observed were not due to chance on the one hand, and to determine the extent of the relationship between a mechanism and the outcome on the other, it may be necessary to turn to quantitative data analysis. These relationships, or the identification of potential causal mechanisms as explained above, may be investigated through the use of inferential statistics, and in particular, the use of significance tests which can establish relationships between these components, and the use of measures of association or effect sizes which can determine the extent of these relationships. However, without intensive qualitative research, it may not be possible to identify the relevant mechanisms that can be subjected to this kind of extensive quantitative analysis, and again, the realist cycle may require that the findings from the quantitative analysis should be fed back into practice, and inform the prospective intensive research, and so forth. What is advocated here is a dialectical relationship between the two types of analysis where one informs and changes the other as the cycle progresses, with the overall aim of changing the programmes of intervention to reflect the changing circumstances of service users.

There are a number of texts that describe the statistical tests available for these purposes (Argyrous, 2000; Robson, 2002; Rubin and Babbie, 2001). Let us suppose that we have observed a correlation between two variables, for example, that an increase in the number of cases where the child/young person is engaged in the assessment work leads to an increase in the number of cases where the assessment is completed. First, we need to establish if this relationship is equally possible through the luck of the draw or not. Testing for statistical significance means calculating the probability, or odds, of finding due to chance a relationship that is at least as strong as the one we have observed in our findings. That probability will fall 'somewhere between zero and 1.0' (Rubin and Babbie, 2001: 514). For example, a probability of 0.05 means that the chance of finding the relationship by chance is five times out of a hundred, that is, the confidence level is 95%. There are a number of significance tests available, depending on the type of data, and they all indicate a probability level between 0 and 1.0. In social research, the convention is to have a confidence level of less than 0.05 (or $p < 0.05$), although in some types of research $p < 0.01$ may be preferred. The software package SPSS (Foster, 2001) flags up the significance levels at both of these, and also provides the coefficient r that indicates the nature of the relationship between the two variables.

If we discover that there is a significant relationship between the child/young person engaged in the assessment work and completion of the assessment, that in itself does not tell us very much. For example, the extent of the correlation between the two may be very small, and although the relationship may be significant, it may not be important for practice. Therefore, once the significance is established at the required confidence level, the next step is to use the measure of association (or the effect size) between the two variables, and that is the r coefficient also provided by SPSS. When the r is squared, it indicates the extent to which the variation in one variable is explained by the other. For example, an r of .30 when squared equals .09, indicating that the independent variable (such as the child/young person engaged in the assessment work) is explaining nine per cent of the variation in the dependent variable (for example, assessment completed). In this regard, the benchmark is not as high as one would expect. According to Rubin and Babbie (2001: 531), 'interventions whose effect size explain approximately five per cent to ten per cent of outcome variance are about as effective as the average intervention reported in published evaluations'.

Once the significance level is established, the effect size is of importance in realist evaluation in determining the extent to which a mechanism has influenced the outcome. As Robson explains, with a

realist approach, statistical analysis is used to confirm the existence of mechanisms whose operation we have predicted in the contexts set up in an experiment or other study. Large effect sizes provide confidence in their existence; hence they are what you are looking for. Significance levels play a subsidiary role, their inclusion perhaps lacking something in logic but sanctioned by convention. (2002: 402)

Rubin and Babbie (2001: 539) provide a useful guide regarding the effect size, which could be interpreted as follows:

Small	$r = .10$	r squared $= .01$
Medium	$r = .30$	r squared $= .09$
Large	$r = .50$	r squared $= .25$

Having established significance at the .05 level, and a large effect size, we may infer that a mechanism does influence the desired outcome. However, this is not the end of the line with regard to having confidence in our findings. We have to consider the possibility of having made errors. Type I error is where we think the relationship is significant when it could be by chance, and at the .05 level we are accepting that there is a 5% chance of making this error in any case. Therefore, significance testing tells us the probability of committing a Type I error. However, it does not tell us the probability of making another type of error, that is, Type II where we think the relationship is not significant when it actually is. The larger the sample size, the less the chance of making this error, and statistical power analysis deals with the probability of committing this error (Rubin and Babbie, 2001). Cohen (1988: 528–9) provides detailed tables which can determine the statistical power of a significance test according to the significance level, the effect size and the sample size. A statistical power of .80 suggests that there is a 20% chance of making a Type II error, and this is the confidence level suggested by Cohen.

Therefore, for realist evaluators to have confidence in their finding that a mechanism has influenced an outcome, we need to demonstrate the significance level, the effect size, the sample size, and the statistical power. However, this is not the end of our considerations with regard to establishing the mechanism–context–outcome configurations.

We need to know what type of data we have, and what type of significance test is appropriate for the type of data available. Both Robson (2002) and Rubin and Babbie (2001) are helpful in this regard. For example, if both variables are nominal, that is, the numbers are used for classification rather than rank order, then Cramer V test is appropriate. If the variables are ordinal, that is, in rank order, then Spearman Rho will be appropriate, and if one of the variables is continuous (for example, numbers of meetings or sessions), then it may be possible to use the Pearson or Eta tests. Argyrous (2000) and Foster (2001) indicate where these tests can be accessed using SPSS.

Patterns in Relation to the Outcome 'Assessment Completed or Not'

Table 8.1 indicates the significant correlations found between the outcome of 'assessment completed or not' and the other outcomes, content variables, and mechanisms. All of the variables, mechanisms and contexts identified in Chapter 3 were selected, and only those where there was a significant relationship, a sample size of greater than 15 (the starting point of the

Table 8.1 *Significant correlations between assessment completed and other outcomes, content variables and mechanisms*

Other outcomes	Spearman or Eta R	N	Sig. (two-tailed)	R square	Effect size	Power of sig. test (approx.)
Child engaged or not	.632	44	.000	.400	large	.83
Parent engaged or not	.454	44	.000	.206	medium	.56
Content						
Requirements of the model met or not	.675	42	.000	.456	large	.96
No. of days between first and last direct contact	.758	44	.000	.574	large	.97
No. of sessions with either parent during assessment work	.579	44	.000	.336	large	.83
No. of sessions with child/young person during assessment work	.885	44	.000	.783	large	>.995
No. of sessions–child–family background	.888	44	.000	.789	large	>.995
No. of sessions–parent–family background	.594	44	.000	.353	large	.83
No. of sessions–child–current situation	.830	44	.000	.699	large	>.995
No. of sessions–parent–current situation	.582	44	.000	.339	large	.83
No. of sessions–child–actual offence	.610	44	.000	.372	large	.83
No. of sessions–parent–actual offence	.454	44	.005	.206	medium	.56
No. of sessions–child–changing/understanding behaviours	.765	44	.000	.585	large	>.995
No. of sessions–parent–changing/understanding behaviours	.520	44	.000	.270	large	.83
No. of multi-disciplinary meetings	.446	43	.010	.199	medium	.56
Mechanisms						
Parents' relationship–agreement	-.363	37	.027	.132	medium	.45
Child/young person's ability to engage in the work	.408	40	.009	.167	medium	.74
Improvement in the child/young person's ability etc.	.411	38	.010	.169	medium	.72
Improvement in multi-disciplinary relationship	.352	44	.019	.124	medium	.52

power tables in Cohen, 1988, described earlier), and at least a medium effect size are included. The last column indicates the approximate power of the significance test, as in Cohen (1988) and as described above. It was found that whether the child was engaged in the assessment work or not had a large effect, and the statistical power level was also within the .80 or above recommended by Cohen. However, the engagement of either parent only had a medium effect, and the statistical power was low at .56, indicating a lower level of confidence. With regard to the content variables, all of those listed had a large effect size, and a power level of greater than .80, with the exception of (a) number of sessions with parents where the actual offence was discussed and (b) the number of multi-disciplinary meetings, which both had a medium effect and a much lower statistical power.

With regard to identifying potential causal mechanisms, four did shine through, but only partially as the effect sizes were medium and the power levels were less than .80. The four were: (a) parents' relationship–agreement (negative effect or inverse relationship); (b) child/young person's ability to engage in the assessment work; (c) improvement in the child/young person's ability to engage in the work; (d) improvement in multi-disciplinary relationship.

Patterns in Relation to the Outcome 'Engagement of the Child/Young Person in the Programme'

Table 8.2 indicates that there were significant associations between the engagement of the child/young person and the other outcomes of 'assessment completed or not' and the engagement of either parent, with large effect sizes and high statistical power. These findings suggest that the engagement of the child/young person and the engagement of either parent are both related to the completion of the assessment.

Table 8.2 also indicates an inverse relationship between this outcome and the level of the first Child BRIC score with a large effect size (see explanation of this measure in Chapter 6). This indicates that the lower the Child BRIC score (that is, the better the initial assessment of behaviour from the child's own perspective), the more likely it is that the child/young person will engage in the assessment work. However, there is a note of caution in this finding, as the statistical power is rather low, and there is a 47% probability of this observed relationship having occurred by chance.

Patterns in Relation to the Outcome 'Engagement of either Parent in the Programme'

In Table 8.1, most of the content variables had a large effect size, but in Table 8.2 all of these indicated a large effect size and statistical power above .80, including the number of sessions with parents on the actual offence and the number of multi-disciplinary meetings which had indicated a

Table 8.2 *Significant correlations between engagement of the child/young person in the programme and other outcomes, content variables and mechanisms*

Other outcomes	Spearman or Eta R	N	Sig. (two-tailed)	R square	Effect size	Power of sig. test (approx.)
Assessment completed or not	.908	44	.000	.824	large	>.995
Engagement of either parent	.708	46	.000	.501	large	>.995
Level of child BRIC first score	−.509	16	.044	.259	large	.53
Content						
Requirements of the model met or not	.662	44	.000	.438	large	.97
No. of days between first and last direct contact	.788	46	.000	.621	large	>.995
No. of sessions with either parent during assessment work	.557	46	.002	.310	large	.85
No. of sessions with child/young person during assessment work	.877	46	.000	.769	large	>.995
No. of sessions–child–family background	.818	46	.000	.669	large	>.995
No. of sessions–parent–family background	.547	46	.004	.299	large	
No. of sessions–child–current situation	.800	46	.000	.640	large	>.995
No. of sessions–parent–current situation	.559	46	.001	.312	large	.85
No. of sessions–child–actual offence	.703	46	.000	.494	large	>.995
No. of sessions–parent–actual offence	.505	43	.043	.255	large	.85
No. of sessions–child–changing/understanding behaviours	.759	46	.000	.576	large	>.995
No. of sessions–parent–changing/understanding behaviours	.564	46	.000	.318	large	.85
No. of multi–disciplinary meetings	.535	45	.001	.286	large	.85
Mechanisms						
Parents' relationship–agreement	−.397	39	.012	.158	medium	.47
Child/young person's ability to engage in the work	.472	42	.002	.223	medium	.53
Improvement in the child/young person's ability etc.	.503	39	.001	.253	large	.77
Improvement in multi-disciplinary relationship	.464	46	.001	.215	medium	.58

medium effect size previously. Once again, the same four mechanisms shine through, although improvement in the child/young person's ability indicated a large effect size this time. However, the statistical power was again lower than .80 for all of these mechanisms.

In Table 8.3, once again, in relation to the outcome of engagement of either parent in the assessment work, a relationship can be observed with the other outcomes of assessment completed or not and the engagement of the child/young person, with large effect sizes and very high statistical power.

Once again, all of the content variables indicate large effect sizes and statistical power in excess of .80, with the exception of 'requirements of the model met or not' where the effect was medium and power was much lower; 'number of sessions with either parent during assessment work' where the effect size was large but the power lower; and the 'number of sessions with the child on the actual offence' where the effect size was medium and the power was much lower than .80.

With regard to the mechanisms, again three out of the previous four partially shine through, namely: (a) parents' relationship–agreement (negative effect or inverse relationship); (b) child/young person's ability to engage in the assessment work; (c) improvement in multi-disciplinary relationship.

Further, it can be observed that one other mechanism also partially shines through, namely: improvement in support from parents.

Some Conclusions from the Mechanism–Context–Outcome Configurations so far

Tables 8.1 to 8.3 indicate the significant correlations found between the outcomes, content variables and mechanisms. None of the contexts had a significant correlation with any of these outcomes, thereby appearing to confirm the realists' contention that programme outcomes are produced through an interaction between the causal mechanisms that already exist in the circumstances of the service users, and the additional generative mechanisms introduced by the programme's interventions, and that all of these are then triggered in given contexts to produce the outcomes.

Most of the content variables were found to have a large effect size and statistical power greater than .80, but there were also some mixed results. For example, the effect size for the association between engagement of the child/young person and assessment completed was large, but the association with engagement of either parent was only of medium effect size with lower statistical power. On the other hand, the effect size for the association between engagement of either parent and engagement of the child/young person was large, with maximum statistical power. The indications are that whether the assessment is completed or not is associated with the engagement of the child/young person in the assessment work, which is in turn related to the engagement of either parent in the assessment

Table 8.3 *Significant correlations between engagement of either parent in the programme and other outcomes, content variables and mechanisms*

Other outcomes	Spearman or Eta R	N	Sig. (two-tailed)	R square	Effect size	Power of sig. test (approx.)
Assessment completed or not	.607	44	.000	.368	large	.97
Engagement of child/ young person	.708	46	.000	.501	large	>.995
Content						
Requirements of the model met or not	.496	44	.001	.246	medium	.58
No. of days between first and last direct contact	.640	46	.000	.410	large	.98
No. of sessions with either parent during assessment work	.574	46	.000	.330	large	.58
No. of sessions with child/young person during assessment work	.668	46	.000	.446	large	.98
No. of sessions–child–family background	.663	46	.000	.440	large	.98
No. of sessions–parent–family background	.549	46	.000	.302	large	.85
No. of sessions–child–current situation	.609	46	.000	.295	large	.85
No. of sessions–parent–current situation	.625	46	.000	.371	large	.85
No. of sessions–child–actual offence	.424	46	.000	.180	medium	.58
No. of sessions–parent–actual offence	.529	46	.000	.280	large	.85
No. of sessions–child–changing/understanding behaviours	.527	46	.000	.278	large	.85
No. of sessions–parent–changing/understanding behaviours	.534	46	.000	.285	large	.85
No. of multi-disciplinary meetings	.512	45	.014	.262	large	.94
Mechanisms						
Parents' relationship–agreement	-.383	39	.016	.147	medium	.47
Child/young person's ability to engage in the work	.317	42	.041	.101	medium	.25
Improvement in multi-disciplinary relationship	.334	46	.023	.112	medium	.54
Improvement in support from parents	.430	38	.007	.185	medium	.48

work. It can be concluded, therefore, that the Shield team workers need to engage both the child/young person and either parent in order to complete the assessment.

With regard to the content variables, in general, the three outcomes in Tables 8.1 to 8.3 indicated a direct relationship with almost all of the content variables. Whether the requirements of the assessment model were met or not had a large effect on the outcomes of assessment completed and the child/young person engaged with power levels of .96–7, but the effect was only medium on the engagement of either parent, and the statistical power was much lower. It can be concluded, therefore, that the Shield team workers need to meet the requirements of the assessment model in order to engage the child/young person in the programme and in order to complete the assessment.

The content variables also indicate that the number of days between the first and last meeting with the clients, the number of sessions with the child/young person and with either parent, and the numbers of sessions where each of the four components of assessment work are discussed, are almost all directly related to the three outcomes. The only exception was that the number of sessions where the actual offence was discussed with either parent was less related to the completion of the assessment.

The number of multi-disciplinary meetings had a large effect on the engagement of the child/young person and the engagement of either parent, but the effect was less direct on the completion of the assessment. However, given the large effect size on the engagement of the child/young person on the completion of the assessment, indications are that the numbers of multi-disciplinary meetings are important in the completion of the assessment.

With regard to mechanisms, the following three did shine through in relation to all three outcomes: (a) Parents' relationship–agreement (negative effect or inverse relationship); (b) Child/young person's ability to engage in the assessment work; (c) Improvement in multi-disciplinary relationship.

A limitation is that the shining through was only partial for each of these mechanisms, as the effect sizes tended to be medium and the power levels were less than .80. However, the fact that all of these three were significantly related to each of the three outcomes in turn, indicates a greater level of confidence that these were the key mechanisms (in addition to the content variables described above) that influenced the three outcomes.

These findings were investigated further with the calculation of relative risk (Hennekens, Buring and Mayrent, 1987; see also Chapter 5 for a description). It was found that, with regard to the last two of the above three mechanisms, the calculations were significant at the 95% confidence levels, but not for the first one regarding the relationship between parents. Where the child/young person's ability to engage in the work was defined as enabling, the likelihood of completing the assessment increased by 25%. Similarly, where there was an improvement in multi-disciplinary relationships with other professionals, the likelihood of completing the assessment increased by 27%.

All of these findings appear to confirm the practice wisdom of the Shield workers, with one exception. The surprise finding was the 'relationship between the parents and agreement on support for the child'. Where the workers considered this mechanism to be disabling, the findings suggest the opposite was the case – the Shield workers were more likely to engage the clients in the assessment work and more likely to complete the assessment where there was less agreement between the parents. However, as the statistical power was the lowest for this particular mechanism (ranging from a 53% to 55% chance of making Type II errors), and as the calculation of relative risk was found to be not significant, the conclusion with regard to this mechanism will have to be more cautious, and there is a need for further research in the causal properties of this mechanism.

In general, the statistical analysis so far indicates that the potential causal mechanisms in relation to the outcome of assessment completed are more likely to be those related to the work of Shield rather than the existing mechanisms in the clients' circumstances, as activities such as meeting the requirements of the assessment model, the number of sessions with the clients, and the engagement of the clients have larger effect sizes and statistical power in relation to the outcome. At this stage of the analysis, none of the contexts were found to be significant.

What works, for Whom and in What Contexts – Deeper Analysis

Thus far, we have identified some potential causal mechanisms in the process of what works, for whom and in what contexts, in relation to the work of the Shield Project. We have established what appear to be the key content variables (that is, the mechanisms introduced by the Shield workers) and also identified at a lower degree of confidence two mechanisms that appear to be causal mechanisms in relation to the three outcomes, and the possibility of a third one. However, thus far we have investigated only the bivariate relationships, that is, the relationship of each mechanism and context in turn with each outcome. We know that mechanisms and outcomes have multiple effects on each other, and that they can be triggered in multiple contexts. We also know from the realist philosophy of science that the mere identification of mechanisms with causal powers is not sufficient, because we also need to know the conditions (or contexts) in which the causal powers of these mechanisms are activated (Sayer, 2000).

Realist evaluation strategies seek to explain how the programme's causal mechanisms interact with the other causal mechanisms in the circumstances

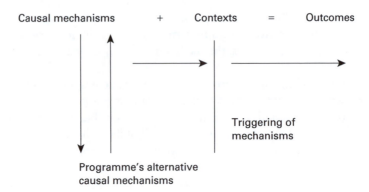

Figure 8.1   *The interaction of causal mechanisms in realist evaluation*

of the service users, and the conditions or contexts in which they are triggered (Figure 8.1). Realist evaluators would aim to achieve retroduction, that is, the identification of the causal mechanisms that influence the outcomes, an explanation of how they are activated, and the contexts in which they are triggered. This is the challenge of realist evaluation for practice, and the foregoing analysis seeks to respond to this challenge. Now we need to deepen the analysis of the concrete, to investigate how the content variables interact with the other mechanisms, and the contexts in which they are triggered to produce the main one of the three outcomes in Tables 8.1 to 8.3, namely, 'whether assessment was completed or not'.

As Sayer explains, practice takes place in a messy and open system, and therefore one has to rely on abstraction and careful conceptualisation, 'attempting to abstract out the various components or influences in our heads, and only when we have done this and considered how they combine and interact can we expect to return to the concrete, many-sided object and make sense of it' (2000: 19).

Thus far, in relation to Shield, we have achieved a partial retroduction through bivariate analysis, as indicated above. Now we need to deepen the analysis of the concrete, to investigate how the content variables interact with the other mechanisms, and the contexts in which they are triggered to produce the main one of the three outcomes in Tables 8.1 to 8.3, namely, 'whether assessment was completed or not'.

Having used the bivariate significance tests, that is, the relationship between each outcome with each mechanism and with each of the mechanisms introduced by the Shield Project's assessment work (referred to here as the content variables), we have identified the causal mechanisms in relation to the content of the work, as well as three additional mechanisms which interact to produce the outcomes, namely the parents' relationship with each other, the child/young person's ability to engage in the work, and improvement in multi-disciplinary relationships. We can now use more sophisticated statistical analysis, which enables us to examine the relationship between three rather than two variables at a time.

In order to identify the interaction between the causal mechanisms and the contexts, and how the outcomes are produced, regression analyses can be used in relation to each of the outcomes (see Argyrous, 2000, and Robson, 2002). These analyses have become more accessible to researchers through SPSS. In this particular application, binary logistic regression was used. This method investigates the relationship between the dependent variable (such as the outcome of assessment completed or not) and a covariate (such as whether the requirements of the assessment model were met or not) when controlled by a third selection variable (such as when a mechanism or a context is present and when it is not present). First, all three outcomes in Tables 8.1 to 8.3 were used in turn as the dependent variable. Second, the variable 'whether the requirements of the model were met or not' was used as the covariate. This particular variable was selected as the earlier significance tests indicated a strong relationship with each of the three outcomes, and as it can be seen as a reflection of the causal mechanisms introduced by the Shield Project workers in the course of the implementation of their model of assessment. Moreover, the calculation of relative risk indicated that, where the requirements of the assessment model were met, the likelihood of completing the assessment was 6.4 times greater than where the requirements were not met. Third, each of the mechanisms and contexts outlined in Chapter 7 was used as a selection variable. This particular method equates to calculating odds ratios within those where the selection variable was positive.

Table 8.4 indicates the results from this simple binary logistic regression where the selection variables were each of the mechanisms. Only the correlations found to be statistically significant at the level $p < 0.05$ in the presence of adverse conditions or disabling mechanisms are listed. The only outcome that appears as the dependent variable in Table 8.4 is 'whether the assessment was completed or not', as none of the correlations were found to be significant when the variables 'child/young person engaged or not' and 'either parent engaged or not' were used as the dependent variable in this analysis. The r square in this table is known as the Nagelkerke R square, and is an estimate of the variation in the outcome 'whether the assessment completed or not' that can be explained by the presence of 'requirements of the model met' as well as the presence of each of the mechanisms listed. All the effect sizes in Table 8.4 were found to be large. The exact value of the $p < 0.05$ is indicated in the significance (sig.) column. The last column is the exponential beta (exp B) which equates to the odds of the assessment being completed in these conditions. Odds ratios have been used before in research with young people who sexually harm others, for example, in Widom (1995) where the likelihood of such young people becoming adult sexual offenders was investigated.

149

Table 8.4   *Binary logistic regression with mechanisms*

Assessment completed or not and mechanisms: requirements of the model met	R square	Sig.	Exp (B)
Support from parents negative	.523	.012	28.0
Parents' agreement negative	.433	.010	18.0
Parents' agreement deteriorated	.484	.001	22.8
Peer negative	.377	.007	13.5
Peer deterioration	.433	.002	18.2

All of the exponential beta values appear to be large. Table 8.4 indicates that where the requirements of the assessment model are met in the presence of these disabling mechanisms or adverse conditions, the assessment is likely to be completed. As explained in Chapter 7, research indicates that the typology of children/young people who sexually harm others includes poor social skills and poor peer relationships (for example, Veneziano, Veneziano and LeGrand, 2000). The results in Table 8.4 indicate that even where the 'ability to make and maintain supportive peer relationships' was considered to be a disabling mechanism, the odds of completing the assessment were favourable, provided that the requirements of the model were met.

The Triggering of the Mechanisms in Relevant Contexts

Thus far, none of the contexts have appeared to be significant in relation to the outcomes. However, as the binary logistic regression analysis when controlling for each context was used, a number of correlations were found to be significant, again only in relation to the outcome 'assessment completed or not', and again selecting only the cases where the requirements of the assessment model were met (Table 8.5). Once again, the R square column indicates that all the effect sizes were large, and the odds ratios as indicated by the exponential beta column are very high. As outlined in Chapter 7, all of these contexts have been found to exist in fair to large proportions in the studies of children/young people who sexually harm others (for example, Burke, 2001; Ryan et al., 1996), and therefore our findings thus far are consistent with the other main research findings in the western world.

In particular, Table 8.5 indicates that where a 'history of sexual abuse in relation to the client' was present, and where the requirements of the assessment model were met, the odds of the Shield Project completing the assessment were very high. Where a history of emotional neglect was present, the odds were again a huge 66:1, but where this context was not reported as present the correlation was not significant. The rest of the high odds ratios were in relation to a 'history of emotional neglect', 'history of the client being physically abused', 'history of school problems', 'history of

Table 8.5   *Binary logistic regression in relation to contexts*

Assessment completed or not and contexts: requirements of the model met	R square	Sig.	Exp(B)
History of young person being sexually abused	.695	.003	81.0
History of emotional neglect	.658	.001	66.0
Learning disability	.546	.009	32.0
History of domestic violence	.546	.002	31.5
History of young person being physically abused	.544	.002	30.0
Parents not together	.511	.001	26.3
History of difficult relationships with peers	.467	.001	21.0
History of social services' involvement	.445	.004	18.0
History of school problems	.397	.003	15.4

difficult relationships with peers', and 'history of domestic violence'. Of particular note are the odds ratios in relation to the presence of a learning disability, and where the parents were not together. Table 8.5 indicates that, provided the requirements of the assessment model were met, the odds of completing the assessment were high even in the presence of considerable previous trauma.

Mechanism–Context–Outcome Configurations – the Interactions of Several Variables

Thus far, in both Tables 8.4 and 8.5, we are selecting the cases where the requirements of the assessment model were met, and therefore this analysis does not indicate the likelihood of meeting the requirements in these adverse conditions – that is, subject of deeper analysis as the next stage in the process of realist investigation. What we have found so far is that there is a significant correlation between the completion of the assessment and each of the requirements of the model met, the child/young person engaged in the work, and the engagement of either parent in the work. We have also indicated the association between each of these outcomes and the presence or absence of each of the contexts and the status of each mechanism with regard to whether it is enabling or not.

In terms of realist evaluation, the causal mechanisms introduced by a programme interact with the causal mechanisms in the circumstances of clients, and these mechanisms are triggered in particular contexts, which suggests that several relevant mechanisms interact in several relevant contexts. Therefore, we now turn to the ways in which the presence of several contexts and mechanisms affect the outcome indicators. In consultation with a statistician, it was decided that binary logistic regression would again be the method for this purpose, but this time several mechanisms and contexts would be entered at the same time in our analysis. The statistician John Varlow describes the method as follows:

This method investigates the relationship between the dependent variable (in this case, whether the assessment was completed or not) and a number of covariates including whether the requirements of the model were met. It is important when building regression models to have a clear idea of what may be influencing the model, since unforeseen interactions between covariates (multicollinearity), even those that do not contribute to outcome, may influence or even negate findings. Classic misconceptions around regression models often lead to all variables being entered as covariates, and invariably producing a long list of non-significant, weak interactions.

The strength of binary logistic regression is in its ability to control for the effects of all key covariates. For instance, we can get an estimate of the relevance of whether the requirements of the model were met, regardless of subjects' gender, age or other contexts/mechanisms. Additionally, contexts or mechanisms initially put into the model with good reason that are excluded through the iterative nature of regression are themselves important. We can, with relative confidence, say that these mechanisms/contexts have no significant role within our hypothesised model. It is an important result, for example, to know that subjects with learning difficulties are equally as likely to complete the assessment than those without. Consequently, any programs that are instigated need not limit acceptance onto them on the basis of learning difficulties. The non-appearance of gender and age in the hypothesised model are in themselves important results since they suggest that such programmes do not have to be targeted at different age/gender groups, saving both time and resources. (email communication with author, 8 July 2002)

The binary logistic regression models presented within this chapter look separately at contexts and mechanisms, since complex interactions between these negate the usefulness of looking at a combined model. The models also utilise a forward–conditional method. Standard forward–entry methodology examines each covariate and if it proves to have a significant effect on the dependent variable, adjusting for covariates already included, it is added to the model. The iterative nature of this procedure results in a list of covariates that were significant at some point in the entry process. Forward–conditional methodology allows for removal of previously significant covariates at later stages of the iterative model as more covariates are entered. The analysis presented here, although utilising forward–conditional methods, can also be duplicated by using alternative forward–entry models included within SPSS.

The tables presented below outline the final stage in our binary logistic regression iterations. The SPSS 'statistics coach' explains that B is the estimated coefficient, with standard error S.E. The ratio of B to S.E., squared, equals the Wald statistic. Exp(B) is the predicted change in odds for a unit increase in the predictor, that is, the odds ratio. As outlined in previous chapters, when Exp(B) is less than 1, increasing values of the variable correspond to decreasing odds of the event's occurrence. When Exp(B) is greater than 1, increasing values of the variable correspond to increasing odds of the event's occurrence. Since context covariates are all yes/no variables, in effect Exp(B) compares the odds of the context having a 'yes' response to that of 'no'.

The first binary logistic regression model (Table 8.6) investigates the impact of contexts (as listed in Table 8.5), as well as the inclusion of 'requirements of the assessment model met or not' as an additional covariant,

Table 8.6 *Binary logistic regression analysis of contexts impacting on the outcome of assessment completed (final step in the forward–conditional method)*

Contexts (and requirements met)	B	S.E.	Wald	Sig.	Exp(B)
History of domestic violence	2.773	1.329	4.351	.037	16.0
History of mental health problems	10.801	60.464	.032	.858	49057.8
Requirements of the model met	13.116	60.470	.047	.828	496701.1

Table 8.7 *Binary logistic regression analysis of contexts impacting on the outcome of engagement of either parent (all three steps in the forward–conditional method)*

Steps	Contexts (and child/ young person engaged)	B	S.E.	Wald	Sig.	Exp(B)
1	Child/young person engaged	2.927	.818	12.803	.000	18.7
2	History of emotional neglect	−2.250	1.134	3.936	.047	0.1
	Child/young person engaged	3.889	1.177	10.918	.001	48.9
3	History of emotional neglect	−2.536	1.189	4.550	.033	0.8
	History of domestic violence	2.478	1.202	4.247	.039	11.9
	Child/young person engaged	4.809	1.464	10.794	.001	122.6

on the outcome of 'assessment completed or not'. In the final step of the forward–conditional method, it was found that, given the presence of all the contexts, the two contexts that influenced the outcome were domestic violence and history of mental health problems, with only domestic violence being statistically significant at the level of $p < 0.05$. Therefore, where domestic violence existed as a context, the odds of the assessment being completed were 16 times higher than where it did not (the other exponential Beta values are based upon small numbers, leading to high values with no statistical significance).

In the second regression model (Table 8.7), the dependent variable is engagement of either parent, as that was found to be significant in relation to 'engagement of the child/young person' with a large effect size (Table 8.2). Again, all the contexts were included, but with engagement of the child/ young person as that was also found to be significantly related to assessment completed (Table 8.1). In the three-step forward–conditional method, child/young person engaged or not is entered in Step 1, history of emotional neglect in Step 2, and history of domestic violence in Step 3. All of these variables are significant, and it appears that the odds of engaging either parent increase almost 19 times when the child/young person is also engaged. These odds increase to almost 49 times when emotional neglect is added to the equation, although emotional neglect has an inverse relationship to both the engagement of the parent and the engagement of the child.

However, when history of domestic violence is added, the odds are much higher at nearly 123 times, again indicating the importance of domestic violence as a context. In the third model, the variables were the same as in the second model, except that the engagement of the child/young person became the dependent variable and the engagement of either parent was used as a covariant. In this model, none of the contexts were found to be significant, and only the engagement of either parent was included in the equation (B = 2.927, S.E. = 0.818, Wald = 12.803, sig. = .000, Exp(B) = 18.7) and was also found to be significant, again confirming the correlation between these two outcomes even when they are interacting with multiple mechanisms and contexts.

In relation to mechanisms, in the fourth binary logistic regression model, assessment completed was the dependent variable, and all the mechanisms in Table 7.16 were added as covariates, along with 'requirements of the assessment model met'. It was found that the only variable included in the equation was 'requirements of the assessment model met' (B = 3.091, S.E. = 0.950, Wald = 10.575, sig. = .001, Exp(B) = 22.0), again confirming our earlier finding (Table 8.4) that the odds of completion of the assessment were high even where the mechanisms were disabling, provided the requirements of the assessment model were met. When the mechanisms were added in the fifth model, with 'child/young person engaged' as the dependent variable and including 'either parent engaged' as a covariant, along with the mechanisms identified in Table 7.16, again the only covariant included in the equation (and also found to be significant) was the engagement of the parent (B = 3.902, S.E. = 1.075, Wald = 13.164, sig. = .000, Exp(B) = 49.5), again confirming the association between these two outcomes. The odds of the child/young person being engaged in the work are more than 49 times higher when parents were also engaged, even where the other mechanisms in the circumstances of the clients were disabling.

Conclusion in Relation to the Realist Evaluation of the Shield Project

In accordance with the principles of realist evaluation, the potential causal mechanisms introduced by the Shield Project (in relation to its assessment work with children/young people who sexually harm others) interact with some other key mechanisms in the circumstances of the clients which are then triggered in some particular contexts. This interaction or activation of the specified mechanisms in the specified contexts may determine whether the Shield Project will complete its assessment or not.

With regard to mechanisms in the circumstances, the following three did shine through in relation to all three outcomes: (a) parents' relationship–agreement (negative effect or inverse relationship); (b) child/young person's ability to engage in the assessment work; (c) improvement in multi-disciplinary relationship.

However, the effect sizes were weak and the statistical power analysis was less than .80 for each of the above three mechanisms. The binary logistic regression analysis has confirmed that these mechanisms were probably not causal mechanisms when investigated in relation to the interaction of the specified mechanisms and contexts with each other and in relation to the outcomes. Indications are that the mechanisms identified in Table 7.16 may not have a bearing on the outcome of the completion of the assessment.

Therefore, in the fifth binary logistic model, the dependent variable was assessment completed, and the covariates were the content variables found to be significant, that is, requirements of the model met, child/young person engaged, either parent engaged, number of sessions with the child/young person, number of sessions with either parent, number of multi-disciplinary meetings, and history of domestic violence (which was the only context found to be significant in our earlier regression models). It was found that the only covariant included in the equation was the number of sessions with the child ($B = 1.273$, S.E. $= 0.411$, Wald $= 9.583$, sig. $= .002$, Exp(B) $= 3.6$), and as the number of sessions are indicators of the implementation of the Shield model of assessment, this confirms our earlier finding that the mechanisms introduced by the Shield Project workers (such as meeting the requirements of the assessment model, engagement of the clients) were the likely causal mechanisms leading to the completion of the assessment. These content mechanisms are triggered in the contexts of prior trauma, particularly domestic violence, and in the absence of emotional neglect.

If most of the content mechanisms are present (that is, the implementation of the assessment model divided into components of family background, current situation, actual offence or sexually harmful behaviours, and changing/understanding behaviours), and triggered in the contexts of prior trauma, then the odds of completing the assessment will be very high, and we can invoke the realist concept of *necessity* (Sayer, 2000: 125). Using the analogy of gunpowder, it can cause an explosion, but only in certain conditions, that is, when it is dry, and when the casual mechanism of a spark is applied (Chapter 3). The generative mechanisms introduced by the Shield workers will not in themselves lead to the outcome of completing the assessment; but in the conditions of the above contexts, and when the Shield Project's requirements of the assessment model are met (that is, the spark), then the assessment will necessarily be completed.

As we have seen from the findings from other studies (Chapter 7) on young people who sexually harm others, although the client groups are heterogeneous, there are a number of mechanisms and contexts that have been found to be common in a fairly high proportion of studies. As we have also found in Chapter 6, the content of the model of assessment of the Shield Project is informed by what is currently known about this client group. For example, Rasmussen, Burton and Christopherson (1992) argued that prior traumatisation was one of a number of precursors to sexual perpetration, with other predisposing factors, including social inadequacy, lack of intimacy and impulsiveness, and the Shield Project workers did identify

155

these authors' work as one of the influences on their model of assessment. It follows, therefore, that the content of the model is such that it is most effective where there are multiple historical problems, and in particular where there is a history of domestic violence.

The purpose of realist evaluation is to investigate what works, for whom and in what contexts in order to develop the human services programmes. The Shield model of assessment can be developed by focusing on engaging with the child/young person, and either parent, as well as with other professionals involved, even in the most difficult circumstances. However, with regard to these circumstances, there appear to be a number of choices. First, the Shield Project's model of assessment could be targeted at clients where the multiple problems highlighted above exist, for example, previous history of trauma. Second, the model could be developed in such a way that it could engage better with the others where such conditions are not present. Third, both of these strategies could be followed, targeting at the most needy, at the same time developing ways of engaging those that appear not to have these complex historical problems. For example, Burton (2000) notes that roughly 30% of boys who act out sexually have no history of sexual victimisation. In this study's sample of 49 cases to date, it was found that 46.9% (Table 7.15) of the children/young people were themselves victims of sexual abuse, or in other words, 53.1% had no reported history of sexual victimisation. Table 8.5 indicates that the odds of completing the assessment are high where this condition exists and the requirements of the assessment model are met. Prior sexual victimisation of sex offenders has been a consistent finding across the adult and juvenile literature, despite considerable differences in sample selection and data collection (Veneziano, Veneziano and LeGrand, 2000). Based on these findings, Burton (2000: 46) concludes that 'focusing on those children when the behaviour is first recognised is justifiable expense and may be critical to the prevention of adolescent sexual offending'. However, a recent meta-analysis does not find a relationship between prior sexual victimisation and later recidivism (Hanson and Bussiere, 1998); but at the same time, the issue is not prior sexual victimisation, but prior traumatisation generally. 'The similarity in the odds ratios of adult arrest for a sex crime across types of childhood maltreatment suggests that the etiologically significant factor in the emergence of abusive sexuality is exposure to trauma, not sexual abuse per se' (Gray et al., 1999). These findings are consistent with the findings from the use of binary logistic regression models above which indicate that, of all the contexts, the presence of a history of domestic violence rather than sexual abuse is significant in the completion of the assessment. Therefore, the Shield Project's effectiveness with children/young people exposed to prior trauma (including domestic violence) may be of crucial importance in helping to reduce recidivism.

With regard to the realist evaluation of what works, for whom and in what contexts, we have found that the Shield assessment model works best under the conditions of prior traumatisation. However, the contradictory findings from other research highlight the problems facing the projects that work with young people who sexually harm others – should they continue to target those who have conditions such as previous histories of abuse, or should they develop other models of assessment and/or intervention to meet the needs of others where such conditions of prior traumatisation are not present? As these findings are from the realist effectiveness cycle that has been integrated into the practice of the Shield Project, the agency does not have to wait for a research report to be written before deciding on the implications of the findings. The agency has decided to do both – to continue with the model of assessment with the cases under the conditions of prior traumatisation, and to introduce a new form of shorter, initial assessment model for the cases where these conditions are not relevant (Kazi, Ward and Hudson, 2002). This change in the content of interventions is an example of the utility of the realist evaluation for the development of effective practice strategies.

9

The Contribution of Realist
Evaluation for Practice

The main contribution of this book is to develop a framework for practice evaluation based on the principles of realist evaluation, and to demonstrate the utility of the realist paradigm in the evaluation of practice within the realities of society. Practice in human services takes place in an open system that consists of a constellation of interconnected structures, mechanisms and contexts. Realism aims to address the significant factors involved in practice, through the realist effectiveness cycle which links the development of the models of intervention with the observed changes in the circumstances in which practice takes place. This link between practice and reality is the evaluation strategy itself. The multi-method data gathering addresses the questions of what actually works, for whom and in what contexts. At each cycle, a better approximation of reality is obtained, as compared with the previous cycle. In this way, realism has the potential to address the main purposes of evaluation – to determine the merit and worth of human service programmes, and to improve these services in the circumstances of practice.

In Chapter 2, we reviewed the main contemporary paradigms in evaluation research as applied to the practice of human services. The boundaries between these paradigms are not firm, and it is not possible to establish them into discrete categories. Nevertheless, the paradigmatic preferences of the inquirer may influence the selection of evaluation questions, the selection of research methods and how they are applied, and the drawing of conclusions from the findings. Each paradigm has its advantages and limitations with regard to practice evaluation, however, each of the main paradigms has also made a definite contribution in developing the strategies for practice evaluation research. For example, empirical practice introduced a focus on outcomes, interpretivist approaches have emphasised the process of practice and a focus on people's in-depth perceptions, and pragmatism emphasises the needs of practice (Kazi, 1999, 2000a; Trinder, 1996). These paradigms enable the transition from a 'black box' evaluation that concentrates on effects to a 'grey box' evaluation that also investigates processes. However, these paradigms tend to remain at the level of establishing 'what works'.

For example, from a 'black box' stance, Sackett et al. (1997: 2) define evidence-based practice within the human services as '... the conscientious, explicit, and judicious use of the current best evidence in making decisions about the care of individual patients'. In their promotion of systematic reviews of social and educational policies and practices, the Campbell Collaboration (http://www.campbell.gse.upenn.edu) suggests that the best evidence is found through randomised field trials, or at least through quasi-experimental designs (Boruch, Petrosino and Chalmers, 1999).

Also from a 'black box' stance, Gambrill (1999a, 1999b) elaborates evidence-based practice in relation to social work as follows:

> Social workers seek out practice-related research findings regarding important practice decisions and share the results of their search with clients. If they find that there is no evidence that a method they recommend will help a client, they so inform the client and describe their theoretical rationale for their recommendations. Clients are involved as informed participants. (1999a: 346)

White accepts that 'what works' is necessary, but argues from a 'grey box' standpoint for a 'research agenda that properly recognises the complex inter-active processes involved in social work interventions, many of which require examination using more interpretive methodological approaches' (White and Stancombe, 2002: 187). Whilst the empirical practice approach is satisfied with the establishment of a causal connection between an intervention and its effects, the interpretivists argue for a more in-depth account of the processes of the same practice. However, both remain at the surface in the sense that their perspectives do not begin from an investigation of the causal mechanisms and the contexts that produce the programme outcomes.

Indeed, it could be argued that non-realist researchers tend not to make the best possible use of the data that may be available. For example, the empirical practice researcher would be satisfied with achieving their gold standard, of establishing that the intervention group faired better than the control group, and would not examine the statistical associations between the outcomes and the different factors such as components of the intervention or the circumstances of the service users, which are usually controlled as extraneous variables (for example, the post-natal study described in Oakley, 1996). On the other hand, the interpretivist researchers may provide an in-depth account of the service users' perceptions regarding the service, but they may fail to establish patterns that may link particular types of service-user circumstances with the level of effectiveness of the services received (such as Everitt and Hardiker's 1996 example of older people). As indicated in Chapter 2, these paradigmatic boundaries are not discrete, and therefore there may be enquirers who do investigate the links between service-user characteristics and outcomes without declaring the influences of realist evaluation (such as Beckett, 2001, who has used cluster analysis, with those at the lower end and those at the top end of desired outcomes).

A contribution of the realist evaluation paradigm may be to enable the evaluation of human service programmes to enter a higher stage, the 'clear box' type of evaluation that investigates the effectiveness of the programmes within an open system. For example, 'what works' is only a starting point, and not the gold standard to strive for, as exemplified by the example of the adult rehabilitation programmes in Chapter 3. One of the 'realist evaluation bloodlines' of Pawson and Tilley (2001: 323) is 'never expect to know "what works", just keep trying to find out'. This is because what may work with some people in certain conditions may not work in different conditions or with different people. Therefore, a contribution of realist evaluation is not only to identify what interventions work, but how they work and in what circumstances. The findings from realist evaluation are used not just to confirm the effectiveness of interventions where they have been found to be effective, but to develop the programmes of intervention to meet the needs of different people in different circumstances. The gold standard for the realist evaluator is not just 'what works', but 'what works, for whom and in what contexts', recognising that an explanation at any one time requires further investigation and further explanation (hence the notion of a realist effectiveness cycle).

Realist Evaluation for Practice: A Framework

The starting point is a partnership between realist evaluators and practitioners. Pawson and Tilley (1997b: 217) regard this relationship as a 'teacher–learner relationship' with practitioners and others to test and explain the 'context–mechanism–outcome configurations'. However, a partnership is advocated here as both the academic evaluator and the practitioners are learners and teachers at the same time, as indicated in the practice examples in Chapters 3–8. This partnership is based on a shared commitment to evaluate practice, and to identify ways in which both internal and external evaluation can be combined together and inform each other. The next step is to identify suitable outcome measures in relation to the programmes of intervention that are to be evaluated. These outcome measures could be selected from published standardised measures (for example, from Corcoran and Fischer, 2000, as used in the Shield Project); created with practitioners (such as in the family centre example in Chapter 5); and/or indicate general outcomes of the programmes, such as whether the programmes were completed, recidivism rates, completion of assessments, and others used in the studies described in this book. Where some outcome indicators are already in place (for example, the adult rehabilitation programme in Chapter 3), a retrospective analysis may be undertaken to establish the extent to which outcomes have been achieved to date, and where possible, to begin to identify the characteristics of service users and the circumstances in which the outcomes are more or less likely to be achieved.

Next, we need to investigate the circumstances of service users in more depth, to enable a deeper investigation of how the outcomes are produced. A contribution of the realist evaluation paradigm is the concept of embeddedness (Chapter 3). Causal powers do not reside in the events or the behaviours of particular objects, variables or individuals, but in the social relations and organisational structures which constitute the open system. One action leads to another because of the actions' accepted place in the whole. Realist evaluation strategies seek to explain how the programme's causal mechanisms interact with the other causal mechanisms in the circumstances of the service users, and the conditions or contexts in which they were triggered (Figure 8.1). At this stage, we need to undertake intensive research with each service user to identify the mechanisms that may enable the outcomes to be achieved, as well as the mechanisms that may be disabling, and the contexts or circumstances in which they may be triggered.

Robson (2000, 2002) indicates that practitioners can rely on their knowledge and experience as well as research findings to help identify the key mechanisms. Both strategies were used in the Shield Project study described in Chapters 6–8, as well as focus-group meetings of practitioners to identify the mechanisms and contexts in the circumstances of individual cases. Another strategy, used in the Lifeline Project in Chapter 4, is that of systematic repeated interviews of service users to help identify the mechanisms and contexts relevant for the outcomes agreed with them (Spurling, Kazi and Rogan, 2000). All of these strategies enable the intensive research with each case, as suggested by Sayer (2000). Qualitative data analysis such as template analysis (Crabtree and Miller, 1999) and matrices (Miles and Huberman, 1994) may be used to identify patterns or demi-regularities across the cases, to help select some common mechanisms and contexts for quantitative analysis (Chapters 4 and 7).

The systematic tracking of outcomes, mechanisms, contexts and programme content variables can be implemented in a realist effectiveness cycle with the use of SPSS databases (Argyrous, 2000; Foster, 2001) in addition to the qualitative strategies. In the studies described in this book (Chapters 3–8), the SPSS databases were developed as part of the partnership between the academic evaluator and the practitioners, and regular analysis and feedback were provided to enable the realist effectiveness cycle to operate in a meaningful way. The regular feedback helped practitioners to improve their programmes of intervention and also helped to better target them to meet the needs of service users in the changing circumstances. The agency's recording systems were adapted to enable a regular update of the databases. The database was not static, but responded to the permeability of the open system (see Pawson and Tilley, 1997b: 218, rule 6) as new mechanisms were added as and when they were discovered. For each mechanism identified, the practitioners were asked to record whether they were enabling or disabling, and to track changes in the form of whether they improved, remained the same or became worse. The contexts recorded included histories of problems as well as current circumstances which take longer to change, such as levels of social deprivation, housing, employment, and the separation of families.

With regard to quantitative analysis as suggested by Lawson (1998) to identify patterns, the use of inferential statistics in the described studies included significance tests, measures of association, odds ratios, calculations of risk, and multiple regression analysis. Whereas in a 'black box' study, the aim would be to determine an intervention's impact, in realist evaluation, inferential statistics may be used with the aim of identifying mechanism–context–outcome configurations. The aim is to identify demi-regularities or patterns, to investigate the characteristics, factors, or mechanisms that lead to more successful or less successful outcomes, and to identify the conditions under which the causal mechanisms may be triggered to produce the outcomes. For example, in the study of family centres (Chapter 5), it was found that non-white parents faired worse in parent-based outcomes, but also that this was not true of child-based outcomes. In the NSPCC Shield Project (Chapters 6–8), it was found that the engagement of the child, the relationship between parents, and the multi-disciplinary relationships may be among the key causal mechanisms, but that the programme's generative mechanism was able to successfully interact with the causal mechanisms in the conditions of a previous history of domestic violence. All of these findings were achieved with the help of a realist evaluation perspective, and particularly under the influence of the concept of realist retroduction. As part of the rules of realist evaluation, Pawson and Tilley (1997b) include the following aims of investigation:

1   what the outcomes are and how they are produced;
2   how the causal mechanisms which generate social and behavioural problems are removed or countered through the alternative causal mechanisms introduced in a social programme;
3   the contexts within which programme mechanisms are activated and in which programme mechanisms can be successfully fired.

The realist investigator will have these aims at the forefront regardless of the type of data that may be available at any given time. For example, in the adult rehabilitation study in Chapter 3, the data available was limited at first, but the realist evaluation perspective influenced the way the data was actually used. This is why the realist investigator may not be satisfied with an explanation of what works, and may strive for deeper explanations. The goal is to understand how the phenomena under study react or change in the presence or absence of other antecedent or concurrent phenomena in an open system. These theories are empirically assessed, and when found to be empirically adequate, are themselves explained in turn, in the cognitive unfolding of explanatory knowledge (Lawson, 1998). That is why a realist effectiveness cycle was used, with a systematic tracking of outcomes, mechanisms and contexts, in a prospective evaluation.

The Replication of Effective Interventions

Replication is a problem in evidence-based practice, but one that is frequently not addressed (Chapter 2). That is because, in the empirical practice approach, the contexts of practice as well as the content of interventions are usually not investigated in depth, and in an interpretivist study, the tendency is to engage in an in-depth study of perceptions and insights in particular situations and in particular ways (Kazi, 2000a; Trinder, 1996). A realist evaluation, such as that of the NSPCC Shield Project, enables greater opportunities for replication, as the investigation is that of mechanisms fired in certain contexts. Programme integrity is also addressed with the systematic tracking of the content of the models of intervention (Chapter 6), thereby providing better opportunities for replication. The concept of necessity (Chapter 3) indicates that certain mechanisms will necessarily be fired in certain conditions; however, that may be true under the closed conditions of an experiment. On the other hand, the realist concept of emergence suggests that mechanisms and contexts can transform themselves, and that new mechanisms may emerge.

Therefore, the realist inquirer would also be aware that if replication were possible, it would neither provide confirmation of an intervention's effectiveness, nor prove that it was not effective, and that is because practice takes place in an open system. As Robson (2002) explains:

> Because we are dealing with open systems, we have to accept that we are dealing with tendencies and probabilities. Causal processes may sometimes, even usually, lead to particular outcomes. But on some occasions, and in some circumstances, they may not. Our hypothesis is that there are one or more mechanisms at work which will trigger these outcomes, and that there are other mechanisms which will interfere so that the outcome does not occur. (p. 40)

The NSPCC Shield Project Study also demonstrates that, in a prospective evaluation where the realist effectiveness cycle is integrated into practice, the changes and transformations in the mechanisms are systematically tracked, and the generative mechanisms introduced by the models of intervention can also be transformed in the changing circumstances, guided by the findings from a prospective realist evaluation. For example, the agency is continuing to implement the model of assessment in the conditions of prior traumatisation where it is demonstrated to be most effective, and at the same time developing a different model of intervention for cases where these conditions are not present. In this way, the realist evaluation framework for practice as presented in this book can provide a bridge to connect evaluation research with practice, and current with future practice.

Some Limitations of Realist Evaluation

A crucial part of realist evaluation is the identification and systematic tracking of causal mechanisms and the contexts in which they may be triggered to produce the outcomes. In the realist view of causation, the notion of underlying *mechanism* is central. 'A mechanism is ... not a variable but an account of the makeup, behaviour, and interrelationships of those processes that are responsible for the outcome. A mechanism is thus a theory – a theory that spells out the potential of human resources and reasoning' (Pawson and Tilley, 1997a: 408).

Therefore, the selection of mechanisms is influenced by the theoretical preferences of the inquirer, and in both the intensive and extensive research, the chosen mechanisms may not be the relevant ones, or the relevant ones may remain hidden because the practitioners and/or evaluators are following preconceived ideas from past experiences which may bear no relation to the current make-up of mechanisms. This is particularly true of open systems, where mechanisms and contexts are transforming themselves and new ones are emerging.

When the mechanisms are identified through an interaction with service users (as in Chapter 4), the power relations between the agency's workers and the service users (as in self-reported levels of drug misuse, for example) may influence the extent to which the service user is motivated to share their true reflections. Where the workers identify the mechanisms from their own experiences and judgements (as in the NSPCC Shield Project, Chapters 6–8), each individual may have a different preference in identifying the relevant mechanisms, or the existence or otherwise of a particular mechanism or context may be based on, or influenced by, information of an essentially self-report nature from the child/young person and either parent. For example, a history of sexual abuse and other types of abuse are many times based on self-report and respondents can over- or under-report their histories of abuse (Murphy et al., 2001). Also, retrospective self-reports of childhood experiences are open to a number of possible biases such as reinterpreting past memories in the context of present experiences (Widom, 1988). Houston (2001: 855) suggests that social workers should be alert to the effects of 'cognitive bias, defence mechanisms, and ideology in shaping people's accounts'.

Nevertheless, these limitations are not just applicable to realist evaluations, but to research generally. For example, the odds ratios calculated by Widom (1995) indicated that sexually-abused children were 4.7 times more likely than non-abused children to be arrested as an adult for a sex crime, and that physically abused children were 4.1 times more likely than non-abused children to be arrested as an adult for a sex crime. However, the limitations with regard to the source of the information relevant to the history of abuse may be the same as in the Shield Project study. Apart from reviewing the findings from relevant research to help in the selection of mechanisms in realist evaluation, the realist effectiveness cycle may act as a self-correcting mechanism, as the quest for explanation of explanations, as indicated earlier, may confirm the existence or otherwise of an expected mechanism. For example, the Shield workers thought that the relationship between parents, and whether they agreed with each other regarding the support needed for the child, would be an enabling mechanism in the Project's assessment work. However, the mechanism–context–outcome configurations reported in Chapter 8 found that the opposite was the case – the assessment model was more likely to work where the parents were not in agreement with each other. As a result of this finding, the workers are considering the implications and reinvestigating their theoretical positions with regard to this finding.

It is possible that the analysis presented in Chapters 6–8 has missed out a crucial mechanism that has not been identified to date, and which may have greater causal powers then those selected for analysis. If this were to be the case, this hypothesis may remain untested, as the analysis is dependent on the entry of factors into the database. However, even if it was found that none of the mechanisms identified had a significant influence on the outcomes, and even if the statistical power analysis (Cohen, 1988) as explained in Chapter 8 confirmed that the likelihood of errors was low, the realist inquirer would still continue the search for the relevant mechanisms until they were found, and even after they were found. In fact, as we have indicated, even after their discovery, the realist effectiveness cycle would not be satisfied but continue to investigate the configurations of causal mechanisms and the conditions in which they may be fired, in a prospective evaluation. The theories about mechanisms are subject to empirical tests, and new ones emerge that require further tests. Therefore, the realist evaluator may not be satisfied with the findings from analysis at any given time; rather, they are also involved in developing an adequate and self-consistent system of concepts with which to understand the world as revealed in the results of repeated analyses.

We now return to the question raised in Chapters 1 and 6 – there are no published studies of realist evaluations following the publication of Pawson and Tilley's (1997b) manifesto, and the publications on realist evaluation to date are rather short on examples and long on theories and possibilities. That may be because the authors, such as Archer, Pawson and Tilley and Sayer, are concentrating on developing realism as a philosophy of science, and some concepts are rather underdeveloped at the level of methodology. For example, as we have noted in Chapter 3, it has been stated that the central mode of realist research is not induction or deduction, but retroduction (Archer, 1998; Lawson, 1998). As the main research methodologies involve induction or deduction or both (Chapter 3), this may give the impression that realists may prefer to use other methods that are related to retroduction. In fact, as the studies in this book have demonstrated, the process of retroduction actually involves induction and/or deduction, based on empirical evidence. The methods used are those that are available in the existing repertoire of both qualitative and quantitative methods, and as yet there is no reported research method that is dedicated solely to realist evaluation. As the main realist authors dedicate themselves to addressing questions at the level of the philosophies of science, the practice of realist evaluation has been rather limited to date. The main contribution has been at the level of perspectives and approaches, rather than the methods of practising evaluation research. This book has initiated a different emphasis by contributing to develop a practice framework for realist evaluation.

The Potential of a Realist Evaluation Perspective

A central reason for starting from the realist perspective, is its focus on explanations (Kazi et al., 2002a). The research question is not just that the programme works, but what it is about the programme that makes it work, and why it works with some people and not with others, as demonstrated in the studies in this book. In the evaluation of practice, the realist approach is integrated into the practice of human services, including the development of recording systems, practices and evaluation of effectiveness. Based on existing knowledge and data accumulation on outcomes, mechanisms and contexts, the programmes are developed as models targeted to achieve the desired outcomes. A multi-method research strategy is applied to test the extent to which these models are analogous with reality, and the data collection and analysis directly contribute to further development of the models, as well as their future targeting within a realist effectiveness cycle. In this way, the content of the programmes, their interaction with pre-existing mechanisms and contexts, and their effectiveness in achieving outcomes, are addressed.

As indicated in Chapter 1, realism is methodological-pluralist, but the methods it can draw upon were developed either within the empirical or interpretivist paradigms that may not have the same ontological depth as realism. There are very few examples of realist evaluation, and as Tolson (1999) explains, the methodological rules are still emerging. A contribution of this book is to demonstrate that, in realist evaluation, the research methods can be selected from the full repertoire available (such as Bryman, 2001; Miles and Huberman, 1994; Robson, 2002; Rubin and Babbie, 2001), drawing upon both qualitative and quantitative methods. There is a tendency among some realists to prefer qualitative strategies, for example, Houston (2001) expresses a preference for the interpretivist methods suggested in White (1997), and also suggests that retroductive analysis is possible through Sheppard's (1995) reflexive methods. Whilst a mixture of qualitative and quantitative methods may be preferred to enable retroduction as demonstrated in the evaluation of the Shield Project, the methods in themselves are not decisive; rather, it is the perspective of the inquirer which determines how the methods are used, and for what purpose. The outcomes of the evaluations are to provide data on what works, for whom and in what contexts, along with explanations of why a programme may work with some people and not with others. The findings from the studies included as examples form the basis for a conclusion that, when compared with other paradigms, the realist evaluation paradigm enables the inquirer to reach deeper in capturing the shifting sands of human service effectiveness, and helps the human service programme to develop as a generative mechanism for change.

References

Aljazireh, L. (1993) 'Historical, environmental, and behavioural correlates of sexual offending by male adolescents: a critical review', *Behavioral Sciences and the Law*, 11 (4): 423–40.

Anastas, J.W. (1999) *Research Design for Social Work and the Human Services*, 2nd edn. New York: Columbia University Press.

Anastas, J.W. and MacDonald, M.L. (1994) *Research Design for Social Work and the Human Services*. New York: Lexington Books.

Archer, M. (1998) 'Introduction', in M. Archer, R. Bhaskar, A. Collier, T. Lawson and A. Norrie (eds), *Critical Realism: Essential Readings*. London: Routledge. pp. 189–205.

Argyrous, G. (2000) *Statistics for Social and Health Research*. London: Sage.

Beckett, R. (2001) 'Findings from the adolescent abusers project: impact on treatment', Keynote presentation at The National Organisation for the Treatment of Abusers (NOTA), international annual conference, Pontypridd, South Wales, September.

Bhaskar, R. (1997) *A Realist Theory of Science*, 2nd edn. London: Verso.

Bhaskar, R. (1998) 'General introduction', in M. Archer, R. Bhaskar, A. Collier, T. Lawson and A. Norrie (eds), *Critical Realism: Essential Readings*. London: Routledge. pp. ix–xxiv.

Bhaskar, R. and Lawson, T. (1998) 'Introduction: basic tenets and developments', in M. Archer, R. Bhaskar, A. Collier, T. Lawson and A. Norrie (eds), *Critical Realism: Essential Readings*. London: Routledge. pp. 3–15.

Blom, B. (1996) *Kurator i primärvård. Utvärdering av kuratorsverksamheten vid Skelleftehamns vårdcentral. (Counsellor in primary health care. Evaluation of the counsellor's role at Skelleftehamns primary health care unit)*. Rapport no. 6. Umeå: Umeå universitet, Institutionen för socialt arbete.

Blom, B. (2001) 'The personal social services in a Swedish quasi-market context', *Policy and Politics*, 29: 29–42.

Bloom, M. (1999) 'Single-system evaluation', in I. Shaw and J. Lishman (eds), *Evaluation and Social Work Practice*. London: Sage. pp. 198–218.

Bloom, M., Fischer, J. and Orme, J. (1999) *Evaluating Practice: Guidelines for the Accountable Professional*, 3rd edn. Boston: Allyn and Bacon.

Boruch, R., Petrosino, A. and Chalmers, I. (1999) 'The Campbell Collaboration: a proposal for systematic, multi-national, and continuous reviews of evidence', Paper presented at the London Meeting, Campbell, 15–16 July (http://www.campbell.gse.upenn.edu).

Briggs, H.E. and Corcoran, K. (2001) (eds) *Social Work Practice: Treating Common Client Problems*. Chicago: Lyceum Books.

Bryman, A. (2001) *Social Research Methods*. Oxford: Oxford University Press.

Burke, D.M. (2001) 'Empathy in sexually offending and non-offending adolescent males', *Journal of Interpersonal Violence*, 16 (3): 222–33.

Burton, D.L. (2000) 'Were adolescent sexual offenders children with sexual behaviour problems?', *Sexual Abuse: A Journal of Research and Treatment*, 12 (1): 37–48.

Carlsson, B. (1995) *Att åtgärda eller behandla. En utvärdering av en organisationsförändring inom IFO i Nässjö och dess konsekvenser för klientarbetet. (Taking measures or to treat. Evaluation of organisational change within the PSS in Nässjö and its consequences for work with clients)*. Rapport no. 6. Göteborg: Göteborgs universitet, Institutionen för socialt arbete.

Cheetham, J. (1998) 'The evaluation of social work: priorities, problems and possibilities', in J. Cheetham and M.A.F. Kazi (eds), *The Working of Social Work*. London: Jessica Kingsley. pp. 9–29.

Cheetham, J., Fuller, R., McIvor, G. and Petch, A. (1992) *Evaluating Social Work Effectiveness*. Buckingham: Open University Press.

Cohen, J. (1988) *Statistical Power Analysis for the Behavioural Sciences*, 2nd edn. New York: Academic.

Cook, T.D. and Campbell, D.T. (1979) *Quasi-Experimentation*. Chicago: Rand McNally.

Corcoran, K. and Fischer, J. (2000) *Measures for Clinical Practice: A Source Book*, vols 1 and 2, 3rd edn. New York: The Free Press.

Crabtree, B.F. and Miller, W.L. (1999) 'Doing qualitative research', 2nd edn. Thousand Oaks, CA: Sage.

Dillenburger, K. (1998) 'Evidencing effectiveness: the use of single-case designs in child care work', in D. Iwaniec and J. Pinkerton (eds), *Making Research Work*. Chichester: Wiley. pp. 71–91.

Drisko, J.W. (1997) 'Strengthening qualitative studies and reports: standards to enhance academic integrity', *Journal of Social Work Education*, 33: 1–13.

Drisko, J.W. (2000) 'Qualitative data analysis: it's not just anything goes', Paper presented at Society for Social Work and Research Annual Conference, Charleston, SC, USA, 30 January.

Dufåker, M. (2000) *Östermalmsgatan 54. Utvärdering av ett stödboende för kvinnor Östermalmsgatan 54. (Evaluation of a women's shelter)*. Rapport no. 45. Umeå: Umeå universitet, Institutionen för socialt arbete.

Duguid, S. and Pawson, R. (1998) 'Education, change and transformation: the prison experience', *Evaluation Review*, 22 (4): 470–95.

Dullea, K. and Mullender, A. (1999) 'Evaluation and empowerment', in I. Shaw and J. Lishman (eds), *Evaluation and Social Work Practice*. London: Sage. pp. 81–100.

Everitt, A. (1996) 'Developing critical evaluation', *Evaluation* 2 (2):173–88.

Everitt, A. and Hardiker, P. (1996) *Evaluating for Good Practice*. Basingstoke: Macmillan.

Fetterman, D.M. (2001) *Foundations of Empowerment Evaluation*. Thousand Oaks, CA: Sage.

Finkelhor, D. (1984) *Child Sexual Abuse: New Theory and Research*. New York: The Free Press.

Fischer, J. and Corcoran, K. (1994) *Measures for Clinical Practice: A Source Book*, vols 1 and 2. New York: The Free Press.

Forsberg, H. (2000) *Lapsen näkökulmaa tavoittamassa. Arviointitutkimus turvakotien lapsikeskeisyyttä kehittävässä projektissa. (Searching the child's perspective. Evaluation in a project for developing child-centredness in shelters)*. Helsinki: Ensi-ja turvakotien liiton julkaisu 24.

Fortune, A.E. and Reid, W.J. (1999) *Research in Social Work*, 3rd edn. New York: Columbia University Press.

Foster, J.L. (1998) *Data Analysis: Using SPSS for Windows*. London: Sage.

Foster, J.L. (2001) *Data Analysis: Using SPSS for Windows, new edn, versions 8–10*. London: Sage.

Fraser, M., Taylor, M.J., Jackson, R. and O'Jack, J. (1991) 'Social work and science: many ways of knowing?', *Social Work Research and Abstracts*, 27: 5–15.

Fuller, R. (1996) 'Evaluating social work effectiveness: a pragmatic approach', in P. Alderson, S. Brill, I. Chalmers, R. Fuller, P. Hinkley-Smith, G. Macdonald, T. Newman, A. Oakley, H. Roberts, and H. Ward (eds), *What Works? Effective Social Interventions in Child Welfare*. Ilford, Essex: Barnardos. pp. 55–67.

Fuller, R. and Petch, A. (1995) *Practitioner Research: The Reflexive Social Worker*. Buckingham: Open University Press.

Gal, M. and Hoge, R.D. (1999) 'A profile of the adolescent sex offender', *Forum on Correctional Research*, 11: 7–11.

Gambrill, E. (1999a) 'Evidence-based practice: an alternative to authority-based practice', *Families in Society*, 80: 341–50.

Gambrill, E. (1999b) 'Evidence-based clinical practice, evidence-based medicine and the Cochrane collaboration', *Journal of Behavior Therapy and Experimental Psychiatry*, 30: 1–14, 153–4.

Gomm, R., Needham, G. and Bullman, A. (eds) (2000) *Evaluating Research in Health and Social Care*. London: Sage.

Gray, A., Pithers, W.D., Busconi, A. and Houchens, P. (1999) 'Developmental and etiological characteristics of children with sexual behaviour problems: treatment implications', *Child Abuse and Neglect*, 23 (6): 601–21.

Guba, E.G. (1990) 'The alternative paradigm dialogue', in E.G. Guba (ed.), *The Paradigm Dialogue*. Thousand Oaks, CA: Sage. pp. 17–27.

Hall, C. (1997) *Social Work as Narrative: Storytelling and Persuasion in Professional Texts*. Aldershot: Ashgate.

Hanson, R.K. and Bussiere, M.T. (1998) 'Predicting relapse: a meta-analysis of sexual offender recidivism studies', *Journal of Consulting and Clinical Psychology*, 66: 348–62.

Hansson, K. (2001) *Familjebehandling på goda grunder: en forskningsbaserad översikt. (Family treatment for good reasons: a research-based overview)*. Stockholm: Gothia, Centrum för utvärdering av socialt arbete (CUS).

Hansson, K., Cederblad, M. and Höök, B. (2000) 'Funktionell familjeterapi – en behandlingsmetod vid ungdomskriminalitet. (Functional family therapy: a method for treating juvenile delinquents), *Socialvetenskaplig tidskrift*, 7: 231–43.

Harre, R. (1984) *The Philosophies of Science: An Introductory Survey*, 2nd edn. Oxford: Oxford University Press.

Hartman, A. (1990) 'Many ways of knowing', *Social Work*, 35 (1): 3–4.

Hennekens, C.E., Buring, J.E. and Mayrent, S.L. (1987) *Epidemiology in Medicine*. Boston: Little, Brown and Company.

Houston, S. (2001) 'Beyond social constructionism: critical realism and social work', *British Journal of Social Work*, 31 (6): 845–61.

Hummel, P., Thomke, V., Oldenburger, H.A. and Specht, F. (2000) 'Male adolescent sex offenders against children: similarities and differences between those offenders with and those without a history of sexual abuse', *Journal of Adolescence*, 23: 305–17.

Humphries, B. (1999) 'Feminist evaluation', in I. Shaw and J. Lishman (eds), *Evaluation and Social Work Practice*. London: Sage. pp. 118–32.

Hunter, J.A., Hazelwood, R.R. and Slesinger, D. (2000) 'Juvenile-perpetrated sex crimes: patterns of offending and predictors of violence', *Journal of Family Violence*, 15 (1): 81–93.

Jenkinson, C. (ed.) (1994) *Measuring Health and Medical Outcomes*. London: UCL Press.

Johnson, G.M. and Knight, R.A. (2000) 'Developmental antecedents of sexual coercion in juvenile sexual offenders', *Sexual Abuse: A Journal of Research and Treatment*, 12 (3): 165–78.

Jordan, B. (1978) 'A comment on "theory and practice in social work"', *British Journal of Social Work*, 8: 23–5.

Kauppila, T. (2001) *Sosiaalityön laadun parantaminen tietotekniikan avulla 1998–2000. Loppuraportti. (Promoting the quality of social work with the help of information technology 1998–2000. Final report)*. Helsinki: National Research and Development Centre for Welfare and Health (STAKES), FinSoc Arviointiraportteja 1/2001.

Kazi, M.A.F. (1996) 'The Centre for Evaluation Studies at the University of Huddersfield: a profile', *Research on Social Work Practice*, 6 (1): 104–16.

Kazi, M.A.F. (1997a) 'Single-case evaluation in British social services', in E. Chelimsky and W.R. Shadish (eds), *Evaluation for the 21st Century: A Resource Book*. Thousand Oaks, CA: Sage. pp. 419–42.

Kazi, M.A.F. (1997b) 'Towards a pragmatic approach to the proper method mix', Paper presented at the 1997 European Evaluation Society Conference 'Evaluation: What Works and for Whom?', Stockholm, 6–8 March.

Kazi, M.A.F. (1998a) *Single-Case Evaluation by Social Workers*. Aldershot: Ashgate.

Kazi, M.A.F. (1998b), 'Putting single-case evaluation into practice', in J. Cheetham and M.A.F. Kazi (eds), *The Working of Social Work*. London: Jessica Kingsley. pp. 187–99.

Kazi, M.A.F. (1999) 'Paradigmatic influences in practice research: a critical assessment', in M. Potocky-Tripodi and T. Tripodi (eds), *New Directions for Social Work Practice Research*. Washington, DC: NASW Press. pp. 56–78.

Kazi, M.A.F. (2000a) 'Contemporary perspectives in the evaluation of practice', *British Journal of Social Work*, 30: 755–68.

Kazi, M.A.F. (2000b) 'Evaluation of social work practice in England', *Journal of Social Work Research And Evaluation*, 1 (2): 101–9.

Kazi, M.A.F. (2000c) 'Single-case evaluation in social work', in M. Davies (ed.), *The Blackwell Encyclopaedia of Social Work*. Oxford: Blackwell. p. 317.

Kazi, M.A.F. and Firth, K. (1999) 'Evaluation of an adult rehabilitation unit in England', Paper presented at the Third Annual Conference of the Society for Social Work at Austin, Texas, 22–24 January.

Kazi, M.A.F. and Firth, K. (2000) 'Integration of single-case and multi-method evaluation procedures in the daily practice of an adult rehabilitation unit', Paper presented at the Evaluation for Practice International Conference, University of Huddersfield, 12–14 July.

Kazi, M.A.F. and Mäntysaari, M. (2002) 'Realist Evaluation for Practice', Invited plenary paper at the 4th Evaluation for Practice International Conference, Tampere, Finland, 4–6 July.

Kazi, M.A.F. and Spurling, L.J. (2000) 'Realist evaluation for evidence-based practice', Paper presented at the 2000 European Evaluation Society Conference, Lausanne, Switzerland, 12–14 October.

Kazi, M.A.F. and Ward, A. (2001) 'Service-wide integration of single-subject designs and qualitative methods: a realist evaluation', Paper presented at the Society for Social Work and Research Conference, Atlanta, January.

Kazi, M.A.F. and Wilson, J. (1996) 'Applying single-case evaluation in social work', *British Journal of Social Work*, 26: 699–717.

Kazi, M.A.F., Manby, M. and Buckley, M. (2001) *Evaluation of Family Centres in Kirklees: An Extensive Use of Single-Case Evaluation*. Huddersfield: Nationwide Children's Research Centre.

Kazi, M.A.F., Mäntysaari, M. and Rostila, I. (1997) 'Promoting the use of single-case designs: social work experiences from England and Finland', *Research on Social Work Practice*, 7 (3): 311–28.

Kazi, M.A.F., Ward, A. and Hudson, G. (2002) *Realist Evaluation of NSPCC Shield Project: Evaluating Practice with Children and Young People who Display Sexually Harmful Behaviours*. Huddersfield: Centre for Evaluation Studies, University of Huddersfield.

Kazi, M.A.F., Blom, B., Morén, S., Perdal, A-L. and Rostila, I. (2002a) 'Realist evaluation for practice in Sweden, Finland and England', *Journal of Social Work Research And Evaluation*, 3 (2): 171–86.

Kazi, M.A.F., Taylor, R., Firth, K., Lickess, S., Henson, A. and Frost, S. (2002) 'Single-subject and realist evaluation of adult rehabilitation programmes', Paper presented at the 6th Annual Conference of the Society for Social Work and Research, San Diego, California, 17–20 January.

Kazis, L.E., Anderson, J.J. and Meenan, R.F. (1989) 'Effect sizes for interpreting changes in health status', *Medical Care*, 27 (3): S178–89.

Kenny, D.T., Keogh, T. and Seidler, K. (2001) 'Predictors of recidivism in Australian juvenile sex offenders: implications for treatment', *Sexual Abuse: A Journal of Research and Treatment*, 13 (2): 131–48.

King, N. (1998) 'Template analysis', in C. Cassell, and G. Symon (eds), *Qualitative Methods and Analysis in Organisational Research*. London: Sage. pp. 118–34.

Kitzinger, J. and Barbour, R.S. (1999) 'Introduction: the challenge and promise of focus groups', in R.S. Barbour and J. Kitzinger (eds), *Developing Focus Group Research*. London: Sage. pp. 1–20.

Klee, R. (1997) *Introduction to the Philosophy of Science: Cutting Nature at its Seams*. New York: Oxford University Press.

Kuhn, T. (1970) *The Structure of Scientific Revolutions*, 2nd edn. Chicago: University of Chicago Press.

Lane, S. (1997) 'The Sexual Abuse Cycle', in G. Ryan and S. Lane (eds), *Juvenile Sexual Offending: Causes, Consequences and Corrections*, 2nd edn. San Francisco: Jossey-Bass.

Langstrom, N., Grann, M. and Lindblad, F. (2000) 'A preliminary typology of young sex offenders', *Journal of Adolescence*, 23: 319–29.

Lawson, T. (1998) 'Economic science without experimentation/Abstraction', in M. Archer, R. Bhaskar, A. Collier, T. Lawson and A. Norrie (eds), *Critical Realism: Essential Readings*. London: Routledge. pp. 144–85.

Lightfoot, S. and Evans, I.M. (2000) 'Risk factors for a New Zealand sample of sexually abusive children and adolescents', *Child Abuse and Neglect*, 24 (9): 1185–98.

Lindqvist, T. (1996) *Miten tukea ihmisten selviytymistä? Sosiaalityko-kurssien evaluaatiotutkimus. (How to support the coping of the unemployed? Evaluation of rehabilitative educational courses)*. Helsinki: Helsingin kaupungin sosiaalivirasto D:1/1996.

Macdonald, G. (1994) 'Developing empirically-based practice in probation', *British Journal of Social Work*, 24: 405–27.

Macdonald, G. (1996) 'Ice therapy: why we need randomised controlled trials', in P. Alderson, S. Brill, I. Chalmers, R. Fuller, P. Hinkley-Smith, G. Macdonald, T. Newman, A. Oakley, H. Roberts and H. Ward (eds), *What Works? Effective Social Interventions in Child Welfare*. Ilford, Essex: Barnardos. pp. 16–32.

Madill, A., Jordan, A. and Shirley, C. (2000) 'Objectivity and reliability in qualitative analysis: realist, contextualist and radical constructionist epistemologies', *British Journal of Psychology*, 91: 1–20.

Malamuth, N.M., Sockloskie, R.J., Koss, M.P., and Tanaka, J.S. (1991) 'Characteristics of aggressors against women: testing a model using a national sample of college students', *Journal of Consulting and Clinical Psychology*, 59: 670–81.

Manicas, P.T. (1987) *A History and Philosophy of the Social Sciences*. Oxford: Blackwell.

Manicas, P.T. (1998) 'A realist social science', in M. Archer, R. Bhaskar, A. Collier, T. Lawson and A. Norrie (eds), *Critical Realism: Essential Readings*. London: Routledge. pp. 313–38.

Manicas, P.T. and Secord, P.F. (1983) 'Implications for psychology of the new philosophy of science', *American Psychologist*, 38: 399–413.

Mäntysaari, M. (1999) *Toimeentulotuki työllistäjänä. Lahden työllistämispalveluprojektin arviointia. (Employment through income support. Evaluating a special service for the unemployed in Lahti)*. Helsinki: Sosiaali-ja terveysalan tutkimus-ja kehittämiskeskus, FinSoc, Sosiaalihuollon menetelmien arviointiprojekti, työpapereita 3.

Mark, R. (1996) *Research made Simple: A Handbook for Social Workers*. Thousand Oaks, CA: Sage.

Mark, M.M., Henry, G.T., and Julnes, G. (2000) *Evaluation: An Integrated Framework for Understanding, Guiding, and Improving Policies and Programs*. San Francisco: Jossey-Bass.

Markström, U. (1998) *Pro-eller jäkt. En utvärdering av Nätkraft, ett arbetsrehabiliteringsprojekt för funktionshindrande. (Project or rush. Evaluation of Nätkraft, a work rehabilitation project for the disabled)*. Skrift no. 3. Umeå: Utvecklings-och fältforskningsenheten (UFFE) vid Umeå socialtjänst.

Marshall, W.L. (1993) 'The role of attachments, intimacy, and loneliness in the etiology and maintenance of sexual offending', *Sexual and Marital Therapy*, 8 (2): 109–21.

Masson, H. (1997/8) 'Issues in relation to children and young people who sexually abuse other children: a survey of practioners' views', *Journal of Sexual Aggression*, 3 (2): 101–18.

Masterman, M. (1970) 'The nature of a paradigm', in I. Lakatos and A. Musgrave (eds), *Criticism and the Growth of Knowledge*. Cambridge: Cambridge University Press. pp. 59–89.

Medawar, P. (1982) *Plato's Republic*. Oxford: Oxford University Press.

Miles, M.B. and Huberman, A.M. (1994) *Qualitative Data Analysis*, 2nd edn. Thousand Oaks, CA: Sage.

Morén, S. (1994a) 'Social work is beautiful: on the characteristics of social work', *Scandinavian Journal of Social Welfare*, 3: 158–66.

Morén, S. (1994b) 'Social work organizations from within', *International Social Work*, 37: 277–93.

Morrison, T. (2000) 'Cracks and collaboration', Keynote presentation at NOTA international annual conference, Dublin, September.

Murphy, W.D., DiLillo, D., Haynes, M.R. and Steere, E. (2001) 'An exploration of factors related to deviant sexual arousal among juvenile sex offenders', *Sexual Abuse: A Journal of Research and Treatment*, 13 (2): 91–103.

Newburn, T. (2001) 'What do we mean by evaluation?', *Children and Society*, 15 (1): 5–13.

Nugent, W.R., Sieppert, J.D., and Hudson, W.W. (2001) *Practice Evaluation for the 21st Century*. Belmont, CA: Brooks/Cole Thomson Learning.

Oakley, A. (1996) 'Who's afraid of the randomised controlled trial? The challenge of evaluating the potential of social interventions', in P. Alderson, S. Brill, I. Chalmers, R. Fuller, P. Hinkley-Smith, G. Macdonald, T. Newman, A. Oakley, H. Roberts and H. Ward (eds), *What Works? Effective Social Interventions in Child Welfare*. Ilford, Essex: Barnardos.

Outhwaite, W. (1987) *New Philosophies of Social Science: Realism, Hermeneutics and Critical Theory*. Basingstoke: Macmillan.

Outhwaite, W. (1998) 'Realism and social science', in M. Archer, R. Bhaskar, A. Collier, T. Lawson and A. Norrie (eds), *Critical Realism: Essential Readings*. London: Routledge. pp. 282–96.

Parton, N. (1994) 'Problematics of government, (post) modernity and social work', *British Journal of Social Work*, 24: 9–32.

Parton, N. and O'Byrne, P. (2000) *Constructive Social Work: Towards a New Practice*. London: Macmillan.

Pawson, R. and Tilley, N. (1997a) 'An introduction to scientific realist evaluation', in E. Chelimsky and W.R. Shadish (eds), *Evaluation for the 21st Century: A Resource Book*. Thousand Oaks, CA: Sage. pp. 405–18.

Pawson, R. and Tilley, N. (1997b) *Realistic Evaluation*. London: Sage.

Pawson, R. and Tilley, N. (2001) 'Realistic evaluation bloodlines', *American Journal of Evaluation*, 22 (3): 317–24.

Phillips, D.C. (1990) 'Postpositivistic science: myths and realities', in E.G. Guba (ed.), *The Paradigm Dialog*. Thousand Oaks, CA: Sage. pp. 31–45.

Pithers, B. and Gray, A. (1997) 'Cluster analysis of children with sexual behaviour problems', Paper presented at the 16th Annual Research and Treatment Conference for the Treatment of Sexual Abusers, Washington, DC, October.

Pithers, W.D., Beal, L.S., Armstrong, J. and Petty, J. (1989) 'Identification of risk factors through clinical interviews and analysis of records', in D.R. Laws (ed.), *Relapse Prevention with Sex Offenders*. New York: Guilford Press. pp. 77–87.

Pithers, W.D., Gray, A., Busconi, A. and Houchens, P. (1998) 'Caregivers of children with sexual behaviour problems: psychological and familial functioning', *Child Abuse and Neglect*, 22: 129–41.

Popkewitz, T.S. (1990) 'Whose future? Whose past? Notes on critical theory and methodology', in E.G. Guba (ed.), *The Paradigm Dialog*. Thousand Oaks, CA: Sage. pp. 46–66.

Popper, K. (1979) *Objective Knowledge*. Oxford: Clarendon Press.

Porter, S. and Ryan, S. (1996) 'Breaking the boundaries between nursing and sociology: a critical realist ethnography of the theory–practice gap', *Journal of Advanced Nursing*, 24: 413–20.

Powell, J. (2002) 'The changing conditions of social work research', *British Journal of Social Work*, 32: 17–33.

Rasmussen, L., Burton, J.E. and Christopherson, B.J. (1992) 'Precursors to offending and the trauma outcome process in sexually reactive children', *Journal of Child Sexual Abuse*, 1 (1): 33–47.

Reid, W.J. and Zettergren, P. (1999) 'A perspective on empirical practice', in I. Shaw and J. Lishman (eds.), *Evaluation and Social Work Practice*. London: Sage. pp. 41–62.

Robson, C. (1993) *Real World Research*. Oxford: Blackwell.

Robson, C. (2000) *Small-scale Evaluation*. London: Sage.

Robson, C. (2002) *Real World Research*, 2nd edn. Oxford: Blackwell.

Rodwell (O'Connor), M. (1998) *Social Work Constructivist Research*. New York: Garland.

Rostila, I. (2000) 'Realistinen arviointitutkimus ja onnistumisen pakot (Realist evaluation and the pressures to succeed)', in R. Laitinen, (ed.), *Arvioinnin arkea ja peruskysymyksiä. (The principles and reality of evaluation)*. Helsinki: Sosiaali-ja terveysturvan Keskusliitto. pp. 9–21.

Rostila, I. (2001) *Sosiaalisen kuntoutuksen mekanismit. Monet-projektin realistinen arviointi.* (*Mechanisms of social rehabilitation. Realist evaluation of the Monet project*). Helsinki: National Research and Development Centre for Welfare and Health (STAKES), FinSoc, Arviointiraportteja 3/2001.

Rostila, I. and Kazi, M.A.F. (2001) 'Realistinen arviointitutkimus toimintamallin kehittämisen välineenä (Realist evaluation as a means of developing models of practice)', in P. Vartiainen (ed.), *Näkökulmia projektiarviointiin. Tasapainottelua taloudellisessa, hallinnollisessa ja sosiaalisessa kontekstissa.* (*Perspectives for evaluating projects. Balancing in economic, administrative and social contexts*). Tampere: Finnpublishers. pp. 69–99.

Rubin, A. and Babbie, E. (1997) *Research Methods for Social Work*, 3rd edn. Pacific Grove, CA: Brooks/Cole.

Rubin, A. and Babbie, E. (2001) *Research Methods for Social Work*, 4th edn. Belmont, CA: Wadsworth.

Ryan, G. (1999) 'Treatment of sexually abusive youth', *Journal of Interpersonal Violence*, 14 (4): 422–36.

Ryan, G. (2000) 'Childhood sexuality: a decade of study. Part II – dissemination and future directions', *Child Abuse and Neglect*, 24 (1): 49–61.

Ryan, G., Miyoshi, T.J.O., Metzner, J.L., Krugman, R.D. and Fryer, G.E. (1996) 'Trends in a national sample of sexually abusive youth', *Journal of the Academy of Child and Adolescent Psychiatry*, 35: 17–25.

Saarnio, P., Tolonen, M., Heikkilä, K., Kangassalo, S., Mäkeläinen, M.-L., Niitty-Uotila, P., Vilenius, L. and Virtanen, K. (1998) 'Päihdeongelmaisten selviytyminen hoidon jälkeen. (The coping of alcoholics after care)', *Sosiaalilääketieteellinen aikakauslehti*, 35: 207–19.

Sackett, D.L., Richardson, W.S., Rosenberg, W. and Haynes, R.R. (1997) *Evidence-based Medicine: How to Practice and Teach EBP.* New York: Churchill-Livingston.

Sayer, A. (1998) 'Abstraction: a realist interpretation', in M. Archer, R. Bhaskar, A. Collier, T. Lawson and A. Norrie (eds), *Critical Realism: Essential Readings.* London: Routledge. pp. 120–43.

Sayer, A. (2000) *Realism and Social Science.* London: Sage.

Schram, D.D., Milloy, C.D. and Rowe, W.E. (1991) *Juvenile Sex Offenders: A Follow-up of Reoffense Behavior.* Olympia, WA: Washington State Institute for Public Policy.

Scriven, M. (1994) 'The fine line between evaluation and explanation', *Evaluation Practice*, 15 (1): 75–7.

Shaw, I. (1996) *Evaluating in Practice.* Aldershot: Arena (Ashgate).

Shaw, I. (1998) 'Practising evaluation', in J. Cheetham and M.A.F. Kazi (eds), *The Working of Social Work.* London: Jessica Kingsley. pp. 201–23.

Shaw, I. (1999) 'Evidence for practice', in I. Shaw and J. Lishman (eds), *Evaluation and Social Work Practice.* London: Sage. pp. 14–40.

Sheldon, B. (1978) 'Theory and practice in social work: a re-examination of a tenuous relationship', *British Journal of Social Work*, 8: 1–22.

Sheldon, B. (1988) 'Single-case evaluation methods: review and prospects', in J. Lishman (ed.), *Evaluation*, 2nd edn. London: Jessica Kingsley. pp. 40–57.

Sheppard, M. (1995) 'Social work, social science and practice wisdom', *British Journal of Social Work*, 8: 1–22.

Smallbone, S.W. and Dadds, M.R. (2000) 'Attachment and coercive sexual behaviour', *Sexual Abuse: A Journal of Research and Treatment*, 12 (1): 3–15.

Smallbone, S.W. and Dadds, M.R. (2001) 'Further evidence for a relationship between attachment insecurity and coercive sexual behaviour in non-offenders', *Journal of Interpersonal Violence*, 16 (1): 22–35.

Spurling, L.J., Kazi, M.A.F. and Rogan, M. (2000) *Developing Models for the Social Inclusion of Drug Users: First Annual Report.* Huddersfield: Lifeline/SHAP/University of Huddersfield.

Sundman, P. (1993) *Avioliitto-ja perheneuvonnan vaikuttavuus.* (*The effectiveness of family counselling*). Helsinki: Helsingin kaupunki, Sosiaaliviraston julkaisusarja A7.

Taylor, C. and White, S. (2000) *Practising Reflexivity in Health and Welfare.* Buckingham: Open University Press.

Tesch, R. (1990) *Qualitative Research: Analysis Types and Software Tools*. New York: State University of New York Press.

Thyer, B.A. (1998) 'Promoting evaluation research on social work practice', in J. Cheetham and M.A.F. Kazi (eds), *The Working of Social Work*. London: Jessica Kingsley. pp. 171–85.

Tolson, D. (1999) 'Practice innovation: a methodological maze', *Journal of Advanced Nursing*, 30 (2): 381–90.

Trinder, L. (1996) 'Social work research: the state of the art (or science)', *Child and Family Social Work*, 1: 233–42.

University of Leeds (1992) *Effective Health Care*, Bulletin no. 2, March.

Veneziano, C., Veneziano, L. and LeGrand, S. (2000) 'The relationship between adolescent sex offender behaviours and victim characteristics with prior victimisation', *Journal of Interpersonal Violence*, 15 (4): 363–74.

Vizard, E., Monck, E. and Misch, P. (1995) 'Child and adolescent sex abuse perpetrators: a review of the research literature', *Journal of Child Psychology and Psychiatry*, 36: 731–56.

Wainwright, S.P. (1997) 'A new paradigm for nursing: the potential of realism', *Journal of Advanced Nursing*, 26: 1262–71.

White, S. (1997) 'Beyond retroduction? Hermeneutics, reflexivity and social work practice', *British Journal of Social Work*, 27: 739–53.

White, S. (1998) 'Analysing the content of social work: applying the lessons from qualitative research', in J. Cheetham and M.A.F. Kazi (eds), *The Working of Social Work*. London: Jessica Kingsley. pp. 153–69.

White, S. and Stancombe, J. (2002) 'Colonising care? Potentialities and pitfalls of scientific-bureacratic rationality in social care', *Journal of Social Work Research and Evaluation*, 3 (2): 187–202.

Widom, C.S. (1988) 'Sampling biases and implications for child abuse research', *American Journal of Orthopsychiatry*, 58: 260–70.

Widom, C.S. (1995) *Victims of childhood sexual abuse, later consequences: National Institute of Justice – Research in Brief*. Washington DC: National Institute of Justice. pp. 1–8.

Worling, J.R. and Curwen, T. (2000) 'Adolescent sexual offender recidivism: success of specialized treatment and implications for risk prediction', *Child Abuse and Neglect*, 24 (7): 965–82.

Zolondek, S.C., Abel, G.G., Northey, Jr., W.F. and Jordan, A.D. (2001) 'The self-reported behaviours of juvenile sexual offenders', *Journal of Interpersonal Violence*, 16 (1): 73–85.

Index

Adult rehabilitation services 7, 22, 34–40, 162
Aljazireh, L. 113
Anastas, J. 4, 5, 26
Anderson, J. 71
Archer, M. 4, 24, 60, 165
Argyrous, G. 72, 138, 140, 161
Australia 113

Babbie, E. 62, 66, 71, 88, 89, 138, 139, 140, 166
Barbour, R. 97, 103
Barton Services 35, 39–40
Beckett, R. 112, 159
Bhaskar, R. 1, 4, 5, 28
Binary logistic regression 8, 150, 151
  def. 152
  models of 153–5, 156
Bivariate tests 8, 147, 148
Blom, B. 11
Bloom, M. 11, 14, 36, 65
Boruch, R. 159
Briggs, H. 30
Bryman, A. 166
Buckley, M. 64, 66, 71
Bullman, A. 90
Burke, D. 112, 113, 115
Burton, D. 113, 128, 156

Calderdale and Huddersfield NHS Trust 34
Campbell Collaboration 159
Campbell, D. 4, 59
Carlsson, B. 11, 20
Cederblad, M. 11
Centre for Evaluation Studies 21, 31, 34, 42, 97
Cheetham, J. 10, 11, 17
Cohen, J. 140, 142, 165
Comparison group design 26, 30, 65
Constructivist evaluation 11, 13, 18
Contexts 8, 10, 16, 31, 43, 45, 56, 103, 108, 113–14, 127–9, 130
  def. 27, 56, 100, 111
Cook, T. 59

Corcoran, K. 30, 66, 101, 160
Crabtree, B. 44, 161
Critical evaluation 10
Critical realism 4, 18
Critical theory 3, 11, 18, 20
Curwen, T. 113, 115

Dadds, M. 113
Dartmouth COOP Charts 39–40
Dillenburger, K. 11, 14
Drisko, J. 45, 103
Drug using community 42–3, 49
Dufåker, M. 11, 20
Duguid, S. 8, 21, 34, 63, 72, 117

Effect sizes, as in measures of association 138–40
  def. 139
  interpretation of 140, 142, 144, 154
Effect sizes, calculating from standardised measures 71, 118–23
Effectiveness, 10, 24
Empirical practice paradigm 6, 7, 11, 13, 14, 20, 22, 97
  contribution of 15, 158
  def. 13
  limitations of 15, 16, 60, 159
Epistemological debates 3, 6, 14, 16
Ethics 19, 67
Evaluation, goal of, 2
  purposes of, 2
  three boxes of 7, 20, 21, 62, 72, 159–60
Evaluation research 1
Evaluation research perspectives 11
  boundaries of 11
Evans, I. 112, 113, 116
Everitt, A. 3, 11, 15, 18, 159
Evidence-based practice, def. 159
External evaluation, def. 2

Fallibilistic realism 4
Family centres 8, 62, 160, 162
  case examples 68–71
  description of 63–4

Feminist evaluation 18, 19, 20
Fetterman, D. 64
Finkelhor, D. 98
Finland, 4
Firth, K. 35
Fischer, J. 30, 36, 65, 66, 101, 160
Focus groups 35, 103, 111, 116, 161
Focus groups, def. 97–8
Forsberg, H. 11, 20
Fortune, A. 15
Foster, J. 34, 71, 72, 139, 140, 161
Fraser, M. 4, 13
Fuller, R. 3, 11, 16

Gal, M. 113
Gambrill, E. 159
Germany 114, 129
Gomm, R. 90
Grann, M. 114, 128
Gray, A. 115, 156
Guba, E. 3, 10, 12, 13, 18

Hall, C. 11, 18
Hanson, R. 115, 156
Hansson, K. 11
Hardiker, P. 3, 11, 15, 18, 159
Harre, R. 5
Hartman, A. 16
Hazelwood, R. 113
Health services 2, 5, 10, 20, 96
Hennekens, C. 146
Henry, G. 5, 6
Hodge, R. 113
Höök, B. 11
Houston, S. 41, 164, 166
Huberman, A. 6, 111, 116, 138, 161, 166
Huddersfield, University of 34, 42, 97
Hudson, G. 95, 97, 157
Hudson, W. 62, 65, 89
Human services 1, 2, 7, 10, 24
Hummel, P. 114, 129
Humphries, B. 11, 14, 19
Hunter, J. 113

Inferential statistics 8, 34, 63, 117, 118, 137, 138, 162
Internal evaluation, def. 2
International Association for Critical Realism (IACR) 5
Interpretivist paradigm 3, 6, 7, 11, 12, 19, 20, 22, 43, 60, 158, 166
    def. 18
    limitations of 19, 59–60, 159
Interventions 1, 8, 13, 14, 17, 24, 27, 28, 30, 34, 63, 115, 118

Interventions cont.
    as generative mechanisms 27, 49, 96–9, 155
    content of 49, 100, 125–7, 146
    replication of 163

Jenkinson, C, 39
Johnson, G. 112, 113, 114, 115
Jordan, A. 44
Jordan, B. 15
Julnes, G. 5, 6
Jyväskylä, University of 4

Kauppila, T. 11
Kazi, M. 1, 3, 5, 11, 12, 14, 21, 31, 34, 42, 62, 63, 64, 66, 129, 157, 158, 163, 166
Kazis, L. 71
Keogh, T. 113, 115
Kenny, D. 113, 115
Kind, N. 44
Kirklees Metropolitan Council 8, 43, 62, 63
Kitzinger, J. 97, 103
Klee, R. 22
Knight, R. 112, 113, 114, 115
Kuhn, T. 4

Lane, S. 98
Langstrom, N. 114, 128
Lawson, D. 44, 45
Lawson, T. 6, 24, 25, 26, 28, 31, 34, 96, 104, 117, 130, 137, 138, 162, 163
LeGrand, S. 113, 156
Lifeline 42, 44, 160
Lightfoot, S. 112, 113, 116
Lindblad, F. 114, 128
Lindqvist, T. 11

Macdonald, G. 3, 11, 14, 16, 26
MacDonald, M. 4
Madill, A. 44
Malamuth, N. 114
Manicas, P. 4, 12, 23, 56, 61
Manby, M. 64, 66, 71
Mäntysaari, M. 4, 11, 14
Mark, M. 2, 5, 6, 56
Mark, R. 4
Markström, U. 11
Marshall, W. 113
Masson, H. 112, 115
Masterman, M. 4
Matrices 46–56, 57–8, 111, 116, 138, 161
    def. 111

Mechanism–context–outcome patterns 7, 8, 44, 56, 62, 89–93, 117, 131–2, 138
  statistical analysis 72–83, 117, 138, 138–40, 142, 144
Mechanisms 1, 8, 26, 43, 56, 59, 108
  causal mechanisms 1, 7, 9, 24–5, 56, 59–60, 94, 95, 104, 105–6, 137, 147, 160
  def. 31, 111, 164
  identifying 26–7, 42, 44, 46, 49, 95, 103, 110, 113–14, 130, 137, 140, 148, 160
  limitations in the identification of 93–4, 104, 146, 147
  systematic tracking of 100, 103–4, 129–32, 137, 163
Medawar, P. 15
Meenan, R. 71
Miller, W. 44, 161
Miles, M. 6, 45–6, 111, 138, 161, 166
Milloy, C. 113
Misch, P. 112, 115
Monck, E. 112, 115
Morén, S. 10
Morrison, T. 115
Mullender, A. 11
Murphy, W. 116, 164

National Society for Prevention of Cruelty to Children (NSPCC)
  case examples from 104–8
  description of 96–9
  Shield Project 8, 95, 160, 162, 163, 164–5
New Zealand 113
Newburn, T. 3
Non-realist position 13
Nordic 11, 13, 14, 16, 21
NUD*IST 43
Nugent, W. 62, 65, 89

Oakes Villa Rehabilitation Service 35–9, 40–1
Oakley, A. 14, 15, 159
O'Byrne, P. 11, 18, 20
Odds ratios 90, 115, 149–51, 164
  def. 90
One-group pre-test post-test design 8, 62, 65, 71–83, 89, 118
Ontology 10, 13, 17, 18
  def. 22
Open system 10, 25, 49, 160, 161
Orme, J. 36, 65
Outcomes 8, 14, 15, 20, 22, 24, 30, 34, 43, 44, 45, 46, 60, 62, 65–6, 100, 101–3, 117, 124, 140
  def. 111

Outhwaite, W. 10, 14, 24, 28, 60
Outlook team, Lifeline 42, 43, 44, 49, 59, 60, 61

Paradigm, def. 3–4
Paradigmatic preferences 10, 158, 163, 166
Paradigms 3, 10, 12, 14, 16, 20, 22, 32
Parton, N. 2, 11, 18, 20
Pawson, R. 1, 4, 5, 6, 8, 9, 20, 21, 23, 25, 26, 28, 34, 44, 62, 63, 66, 72, 95, 96, 110, 130, 160, 161, 162, 164, 165
Petch, A. 3, 11
Phillips, D. 4
Pithers, B. 113, 129
Popkewitz, T. 19
Popper, K. 12, 19
Porter, S. 5, 59
Positivism 10, 14
Positivism, foundationist 14
Positivism, varieties of 14
Post-positivism 10, 11, 19, 20, 32
Powell, J. 2, 13, 20
Practice 1, 4, 10, 22
Practice effectiveness 3
Practitioner research 3, 11, 13, 28
Practitioner-evaluators 1
Pragmatist paradigm 11, 13, 16, 20, 22, 158
  def. 16
  limitations of 17, 18
  methods 17
Process outcomes 8

Qualitative methods 6, 7, 8, 16, 17, 31, 33, 42, 43, 56, 59, 97, 101, 103–4, 106, 116, 131, 137, 138, 161, 166
Quantitative methods 6, 7, 8, 16, 17, 31, 33, 63, 93, 101–3, 104, 106, 116–17, 131, 137, 138, 161, 166
Quasi-experimental design 59, 159

Randomised controlled trials 14, 15, 159
Rasmussen, L. 114, 155
Realism 4, 13, 16
Realist effectiveness cycle 1, 7, 8, 33, 42, 56, 61, 62, 131, 161, 163, 165
  def. 28–30
  implementation of 30–1, 99–101, 106, 108, 137, 138, 157
Realist ethnography 59
Realist evaluation 1, 4, 5, 7, 20, 21
  application of 27–8, 60, 158
  causality and explanation 24–6, 60–1, 109, 137, 147–8, 157, 160, 162
  contribution of 160–1, 166–7
  embeddedness 23, 27, 49, 161

Realist evaluation *cont.*
  emergence 24, 130, 137, 160
  def. 4, 5, 137
  framework for 160–2
  induction and deduction 24, 26, 165–6
  intensive and extensive research 32–3,
      101, 108–9, 110, 137, 161
  investigating demi-regularities or patterns
      32–34, 109, 117, 137, 140, 161
  limitations of 9, 164–6
  methodologies for 31–3, 109, 117,
      137–40, 158, 166
  methodology, underdevelopment of 5,
      6, 7, 22, 96, 165
  necessity 26, 155
  ontology of 22–5
  principles of 22–6
  purposes of 62, 95, 99–100, 101,
      110, 115, 117, 132, 137–8,
      147–8, 156, 160, 162, 166
  rules of 27–8, 95–6, 130, 160, 162
  stratified reality 24, 26, 49, 130
  utility of 157, 158, 161, 163
Realist paradigm 1, 5, 6
Realist, purpose of, 1
Referential realism 4
Reid, W. 11, 12, 13, 14, 15
Relative risk, calculation of 90, 146–7
Relativism 17
Reliability, of qualitative data 103–4
  tests 37, 66, 88, 101, 122
Retroduction, 32, 44, 56, 60, 95, 162,
      166, 167
  def. 24–5, 148
Robson, C. 1, 2, 6, 95, 110, 138, 139,
      140, 160, 163, 166
Rodwell, M. 103
Rogan, M. 32, 42, 43, 56
Rostila, I. 4, 5, 11, 14
Rowe, W. 113
Rubin, A. 62, 66, 71, 88, 89, 138, 139,
      140, 166
Ryan, G. 98, 115, 129
Ryan, S. 5, 59

Saarnio, P. 11
Sackett, D. 159
Sayer, A. 1, 4, 6, 23, 24, 26, 31, 60, 61,
      96, 104, 147, 155, 165
Schram, D. 113
Scientific realism 4, 13
Scriven, M. 20, 21, 64
Secord, P. 4
Seidler, K. 113, 115
Service user perspectives 7, 19, 84–7

Sexual harm 8, 112–15, 128–9
Shaw, I. 3, 4, 10, 11, 15, 18, 19
Sheldon, B. 11, 14, 15
Shirley, C. 44
Sheppard, M. 167
Sieppert, J. 62, 65, 89
Significance tests 138–40
  def. 139
  types of 140
Single-case designs 14, 64–5, 67
  aggregation of results 65, 71–83,
      89, 108–9, 118
  examples of 68–71
Single-case evaluation 8, 14, 19, 36–7, 62, 64–5
  def. 65, 101
Single–subject designs 96
Single–system designs 13
Slesinger, D. 113
Smallbone, S. 113
Social constructionism 17, 18, 20
Social work 1, 3, 10, 14, 15, 17, 20, 97
Social work effectiveness 3
Social work practice 1, 2
Social work research 3
Spearman tests 38–40
SPSS 34, 63, 71, 109, 139, 140, 161
Spurling, L. 42, 43, 49, 56, 160
STAKES, Finland 31
Stancombe, J. 21
Standardised measures 8, 60, 66, 101–3,
      117–24, 160
Statistical power analysis 140, 142, 144,
      147, 154, 165
Stirling, University of 16, 17
Sundman, P. 11
Sweden 114, 128

Taylor, C. 20, 103
Template analysis 7, 59, 161
  def. 44–6
Tesch, R. 45
Thyer, B. 11
Tilley, N. 1, 4, 5, 6, 8, 9, 20, 23, 25, 26, 28,
      44, 62, 66, 95, 96, 110, 130, 160, 161,
      162, 164, 165
Tolson, D. 5, 6, 166
Transcendental realism 4
Trinder, L. 11, 12, 13, 16, 158, 163

Umea University, Sweden 31
USA 14, 112, 115, 128, 129
Utility, 8, 157

Values 19
Varlow, J. 151

Veneziano, C. 113, 156
Veneziano, L. 113, 156
Vizard, E. 112, 115

Wainright, S. 5
Ward, A. 95, 97, 98–9, 130, 157
White, S. 12, 14, 18, 20, 103, 166

Widom, C. 114, 116, 149, 164
Wilson, J. 11, 14
Worling, J. 113, 115

Zettergren, P. 11, 12, 13, 14
Zolondek, S. 113, 128